THE FRENCH WAR ON AL QA'IDA IN AFRICA

In January 2013, France intervened in its former African colony, Mali, to stop an Al Qa'ida advance on the capital. French special forces, warplanes, and army units struck with rapid and unexpected force. Their intervention quickly repelled the jihadist advance, and soon the terrorists had been chased from their safe haven in Mali's desolate north – an impressive accomplishment.

Although there have been many books on the U.S. wars in Iraq and Afghanistan, there are almost none on the recent military interventions of America's allies. Because it was quick, effective, and relatively low cost, the story of France's intervention in Mali contains valuable lessons for future strategy.

Based on exclusive interviews with high-level civilian and military officials in Paris, Washington, and Bamako, *The French War on Al Qa'ida in Africa* offers a fast-paced, concise strategic overview of this conflict. As terrorist groups proliferate across North Africa, what France accomplished in Mali is an important reference point for national security experts.

Christopher S. Chivvis is Associate Director of the RAND International Security and Defense Policy Center and teaches at the Johns Hopkins Paul H. Nitze School of Advanced International Studies. Chivvis has worked in the Pentagon; published widely, including in *Foreign Policy*, *The National Interest*, and *The New York Times*; and appears frequently in media outlets such as CNN, BBC, and Al Jazeera. His previous books include *Toppling Qaddafi*, on NATO's military intervention in Libya, and *The Monetary Conservative*, a biography of Jacques Rueff.

The French War on Al Qa'ida in Africa

Christopher S. Chivvis
RAND Corporation

CAMBRIDGE
UNIVERSITY PRESS

CAMBRIDGE
UNIVERSITY PRESS

One Liberty Plaza, 20th Floor, New York, NY 10006, USA

Cambridge University Press is part of the University of Cambridge.

It furthers the University's mission by disseminating knowledge in the pursuit of education, learning, and research at the highest international levels of excellence.

www.cambridge.org
Information on this title: www.cambridge.org/9781107546783

First published 2016
Reprinted 2016

Printed in the United States of America by Sheridan Books, Inc.

A catalog record for this publication is available from the British Library.

Library of Congress Cataloging in Publication Data
Chivvis, Christopher S., author.
The French war on Al Qa'ida in Africa / Christopher S. Chivvis, Rand Corporation.
  pages cm
Includes bibliographical references and index.
ISBN 978-1-107-12103-4 (hardback) – ISBN 978-1-107-54678-3 (pbk.)
1. Qai'da (Organization)   2. National security–Mali.   3. Jihad.   4. Islamic fundamentalism–Africa.   5. France–Military policy.   6. France – Military relations – Mali.   7. Mali–Military relations–France.   I. Title.
DC59.8.M42C47   2016
327.4406623–dc23   2015022565

ISBN 978-1-107-12103-4 Hardback
ISBN 978-1-107-54678-3 Paperback

For Uma and Usha

CONTENTS

FIGURES

TABLES

PREFACE

In the last few years, the world has witnessed a deeply troubling spread of violent extremist groups across North Africa and the Middle East. Al Qa'ida has proven tenacious and rise of the so-called Islamic State of Iraq and al Sham (ISIS) has meanwhile opened a whole new era in the history of U.S. counterterrorism efforts, in the Middle East as well as North Africa. From Iraq to Syria to Libya, the United States, its allies, and its partners have confronted the challenge of developing a military strategy that can be both effective against such groups and also politically saleable to domestic populations reluctant to engage again in large-scale counterinsurgency missions of the type the United States undertook in the decade after the 9/11 attacks. The French found such a strategy in their 2013 intervention against al Qa'ida in Mali. France was able relatively quickly, and at a relatively low cost, to eliminate a major al Qa'ida safe haven, restore Mali's integrity, and deal a major blow to the regional terrorist groups that threatened Mali, France, and many other countries. Mali is a poor, weak country with multiple conflicts that have yet to be resolved. It could again descend, as Libya did after the 2011 NATO intervention there, into civil war. But there is little question that the French intervention had an overall positive effect.

Most literature on intervention strategy in the United States focuses on the U.S. experience alone. By bringing the experience of a key ally to light for an American audience, I hope this book will add a valuable perspective to counter-terrorism strategy debate within the U.S. policy and academic community.

I am as grateful as ever, if not more so, for the willingness of many people to contribute valuable time and support to the research and thinking that went into this project. In Paris, I was very lucky to have several of the most knowledgeable experts in the field of French strategic studies and African affairs give time to the project, including Etienne de Durand, Camille Grand, Philippe Gros, Nathalie Guibert, Marc Hecker, Isabelle Laserre, Antonio Missiroli, and Jean-Jacques Patry. In the United States, Jolyon Howorth, Leo Michel, and Douglas Porch contributed sound advice on French military affairs.

The French government was particularly generous in its willingness to talk on and off the record about this story, and I owe much gratitude to Gen. Bernard Barrera, Jean-Vincent Berte, Gregory Chauzal, Sébastien Chenebeau, Xavier Collignon, Ambassador François Delattre, Pierre Esnault, Hélène Le Gal, Frédéric Garnier, Michel Goya, Gen. Maurice de Langlois, Jean-Christophe Noel, Jean-François Pactet, Gen. Jean-François Parlanti, Gen. Jean-Paul Perruche, Frédéric Pesme, Nicolas Roche, Gen. Grégoire de Saint-Quentin, Pierre Schill, Gen. Olivier Tramond, and Justin Vaïsse. Gen. Steen Harboe Hartov and Karsten Fledelius Jensen also contributed helpful insights on the role of non-U.S. partners in the operation.

No less important was the help of several current and former U.S. officials, especially Jim Schear and Michael Sheehan, both of whom read the manuscript in full and provided excellent guidance. Thanks are also due to Alexis Arieff, William Bellis, Paul Belkin, Amb. Johnnie Carson, Sally Donnelly, Gen. Carter Hamm, Martin Kindl, Amb. Beth Leonard, Brendan McAloon, Bradley Mitchell, Rick Moody, Bisola Ojikutu, Kristen Pappas, Ahren Schaefer, Chris Skaluba, Jim Townsend, Andrea Walther.

In Bamako, I am grateful to the several officials from the EUTM who took the time to sit down and take me through their effort. The late Modibo Goita and his excellency Dioncounda Traoré were extremely generous with their time and efforts on my behalf in Bamako.

At RAND I've benefited especially from the comments of Jim Dobbins, Adam Grissom, Seth Jones, and Andy Liepman, as well as Nathan Chandler's excellent research skills. Andy Hoehn, Susan Marquis, Karl Mueller, Dick Neu, Eric Peltz, Michael Rich, Charlie Ries, and Jack Riley also played helpful roles in bringing this book to fruition. The work of other RAND scholars, especially Stephanie Pezard and Michael Shurkin provided a useful foundation for this work. Christina Bartol and Sunny Bhatt were helpful with key aspects of the book production process. Jessica Bogart did the maps. My father, Dr. Arthur B. Chivvis very helpfully read the whole manuscript in its final stage. Thanks also to Alexandra de Borchgrave, David Calleo, an anonymous reviewer for Cambridge University Press, and, last but not least, John Berger and his team at Cambridge University Press for their willingness to work with me and with RAND on the project.

Most of all, thanks to my wife Sumona Guha and my daughters, Uma Kamala and Usha Kate, who were always supportive of my work, despite the extended overseas travel. I can only hope that when my girls reach my age, we will be a little further along in understanding how to deal with the kind of threats and challenges this story presents. Perhaps the outlook will be a little rosier than it is today. The book is dedicated to them.

ABBREVIATIONS

AFISMA	African-led International Support Mission in Mali
AQIM	Al Qa'ida in the Islamic Maghreb
ATT	Amadou Toumani Toure
CIA	U.S. Central Intelligence Agency
DCRI	Direction Centrale du Renseignement Intérieur (Central Directorate of Homeland Intelligence)
DGSE	Direction Générale de la Sécurité Extérieure (General Directorate for External Security)
DoD	U.S. Department of Defense
ECOWAS	Economic Community for West African States
EU	European Union
EUFOR	European Union Force
GDP	Gross Domestic Product
GIA	Groupe Islamique Armé (Armed Islamic Group)
GPS	Global Positioning System
GSPC	Groupe Salafiste pour la Prédication et le Combat (Salafist Group for Preaching and Combat)
GTIA	Groupe Tactique Interarmes (Joint Tactical Group)
HCUA	High Council for the Unity of the Azawad
IBK	Ibrahim Boubacar Keita
IED	Improvised Explosive Device
IFOR	Implementation Force

ISAF	International Security Assistance Force
ISIS	Islamic State of Iraq and al Sham
JCET	Joint Combined Exchange Training
KFOR	Kosovo Force
kWh	Kilo-Watt Hours
MAA	Arab Movement of the Azawad
MINURCA	United Nations Mission in the Central African Republic
MINURCAT	United Nations Mission in the Central African Republic and Chad
MINUSMA	United Nations Multidimensional Integrated Stabilization Mission in Mali
MNLA	Mouvement Nationale pour la Liberation de l'Azawad (National Movement for the Liberation of Azawad)
MUJAO	Mouvement pour l'Unicité et le Jihad en Afrique de l'Oues (Movement for Unity and Jihad in West Africa)
NATO	North Atlantic Treaty Organization
OEF	Operation Enduring Freedom
RAF	Royal Air Force
RCE	Regional Command East
RPG	Rocket-Propelled Grenade
SFOR	Stabilization Force – Bosnia
SOCOM	U.S. Special Operations Command
TRANSCOM	U.S. Transportation Command
UAV	Unmanned Aerial Vehicle
UN	United Nations
UNAMIR	United Nations Assistance Mission for Rwanda
UNIFIL	United Nations Interim Force in Lebanon
UNMIBH	United Nations Mission in Bosnia and Herzegovina
UNOCI	United Nations Operation in Côte d'Ivoire

UNOSOM	United Nations Operation in Somalia
UNPROFOR	United Nations Protection Force – Former Yugoslavia
UNTAC	United Nations Transitional Authority in Cambodia
USAID	United States Agency for International Development

1   FRANCE, MALI, AND AFRICAN JIHAD

PANETTA GETS A PHONE CALL

It was Friday, January 11, 2013 morning in Washington afternoon in Paris and Bamako. U.S. Secretary of Defense Leon Panetta took an emergency telephone call from French Defense Minister Jean-Yves Le Drian. Le Drian had requested the call through his defense attaché Bruno Caitucoli only a few hours earlier. The normally collected Caitucoli had been visibly concerned. No one was sure exactly what had prompted the emergency call.[1] Their French counterparts had been focused on a developing crisis in their former West African colony of Mali for the last few days, but U.S. officials had several more pressing national security issues on their minds – especially NATO's controversial drawdown after a decade of war in Afghanistan and a civil war in Syria that was growing bloodier by the day.

The call got off on the wrong foot when Le Drian began by explaining the time had come to take action "rapidly" in Mali,[2] and Panetta took this to be a request that the United States start the process of considering some form of joint intervention – perhaps some modified version of the 2011 intervention in Libya – and responded positively that he was prepared to begin discussing an intervention. "No, Mr. Secretary," replied the French defense minister, "We are not asking for you to consider an operation. I am calling to inform you that we have just begun one."

Secretary Panetta's jaw dropped.[3] At the French Defense Ministry, officials waited for the silence on the other end of the line to break.[4] Terrorist groups closely tied to al Qa'ida had been in control of northern Mali for a year, but that France should act so precipitously, so boldly, and so independently came as a surprise in Washington. For several months France and the United States had been struggling to put together an African-led response to the problem of Mali's north. France's decision to go in alone was a near total about-face. It went against a recent, hard-won Franco-American agreement on how the situation in Mali would be handled and threatened to open new rifts within the U.S. government over the role of military force in resolving the crisis.

But Secretary Panetta's fierce antiterrorist convictions immediately overcame any initial hesitations. "We're with you, this is a common fight," he told Le Drian.[5] Defeating al Qa'ida was a core interest shared by France and the United States. The two nations had been waging a global war against it worldwide for more than a decade. Anything France could do to further the common cause was clearly in the U.S. interest. Panetta thus pledged "whatever" American support France needed.[6] Unfortunately, it would turn out to be harder than expected to follow through on that pledge, and would generate friction on both sides of the Atlantic – as well as in the field – before it could be worked out.

In the meantime, thousands of miles away from both capitals and hundreds of miles northwest of the Malian capital of Bamako, in the sandy, semiarid plains outside the town of Mopti, two French special forces Gazelle helicopters were already in a fierce firefight with hundreds of al Qa'ida associates on the ground. The French special operations troops had taken off only an hour earlier from Burkina Faso, where they were stationed as part of the regional French counterterrorism operation *Sabre*. Terrified by reports of an advancing vanguard of al Qa'ida fighters, the Malian army had fled the scene, leaving the French and their two helicopters the only barrier that stood between al Qa'ida and Bamako, a city of more than a million with an international airport and daily direct flights to Paris. By the time Secretary Panetta and Minister Le Drian spoke, the first French soldier had already been killed in action. The French war on al Qa'ida in Africa and what would become operation *Serval* – "wildcat" – was under way.

A little more than two years before, the Arab Spring had unleashed turbulent political and social forces across North Africa, buffeting the region into crisis. Although global attention had focused primarily on the impact of the Arab uprisings further east in Egypt and Syria, the shockwave of the revolts against traditional authority was also felt far to the west, nearly reaching Africa's Atlantic shores. The jihadist threat to the states of the Maghreb and Sahel regions, which include the states along Africa's Mediterranean coast and Sahara desert, had been growing for years. Now, regional Salafi jihadist groups wanted to seize the opportunity created by the Arab Spring to realize their dream of an Islamic caliphate governed by an extreme and brutal interpretation of *shari'a* law. As in Syria, where al Qa'ida–linked groups had used the uprising against President Bashar al Assad to expand their influence and control, North African jihadists had profited from turmoil in Egypt, Libya, and Tunisia to extend their influence and strengthen their operating bases in the region. In the process they had also established links with regional groups in sub-Saharan Africa, including the increasingly violent and destabilizing Nigerian group Boko Haram. (See Annex 1 for a list of African jihadist groups.)

The expansion of terrorist groups linked to al Qa'ida and the fracturing of security in the Sahel and Maghreb reached an apotheosis in Mali in 2012. For decades, this former French colony had faced sporadic revolts from the nomadic Tuareg people who inhabited its deserted north. When the Tuareg's regional benefactor, Muammar Qaddafi, succumbed to a NATO-backed revolt in 2011, bands of Tuareg revolutionaries returned to Mali to fight again for independence. Using a strategy that had worked for al Qa'ida in Afghanistan and in Iraq, al Qa'ida's North African affiliate successfully folded itself into the Tuareg revolt, and over the course of 2012 established control over half of Mali's territory and brutally implemented *shar'ia*. Jihadists from far and wide were reported flocking to this new "Malistan," which increasingly looked like an African version of the safe haven al Qa'ida had once enjoyed in Pushtun areas thousands of miles away along the Afghanistan-Pakistan border – and in several ways presaged the larger "caliphate" the Islamic State of Iraq and al Shām (ISIS) would build in Iraq and Syria a year later.

Key international actors, including the United States and France, largely agreed on the threat but were divided over what to do about it.

The jihadists' push south in early 2013 changed the picture. Fearful of what an African al Qa'ida stronghold would mean for France – not to mention French West Africa itself – French President François Hollande ordered his military to step in, hunt the terrorists down, and help restore Mali's democracy.

This was a risky move that surprised many onlookers. It became the largest French unilateral military operation in Africa since the Algerian war half a century earlier. Within a few months, however, the French had successfully prevented the jihadists from taking over the country and killed or chased a great many of them out. This book is about the challenge of Salafi jihadists in North and West Africa, how and why the French have used their military to meet this challenge, the success they have had, its limits, and the lessons that can be gleaned from the experience so far.[7]

AL QA'IDA'S AFRICAN AMBITION

The French intervention in Mali was an initial western response to the recent proliferation of anti-Western terrorist groups across North and West Africa. These groups are now active from Libya, where ISIS made startling gains in late 2014 and 2015 through the Sahel, where al Qa'ida has long had a foothold, and into Nigeria, where Boko Haram has been a serious menace to the local population. These groups have widespread access to weapons and subscribe to a violent, anti-Western and anti-modern ideology. They are already a serious problem and could become a much larger one if more is not done to contain and dismantle them.

Al Qa'ida in the Islamic Maghreb has been particularly problematic for the French. "Africa will be our neighborhood Afghanistan," said Jean-Claude Cousseran, the former head of the Direction Générale pour la Sécurité Exterieure – the French counterpart to the CIA – as the situation in Mali deteriorated in the spring of 2012. The Sahel in particular was an "African powder keg" right on Europe's doorstep.[8] Al Qa'ida's North African affiliate was in the vanguard of a broader African jihadist movement that has become one of the most problematic in the world.

Africa's often troubled modern history; geography; and political, social, and economic conditions make excellent culture for the growth of terrorist groups.[9] Poverty; weak institutions; ethnic, religious, and tribal conflicts; corruption; an abundance of small arms; deeply rooted (albeit varied) conservative Islamic traditions; lingering postcolonial anti-European sentiment; and proximity to both Europe and the Middle East have made Salafi jihadist terrorism a force in Africa since well before 9/11, when Osama Bin Laden ran al Qa'ida operations from Sudan. Bin Laden's first major attacks were on the U.S. embassies in Dar Es Salaam, Tanzania, and Nairobi, Kenya, in 1998. Although al Qa'ida's leader eventually decamped for Afghanistan as pressure on him grew, Africa remained fertile ground for those inspired by his message. Terrorist attacks continued, for example, in Kenya in 2002, as well as in Somalia, Algeria, Nigeria, and elsewhere. Groups multiplied and spread to Somalia, Nigeria, and the countries of the Sahel and Maghreb.

After Bin Laden's death in 2011, Africa's importance as a proving ground for al Qa'ida reemerged. Globally, al Qa'ida–linked groups have proliferated in recent years.[10] Although the connections between them are shifting and often tenuous, Africa and the Middle East have been the regions most seriously affected by this trend. Boko Haram is a serious threat to Nigeria, Cameroon, Niger, and other countries nearby. Shabab is still entrenched in southern Somalia – well enough to stymie an October 2013 U.S. Navy Seal team strike aimed at taking out one of their leaders. In North and West Africa, al Qa'ida in the Islamic Maghreb – the main group implicated in Mali – increased its regional reach in the messy aftermath of Libyan dictator Muammar Qaddafi's fall in 2011. Loosely affiliated Libyan, Tunisian, and Egyptian jihadist groups have meanwhile sought to destabilize the Maghreb in hope of seizing the reins of the 2011 Arab uprisings to establish extreme forms of Islamic law. More recently, ISIS has established a foothold in Libya, taking over whole towns. This, in turn, threatened an expansion of the war that has ravaged Syria and Iraq to the Maghreb and forced European officials to stretch their limited resources even further in fear of terrorist threats emanating directly from Libya's shores.

The growing threat from African jihadists was driven home for many Americans in 2012, when Ansar al Shar'ia, a local Libyan jihadist

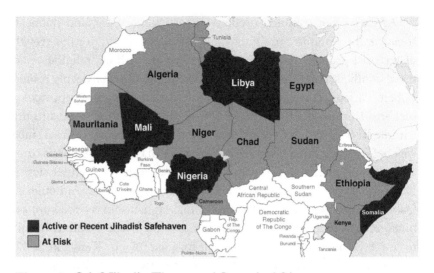

Figure 1. Salafi Jihadist Threatened States in Africa.
Source: Author assessment based on reported jihadist activities and political and economic conditions. Note that in most cases, the whole country is not at risk, only parts of it.

group, overran the U.S. diplomatic facilities in Benghazi, Libya, killing U.S. Ambassador Chris Stevens.[11] The Benghazi attacks were too often portrayed inaccurately in the media and by some members of the U.S. Congress as a straightforward al Qa'ida plot, but whatever al Qa'ida's involvement, the tragedy was a clear sign of the enduring appeal of jihadism in the region.[12]

Soon after Benghazi, as French forces moved into Mali, a recent defector from al Qa'ida in the Islamic Maghreb, Mokthar Belmokthar, took more than a hundred hostages at a gas plant near In Amenas in southern Algeria. In August 2013, the Somali group al Shabab took dozens of innocent civilians hostage at the Westgate shopping mall in Nairobi, sparking a standoff that lasted for several days in which more than sixty people were killed.[13] In 2014, the Nigerian group Boko Haram took hundreds of schoolgirls captive, drawing worldwide attention. Smaller-scale terrorist attacks in Africa had also grown more frequent in recent years, including guerilla assaults on government buildings and kidnappings of Europeans and Africans alike.

To be sure, jihadists in Africa are not a monolithic threat. Africa is an enormous, extremely diverse continent with more than a billion inhabitants, of which these groups make up some ten thousand adherents at most, spread out over millions of square miles, much of which is uninhabitable even for seasoned jihadists like Belmokhtar. There are important differences between al Shabab, Boko Haram, al Qa'ida in the Islamic Maghreb, ISIS, and the jihadist groups in Libya, Tunisia, and Egypt, as well as rifts within these groups themselves. Their allegiances can also be very fluid – a pattern that would be replicated when they occupied northern Mali. Their relationship with "core" al Qa'ida leaders such as Ayman al Zawahiri is tenuous at best. Although al Qa'ida and ISIS have both sent emissaries to liaise with the African groups and Bin Laden often advised the Africans on strategy, leaders like Zawahiri have limited influence over what the Africans do. The emergence of ISIS as a regional and global competitor to al Qa'ida further complicates the picture. To date, African terrorist groups have targeted their own countrymen far more avidly than they do Westerners. Even if they share a common hatred for democracy and Western civilization, they have not been very successful in attacking targets in Europe, let alone the United States.

Nevertheless, if the currents are diverse, they are growing stronger and in some cases cooperating more and more. There is an unpredictability about them that is unnerving, especially when viewed in light of the startlingly rapid transformation of rump al Qa'ida in Iraq into the malignant growth that is ISIS. Even as these groups splinter and morph into a miasma of varying shades of ill and lethality, it is impossible not to acknowledge a serious security challenge that should and does concern Western capitals. Access to cell phones, computers, and especially the Internet, and the phenomenon of increasing movement of would-be jihadists across and between continents, mean that the trajectory and violent potential of even small groups cannot be ignored.

Moreover, African jihadists are catalyzing the spread of vitriol and violence across one of the poorest and most fragile parts of the world (see Figure 1). They are unquestionably a real menace to regional security, and if left unchecked, the problem could metastasize, threatening the United States and France in particular. Without an effective international strategy, it is not unthinkable that North and West Africa could eventually rival the Middle East as a center of global jihad.

Understanding what France has and has not done in the region so far is an essential part of planning for the road ahead. *Serval* was only the beginning of what will need to be a long-term strategy to address a tangled security threat likely to persist for years. Eighteen months after the initial intervention, France transitioned to a new operation, *Barkhane*, that kept 3,000 troops on semipermanent bases across Mauritania, Mali, Burkina Faso, Niger, and Chad specifically for counterterrorism operations. France and its allies also launched a new program to train local security services in the hope that they will eventually be able to combat Salafi jihadist groups themselves. It will be a long haul.

THE MOST INTERVENTIONIST COUNTRY IN THE WORLD?

Secretary Panetta was not the only one surprised by France's decision to intervene in Mali. In 2013 there were many signs that France would be unfavorable to military action. The French-backed aerial intervention that helped topple Muammar Qaddafi in 2011, was increasingly drawing fire as postwar Libya fell apart and then spiraled downward into anarchy. Hollande's mercurial predecessor, Nicolas Sarkozy, had sent highly capable French forces to fight in Afghanistan's dangerous eastern province of Kapisa in 2008, but four years later, facing a tough reelection campaign and low and declining public support for the mission, had withdrawn them despite protests from the United States, Britain, and other allies. Before that, French leaders, had of course been some of the most vociferous opponents of the U.S.-led Iraq war. In 2013, a French intervention in Mali seemed even more unlikely given the campaign promises Hollande had made to avoid a return to France's neocolonial role in Africa – often referred to pejoratively as *Françafrique*. Indeed, the Socialist Hollande was widely expected to make deep cuts to the French defense budget in response to the strain of the European financial crisis. Just a few months before France sent forces in, as Mali was falling apart, most French officials thought an intervention impossible. "To send in the French Army?

No one wants that. *Françafrique* is over!" said one senior official, for example.[14] As in so many other NATO capitals, the mantra in Paris was, "no boots on the ground."

It is thus no surprise Secretary Panetta was caught off guard by the news that French forces were already in action in Mali. But France halted speculation that the days of European military intervention had ended in the Hindu Kush. Over the course of the next several months, French forces would surge north into Mali's vast desert expanses, drive the jihadists back, hammer their northern base along the Algerian border, kill hundreds of them, and splinter them into neighboring countries.

Coming at the time when the United States and Great Britain, not to mention most continental European countries, were recoiling from the possibility of intervention anywhere, France's willingness to intervene, first in Libya and then in Mali, suggested that France was different. When Hollande backed military strikes against Syria later that year, despite U.S. and U.K. reversals on the issue, and then intervened again in the Central African Republic, articles dubbing France "the most interventionist country in the world" rolled off the presses.[15] Two very different French presidencies, one socialist, one conservative, had chosen to risk French lives in North Africa, and, for the most part, the French public supported these interventions. Not even a decade since French President Jacques Chirac broke with the United States and Britain over the invasion of Iraq, it looked like France was going through a neoconservative moment, ready to use its military to promote not only its security interests, but also democracy and human rights.

That France was the most interventionist country in the world may have been an exaggeration, but historically, France has been no more timid to intervene militarily than any other major power. The intervention in Mali was one in a long history of French military interventions in Africa and elsewhere in the world. (Table 1 shows post–Cold War French interventions in which more than 500 troops were involved.) Complex and deep historical forces pulled France toward military action in Mali. Several other factors also drove the French to intervene, including recent terrorist attacks in France, a perception of U.S. retrenchment from Europe, and the fact that because France had

Table 1. Major post–Cold War French military and peacekeeping deployments, by peak force levels and year

Intervention location	Mission(s)/Operation(s)	Peak Force Level	Peak Force Year
Cambodia	UNTAC	1,400	1991
Croatia	UNPROFOR I & SFOR	2,900	1991
Iraq	Operation Desert Storm, Operation Desert Shield, Operation Salamandre, Operation Daguet	15,200	1991
Somalia	UNOSOM, Operation Restore Hope	1,100	1992
Adriatic Sea	Operation Sharp Guard (NATO)	3,200	1993
Rwanda	UNAMIR, Operation Turquoise, Operation Amaryllis, & Operation Noroit	3,000	1994
Bosnia	UNPROFOR II, UNMIBH, IFOR, SFOR, SFOR II, EUFOR II, Operation Althea, Operation Astree	7,500	1995
Albania	Operation Alba (Italian led)	1,000	1996
Kosovo (Yugoslavia/ Serbia & Montenegro)	KFOR & Operation Joint Guardian	5,100	2000
Cote d'Ivoire	Operation Licorne & UNOCI	3,900	2002
DRCongo	Operation Artemis (EU)	900	2003
	EUFOR Congo	500	2006
Chad	Operation Epervier, EUFOR Tchad/RCA, & MINURCAT	1,500	2007
Lebanon	UNIFIL I, UNIFIL II, Operation Baliste	2,200	2008
Afghanistan	ISAF/NATO, Operation Enduring Freedom, Operation Pamir, Operation Herakles, Operation Epidote, Operation Ares	3,900	2011

Location	Operation(s)		Year
Libya	Operation Harmattan; Operation Unified Protector (NATO)	Air power	2011
Gulf of Aden	Operation Atalanta (EU)	Naval power	2012
Mali	Operation Serval	4,000	2013
Central African Republic	Operation Sangaris, Operation Boali, MINURCA, MINURCAT, & EUFOR Tchad/RCA	2,000	2014

Source(s):

1) IISS, *The Military Balance*, multiple years: 1991, p. 58; 1992, pp. 43–44; 1993, pp. 44–45; 1994, pp. 48–49; 1995, pp. 47–48; 1996, p. 55; 1997, p. 53; 1998, pp. 52–53; 1999, pp. 55–56; 2000, pp. 60–61; 2001, pp. 55–56; 2002, pp. 41–42; 2003, pp. 41–42; 2004, pp. 50–51; 2005, pp. 65–66; 2006, pp. 73–74; 2007, pp. 114–116; 2008, pp. 122–124; 2009, pp. 122–124; 2010, pp. 132–134; 2011, pp. 108–109; 2012, pp. 115–116; 2013, pp. 136–137; 2014, pp. 67, 98–99.
2) French Ministry of Defense, "Sanagaris: Situation Update of Thursday, 15 May".
3) French Ministry of Defense, "Operation Serval: update on 4 February 2013".
4) Shaun Gregory, "The French Military in Africa: Past and Present," African Affairs, Vol. 99, No. 396, July 2000, pp. 439–440.
5) James Dobbins, Seth G. Jones, Keith Crane, Christopher S. Chivvis, Andrew Radin, F. Stephen Larrabee, Nora Bensahel, Brooke Stearns Lawson and Benjamin W. Goldsmith, *Europe's Role in Nation-Building: From the Balkans to the Congo*, Santa Monica, CA: RAND Corporation, MG-722-RC, 2008, pp. 112–113.
6) James F. Miskel and Richard J. Norton, "The Intervention in the Democratic Republic of Congo," *CivilWars*, Vol. 6, No. 4, Winter 2003, p. 8.
7) French Delegation to the EU Political and Security Committee, *Brief Guide to European Security and Defense Policy (ESDP)*, December 2005, p. 32.
8) William J. Taylor Jr and James Blackwell, "The Ground War in the Gulf," *Survival*, Vol. 33 No. 3, 1991, pp. 230–245.
9) Joseph P. Englehardt, "Desert Shield and Desert Storm: A Chronology and Troop List for the 1990–1991 Persian Gulf Crisis," Strategic Studies Institute, U.S. Army War College, Carlisle, PA, March 25, 1991.
10) Michael Clodfelter, *Warfare and Armed Conflicts: A Statistical Reference to Casualty and Other Figures, 1500–2000*, second edition, Jefferson, NC: McFarland & Company, Inc., 2002, p. 656.

opted out of the Iraq war, public fatigue with overseas operations was also much less than in the United States and Britain.

After Mali, France was poised to continue to play a key role in African security. That role now seems likely to include further interventions against al Qa'ida and similar groups, provided the French can muster the necessary resources and sustain public confidence. The Mali intervention showed that even if France may no longer be the great power it once was on the global stage, it remains a major power not only in Europe, but also in Europe's neighboring regions, which continue to demand international attention and can use French help.

FRENCH COUNTERINSURGENCY STRATEGY IN MALI

The most important reason for studying French strategy in Mali is that it worked fairly well. As the conclusions to this book detail, France certainly did not solve in a fell swoop the challenge posed by Salafi jihadist groups in North Africa. Mali remains very unstable, and problems there will persist. French operations did, however, strike a major blow to groups they targeted, including al Qa'ida's regional affiliate and its allies. *Serval* prevented these groups from terrorizing Bamako and chased most of them from the country, killing hundreds and at least one important leader – a significant blow. In doing so, French forces denied the jihadists a safe haven from which to organize, plan further attacks, extend their links with other African terrorist groups, and enrich themselves from smuggling. This accomplishment was all the more important given the investment the jihadists had made in setting up the safe haven in the first place. The French thus returned Mali to its territorial integrity, thereby permitting national elections, themselves a necessary precursor for progress on other much-needed reconstruction tasks. They managed to do this while also avoiding the local and international backlash the United States faced after its 2003 invasion of Iraq.

French strategy relied on all branches of the French military and included precision strike, small special forces teams, conventional ground forces, and naval assets. The fact that the French were positioned and willing to move quickly into combat and attack with audacity greatly contributed to their initial success. As French aircraft and special forces struck behind enemy lines in the early days of the operation, French ground troops sped to Bamako, and then turned quickly into the vast reaches of northern Mali. As special forces hopscotched across the jihadist held areas, pushing them out, the conventional forces moved in to consolidate the French hold, in some cases clearing the enemy out themselves.

Meanwhile, the French pushed for immediate relief from an international force. A UN mission began deploying within weeks after the French landed on the ground. Although it was not without weaknesses, some serious, the presence of a larger UN force allowed the French to begin drawing down in order to focus on counterterrorism operations against the more diffuse regional threat that emerged in the wake of their intervention. A French force of 1,600 was still deployed in Mali as part of the operation a year and half after it had begun, but France was relieved of some of the burden it had been carrying and many of the financial, political, and other risks that can come with long-term, large-scale ground force deployments.

The French accomplished all this with 4,500 troops, within eighteen months. Only eight soldiers were killed, and the price tag for 2013 was 647 million euros.[16] For a summary at how this compares with the resources devoured by the Iraq and Afghanistan wars, see Table 2.

The French succeeded with a relatively small force in part because they enjoyed several natural advantages. They were familiar with the territory, and jihadist support among the local population was limited. The French were careful to preserve that advantage. Although the jihadists were vicious and numerous enough to scare off the Malian Army, their ranks were far smaller than those of the Taliban, al Qa'ida in Iraq, ISIS, or other recent U.S. foes. They were also much less well armed than the French initially expected and, in comparison with insurgents in some other parts of the world, lacked the benefit of a dense jungle canopy to hide their movements and cover their operations. They moreover made a number of critical strategic errors that greatly helped the French, most of all when they massed their forces in the open and headed for Bamako, exposing themselves to French airstrikes and justifying the French intervention in the eyes of the international community.

Table 2. Comparative force levels and cost: Afghanistan, Iraq, & Mali

	Peak Total International Troop Strength	Population[a]	Peak Force to Population Ratio (Troops per 1,000)	Total Cost
Afghanistan	142,400[b] (May 2011)	29,105,480 (2011)	4.9	$745 billion (through FY2014 request)[c]
Iraq	182,700[d] (October 2007)	28,740,630 (2007)	6.4	$823 billion (through FY2012 request)[e]
Mali	10,800[f] (4,500 French) (2013)	15,301,650 (2013)	0.7	$876 million[g] (2013 only)
Libya	8,000[h] (2011)	6,103,233 (2011)	n/a	$3.1 billion[i] (2011 only)

Sources:

a) Population data from: World Bank, World Development Indicators 2014. Available at: http://data.worldbank.org

b) O'Hanlon, Michael and Ian Livingston, "Afghanistan Index," Brookings Institution, May 14, 2014. Available at: http://www.brookings.edu/~/media/Programs/foreign%20policy/afghanistan%20index/index20140514.pdf

c) The sum of $744.6 billion through the FY2014 request includes $707 billion for the Defense Department and $37.4 billion for the State Department and USAID. O'Hanlon, Michael and Ian Livingston, "Afghanistan Index," Brookings Institution, May 14, 2014. Available at: http://www.brookings.edu/~/media/Programs/foreign%20policy/afghanistan%20index/index20140514.pdf

d) O'Hanlon, Michael and Ian Livingston, "Iraq Index: Tracking Variables of Reconstruction & Security in Iraq," Brookings Institution, January 31, 2011. Available at: http://www.brookings.edu/~/media/Centers/saban/iraq%20index/index20130726.pdf

e) The sum of $823.2 billion through the FY2012 request includes $768.8 billion for the Defense Department and $54.8 billion for the State Department, USAID, and Veterans Affairs. O'Hanlon, Michael and Ian Livingston, "Iraq Index: Tracking Variables of Reconstruction & Security in Iraq," Brookings Institution, January 31, 2011. Available at: http://www.brookings.edu/~/media/Centers/saban/iraq%20index/index20130726.pdf

f) Includes approximately 4,500 French troops under "Operation Serval" and approximately 6,300 African troops under the banner of ECOWAS' "Africa-led International Support Mission in Mali (AFISMA)" as well as Chadian forces. See, for instance: French Ministry of Defence, "Serval: Situation Update on Operations, Monday, 18 March," press release updated on 3/20/2013, as well as French Ministry of Defence, "Serval: Situation Update on Operations, 29 March," press release updated on 4/3/2013, available at: http://www.defense.gouv.fr/english/portail-defense/une-histoirisee

g) Jean-Dominique Merchet, "Le Mali coutera 647 million d'euros cette année," *l'Opinion*, October 13, 2013.

h) (no ground forces) NATO, "Operation UNIFIED PROTECTOR: Final Mission Statistics," factsheet, November 2, 2011, available at: http://www .nato.int/nato_static_fl2014/assets/pdf/pdf_2011_11/20111108_111107-factsheet_up_factsfigures_en.pdf

i) This figure represents an estimate and should be treated as a conservative figure. Obtaining a reliable estimate for total costs of foreign contributions to the 2011 war in Libya is exceedingly difficult because each partner nation individually paid the costs incurred by their deployed forces as part of Operation Unified Protector. This aggregated estimate of $3.1 billion includes only the cost of operations by the major contributing nations. It excludes smaller costs incurred by Belgium, Bulgaria, Greece, the Netherlands, Norway, Qatar, Romania, Spain, Sweden, Turkey, and the UAE. Conversion rates have been generated by the "Oanda Currency Converter" using the mission end date of October 31, 2011. Costs incurred to major partners include:

United States: $1.1 billion. Note that this total does not include costs incurred by the U.S. State Department and U.S. intelligence communities. Vice President Joe Biden has stated that the cost to the United States was $2 billion. See: Garamone, Jim, "Obama: Gadhafi's Death Marks End of Painful Era for Libya," U.S. Department of Defense News Article, October 20, 2011, available at: http://www.defense.gov/News/NewsArticle .aspx?ID=65737.

United Kingdom: $516 million (or £320 million, including cost of munitions replacements). See: Berman, Gavin, "The Cost of International Military Operations," UK House of Commons Library, July 5, 2012, p. 9.

France: $520 million (or 368 million euros). See: Svitak, Amy, "The Cost of Operation *Serval*," Aviation Week, April 26, 2013.

Canada: $350 million (or $347 million Canadian dollars). See: "Libya Mission's Final Costs Reach $347M," CBC News, May 11, 2012.

Italy: $283 million (or $200 million euros). See: "Italy Removes Aircraft Carrier from Libya Campaign," Defense News, July 7, 2011.

Denmark: $110 million. See: "Denmark's Contribution to Unified Protector Cost US$110 Million," DefenceWeb, January 17, 2012.

NATO AWACS: $61 million (or 43.4 million euros; this figure is based on NATO's operational cost estimate of 6.2 million euros/month, multiplied by approximately 7 months of deployed forces). See: NATO, "Operation UNIFIED PROTECTOR: Final Mission Statistics," factsheet, November 2, 2011.

These factors made the operation easier. But French strategy was also important to success. First, the French were willing to move quickly and take on considerable risks, especially with regard to their logistical chains, which spun out far across the desert, risking enemy ambushes. The speed of the French advance was facilitated by the relative weakness of the jihadists, but it was also possible because France had forces pre-positioned in the region that it was willing to divert quickly and on the fly in order to surprise the enemy and throw it back on its heels. Especially at the outset of operations, such improvization was important to French success.

Second, no less important than speed and risk, the French worked hard to put into place an international stabilization force as quickly as possible so that they could draw down and focus elsewhere. In 2001, U.S. forces used a similar lightning-fast strategy to intervene with equally stunning success against al Qa'ida and its Taliban protectors in Afghanistan. Unlike the French, however, the United States withdrew soon after chasing al Qa'ida across the border into Pakistan, leaving behind only a small international stabilization force in Kabul. Likewise, in 2003, U.S. forces intervened in Iraq and quickly overthrew Saddam Hussein, but then failed to get control of security and were forced into a costly and protracted counterinsurgency campaign. In 2011 in Libya, NATO forces helped rebels topple Muammar Qaddafi, but offered no post-conflict stabilization or peacekeeping forces, greatly contributing to the country's spiral downward into anarchy.

In contrast, in Mali, the French were careful to leave behind an international stabilization force to reduce the chances that a new insurgency would break out and their initial gains be wiped away. The UN force allowed the French to shift focus elsewhere and reduced the chances of their troops becoming mired in a long and bloody counterinsurgency operation.

The UN force has functioned far from perfectly, and Mali still has many troubles and challenges. It remains an extremely poor country, with weak democratic institutions. Moreover, the original ethno-regional conflict that enabled al Qa'ida to infiltrate the North has yet to be resolved, to the frustration of a great many foreign observers.

Yet the gains made by *Serval* were unquestionably a critical step in the right direction. Provided that all-out war does not return – and against this there can be no guarantees – what the French did should be remembered as a key step toward stabilizing this fragile region and reducing the danger posed by the spread of Salafi jihadist groups across it.

After the wars in Iraq and Afghanistan, the United States increasingly drew into introspection reminiscent of the post-Vietnam decade. Both public support and available resources for intervention were poised to decline from the record levels they reached in the years immediately following the 9/11 attacks. For three years, the lack of public support for any U.S. military role in bringing the tragic civil war in Syria to an end made this clear. Honest reflection on the lessons of the American experience in Iraq and Afghanistan is sorely needed, and public reticence about the use of force is a sign of a healthy democracy. But this does not change the fact that the complex crises of today's world will continue to call for complex solutions – solutions that will often require the application of military power. While America must seek to avoid the mistakes of the past, it cannot simultaneously defend its values and interests and eschew the use of force on all occasions. The continued challenge of globalization, weapons proliferation, virulent jihadist ideologies, and social and political upheaval in Africa, the Middle East, and elsewhere will simply not permit a strict policy of nonintervention. President Obama's belated decision to take action against ISIS in Syria in the fall of 2014 makes this clear. Learning how to calibrate the use of force to the threats and crises of the future is a major challenge – one that may require a shift in the attitude that U.S. military and national security experts take toward the use of force and especially its role in the broader political processes that are shaping the global security environment. Limited war should not mean under-resourcing operations so that they fall short of key objectives. But the French experience in Mali clearly shows that not all successful interventions need involve the force levels the United States reached in Iraq and Afghanistan. Again, success in Mali was possible at lower levels, in large part because the challenge was less than in Iraq and Afghanistan, but it was still success. Under some conditions smaller-scale military power can thus be effective in furthering broader political and security objectives.

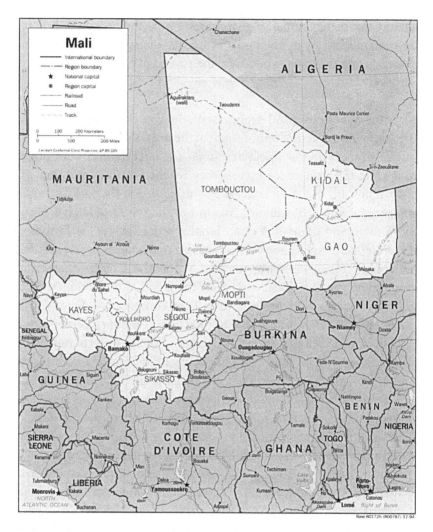

Figure 2. Mali.
Source: U.S. Central Intelligence Agency.

The in-depth study of past cases is critical to understanding the limits and possibilities of future applications of military force because it allows us to put operations in a broader political and military context. It also provides a basis for recognizing when an emerging new crisis that bears similarities to a past case may actually be quite different; the greatest benefit of understanding past cases may in fact be to counter poor historical analogies and the misguided policies they can encourage.[17] Recent cases are in many ways the most important in this regard. But studying them immediately presents challenges of documentation, perspective, and judgment. Interventions that look like successes at the start – Afghanistan and Iraq, for example – can quickly turn sour if policy missteps are made – and sometimes even if they are not.

The following account speculates on but does not draw conclusions about French success in achieving long-term strategic goals. It does, however, demonstrate how and why the French were able to achieve their operational goals with relatively limited resources. Chapter 2 explains the growth of al Qa'ida in the Islamic Maghreb in the years prior to the French intervention. Chapter 3 examines the French and U.S. response to the threat in the period between 2007 and 2011. Chapter 4 explains how Mali collapsed in 2012, while Chapter 5 examines the initial French policy response. Chapter 6 looks at the French decision to intervene and the first military operations. Chapter 7 examines in depth how operations played out. Chapter 8 surveys what happened after the initial intervention. Chapter 9 draws conclusions, assessing the degree of success the French had, its implications for other interventions against Salafi jihadist groups, in Africa and beyond, and the needs for the future.

2 AL QA'IDA'S NORTH AFRICAN FRANCHISE

On April 30, 2011, a U.S. Navy SEAL team killed Osama Bin Laden in his compound in Abbottabad, Pakistan. The death of America's number-one enemy of more than a decade was lauded by many as the end of an era, which it was. Seasoned analysts, however, pointed out that while Bin Laden's death was a serious blow to core al Qa'ida, it was not a death knell for the organization as a whole. In recent years, al Qa'ida had evolved and grown increasingly diffuse and disaggregated through franchise operations, pursuing what former U.S. Director of National Intelligence John Negroponte described as a "mergers and acquisition strategy" aimed at "acquiring" Salafi jihadist groups across South Asia, the Middle East, and Africa.[1] With affiliates in Yemen, Iraq, and Somalia, al Qa'ida in the Islamic Maghreb was one of the key groups that Bin Laden and his deputies had worked to bring into the fold.

AL QA'IDA'S ALLURE

Al Qa'ida's North African franchise was born out of Algeria's bloody civil war of the 1990s. In 1998, after several years of gruesome violence, some of the Islamists waging war against the secular Algerian government left the mainstream Armed Islamic Group to found a group known as the Salafist Group for Preaching and Jihad. Although the Algerian civil war was by then in its final stages, the Salafist Group for Preaching and Jihad survived and continued to resist what it considered the illegitimate apostates ruling in the capital, Algiers.[2]

The group was initially headed by a man named Hassan Hattab. From his perch in the Kabylie mountains along the Mediterranean coast to the east of the Algerian capital, Hattab organized attacks against government buildings in Algiers and elsewhere in the name of restoring a purely Islamic government. His efforts found little support among a population that had grown weary of violence after a decade of civil war, however, and ended up having limited overall impact.

Others in the group soon began to look to Bin Laden's movement for support and inspiration. In the post–9/11 world, alignment with al Qa'ida offered the possibility of regeneration through broader attention, recognition, and legitimacy. One of the Algerian group's central figures at the time, Abdelmalek "el-Para," was viewed by some Westerners as a possible North African Bin Laden.[3] According to testimony given by Belmokhtar's one-time public relations officer, Ghrika Noureddine, before a criminal tribunal in Algiers, Hattab organized for emissaries from Bin Laden to visit the southern emir as early as 2001.[4]

Hattab, however, eventually came to the conclusion that a strong link with al Qa'ida might distract the group from its core mission, which lay in Algeria.[5] He may also have been more inclined toward eventual negotiation with the government than some of his more hardcore brothers-in-arms. In 2003, however in large part as a result of his resistance to the idea, Hattab was ousted.

Under the new leadership of Nabil Sahrawi, the group increasingly gravitated toward al Qa'ida. When Sahrawi was killed by Algerian security services in 2004, he was succeeded by Abdelmalek Droukdal, who shared his enthusiasm for closer ties to Bin Laden. Born in 1970 in the town of Maftah near Algiers, Droukdal joined the radical Algerian Islamist movement in 1993. He holds a degree in chemistry from the University of Blida, a background that made him more useful as a bomb maker and back-room figure than front-line fighter in the 1990s. This in turn likely increased his chances of his survival and encouraged his promotion through the ranks.[6] Droukdal was a long-time enthusiast for a closer relationship with al Qa'ida and eagerly continued the course that Sahrawi had begun. Negotiations over a possible alliance began at least as early as 2005, when one of Droukdal's henchmen solicited the support of al Qa'ida in Iraq, then reaching the height of its violence against U.S. forces there. Negotiations over closer ties between the two groups continued through much of 2005 and 2006.[7]

A formal link with Bin Laden's organization was by no means fore-ordained or automatic, however. Bin Laden needed not only to verify the piety of the postulant organization, he also needed to be sure that it had not been infiltrated by the Algerian secret service.[8] Moreover, there were other groups in the region that al Qa'ida could have chosen to carry his torch. The Libyan Islamic Fighting Group, for example, already had close ties with al Qa'ida, and there was also the Moroccan Islamic Fighting Group and the Tunisian Islamic Fighting Group.

Droukdal's group, however, had demonstrated its ability not only to attack Western targets in the region, but also to expand its reach beyond Algeria with attacks, for example, in Mauritania in 2005.[9] In 2006, on the fifth anniversary of the 9/11 attacks, Ayman al Zawahiri, Bin Laden's deputy, announced an alliance between the two move-ments. "This blessed union will be a bone in the throat of the American and French crusaders ... and will bring fear to the hearts of the miscre-ant sons of France," he said.[10]

Two days later, Zawahiri's announcement was confirmed by Droukdal, who expressed, "full confidence in the faith, the doctrine, the method and the modes of action of [al Qa'ida's] members, as well as their leaders and religious guides."[11] In January 2007, Droukdal proclaimed that, after consultation with Bin Laden, the group had offi-cially changed their name: "by joining the Salafist Group for Call and Combat in Algeria to al Qa'ida Organization for Jihad, and after pledg-ing to the lion of Islam in this time, Sheikh Usama bin Laden, may Allah protect from all harm and bad, the old name must be changed. The "Salafist Group for Call and Combat" will be replaced by a new name that will give an impression of the unity and strength in the alli-ance, and the sincerity of the link between the Mujahideen in Algeria and their other brothers in al Qa'ida Organization."[12] The new name was al Qa'ida in the Islamic Maghreb.

Over the course of the next year, al Qa'ida's new affiliate carried out a series of violent attacks against the Algerian government and foreign targets in Algiers. On April 11, 2007 three simultaneous sui-cide car bombings shook the Algerian capital. The explosions hit the government palace and two security stations. Thirty-three people were killed, and more than 200 were wounded. Al Qa'ida hailed the attacks as the beginning of its jihad in the Maghreb, the "Badr of Maghrib" in reference to the Prophet Mohammed's own first battle.[13] On December 11, another coordinated attack struck the Algerian Constitutional Court and Headquarters of the United Nations – a symbol of al Qa'ida's grievances.[14] Forty-one people were killed in the attacks and many more were wounded.

Previously, suicide bombings had been a rare occurrence in Algeria, but in 2007 and 2008 there were sixteen such attacks. Other attacks that first year also involved cell-phone detonated bombs in emulation of recent attacks by al Qa'ida in Iraq. The techniques and targets demonstrated more ambition and greater skill in the most lethal of terrorist methods. Droukdal's decision to ally with al Qa'ida was more than just a name change. The link with core al Qa'ida had made the Algerians demonstrably more lethal and a much more serious threat to civilians in Algeria as well as in France and Europe in general.

In addition to changing tactics, the geographical remit of Droukdal's attacks would also grow. From 2001 to 2006, the vast majority of these attacks were on targets in Algiers and its immediate environs, with only a few outside Algeria at all (Figure 3). Over the next five years, however, the group not only intensified attacks in Algiers, it also managed far more attacks in southern Algeria, Mauritania, Mali, Niger, and Tunisia.

Droukdal was meanwhile quick to express his admiration for al Qa'ida in Iraq's leader, Abu Musab al Zarqawi and fashioned himself on core al Qa'ida's number two, Ayman Zawahiri. Algerians meanwhile travelled to Iraq to join in al Qa'ida suicide attacks on U.S. forces, likely with Droukdal's support and facilitation.[15]

Droukdal also followed al Qa'ida leadership's exhortation to take advantage of modern media to expand his reach and message more broadly in the region. Working through an official media outlet, *Al-Andalus*, Droukdal sought a more public profile, disseminating videos and other propaganda more widely on the Internet, including, for example, a bloodcurdling video in which his soldiers butchered an Algerian gendarme. In keeping with al Qa'ida in Iraq's methods, jihadist commanders were required to film their attacks for future study and

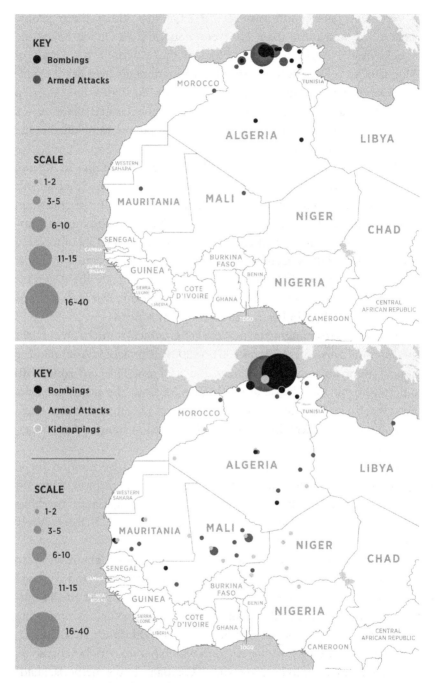

Figure 3. Growth of AQIM Attacks (2001–2006 vs. 2007–2012).
Source: Christopher S. Chivvis and Andrew Liepman, *North Africa's Menace*, Santa Monica: RAND, 2013.

dissemination. The distribution of video footage of successful attacks soon became a central part of their recruitment strategy.[16]

In keeping with the anticolonialism inherent in modern Algeria's political culture, Droukdal also singled out France as "Islam's enemy number one." As one scholar explained, jihadism has long been linked to the Algerian anticolonial movement: "Since 'Abd al Qadir's resistance movement against the French colonization of Algeria in 1832–1847 and Imam Shamil's guerrilla war against Russian expansion into the Caucasus in 1834–1859, popular jihad has become the Islamic version of the anti-colonial struggle."[17] Hence his promise that the link with al Qa'ida would be directed specifically against France, a promise that he would repeat at regular intervals over time. Droukdal would even seek to exaggerate the number of French citizens he killed, in an effort, no doubt, to lend credence to his claim to the leadership of al Qa'ida in North Africa.[18]

The birth of al Qa'ida's North African branch was and would remain a serious security problem for the region, for France, and, by extension, for the United States. Yet the nature of the bond between Droukdal and his new partners holed up in Pakistan was complex and could be (and would be) easily misrepresented as one in which the two groups shared identical objectives, with Bin Laden exercising strict command and control over Droukdal's operations. Instead, the bond was more one of fealty or alliance. Droukdal appears to have taken the al Qa'ida moniker in part to boost his own prestige, attract foot soldiers to his cause, and make his group look more intimidating. Alliance with Bin Laden also offered a doctrinal point of reference and means of sorting out differences within al Qa'ida in the Islamic Maghreb itself. For his part, Bin Laden gained funding and public relations boost from the deal. He clearly saw the Algerians as a means of achieving his objective of expanding in Africa, and almost certainly also viewed the alliance as an opportunity to increase the threat to the United States and other Western countries, put pressure on them to withdraw from Afghanistan, and force them to stretch their counterterrorism resources more thinly around the world. Moreover, the Algerian group had good ties to European Islamist networks including sympathizers beyond France, in Germany, Spain, and the United Kingdom. These northern links could prove quite useful in organizing future attacks against European targets.[19]

Bin Laden approached Droukdal somewhat differently than other important al Qa'ida franchises, in general, giving lower priority to the relationship than that with al Qa'ida in Iraq, which at the time was under duress due to the Anbar Awakening. Moreover, if Droukdal's worldview was akin to core al Qa'ida's and the interests of the groups clearly overlapped, there is no evidence that Droukdal ever took direct orders from al Qa'ida leadership in Pakistan. At the outset, Droukdal clearly sought an alliance with Bin Laden's group, and the leadership of the two groups communicated regularly, both publicly and privately. Bin Laden sought to advise Droukdal on how to coordinate his efforts with other groups in Africa, made recommendations on the timing of the release of hostages, and requested funding from his new franchise – in one missive, he even recommended his Maghrebian brethren plant trees so that they might better conceal themselves from foreign attack. How much Droukdal felt compelled to obey Bin Laden or Zawahiri's instructions, however, is less clear. Excommunication from the world's number one jihadist club would surely have hurt the Algerian jihadist cause, but as time wore on, and pressure on core al Qa'ida grew, Bin Laden arguably needed the support of the Algerians as much as they needed him.

Additionally, it remains unclear to what extent Droukdal fully bought into Bin Laden's strategies and in particular the exhortation to attack the "far-enemy" at its heart in Western capitals. Although its Algerian relative, the Armed Islamic Group, was responsible for murderous attack on the Paris subway in 1995, al Qa'ida in the Islamic Maghreb never managed a successful attack against a target in France, let alone against an American one. There is no question the movement has sympathizers in France and elsewhere in Europe and a number of attempted attacks have been reported, but how closely they were linked to Droukdal remains uncertain. Indeed, despite the rhetoric, Droukdal's actions suggest that he was less preoccupied with making his foreign foes suffer than with waging war against his local enemies from the 1990s – the apostates in power in Algiers. Droukdal would likely have been pleased had an easy way to harm France presented itself, but the extant evidence suggests that he has been less focused on attacking what Bin Laden called "the far enemy," and more focused on a local path to the caliphate.

Nevertheless, the expansion of the al Qa'ida franchise into North Africa was and remains a perilous security threat to the region, one with potential to become a truly serious threat to Europe and America. The inroads made by ISIS in Libya over the course of late 2014 are a challenge to Droukdal insofar as ISIS recruits from a similar base, and if the two groups come to blows in Libya, Mali, or elsewhere. But over-all the concatenation of ISIS and al Qa'ida in the Islamic Maghreb only makes the regional security problem much worse. Both groups seek to target Western diplomats, aid workers, and businessmen in addition to the local population. If they cooperate, their capabilities will grow. If they compete, it may be through attempts at high-profile attacks against both local and Western civilians. ISIS's expansion across Iraq and Syria in 2014 demonstrated how quickly and unexpectedly such groups can gain momentum and attract fighters and other support from abroad, including Europe and America. If North Africa's jihadist groups offer safe-haven and combat opportunities for willing outsid-ers, a similar phenomenon is bound to emerge in North Africa, posing a similar threat to the West.

SMUGGLING AND LEADERSHIP FEUDS

Over the years, al Qa'ida in the Islamic Maghreb's leadership built a fairly elaborate organizational structure to run its operations.[20] At the top of the structure, there is a sixteen-member leadership council, a council of dignitaries, and several executive councils, each respon-sible for specific tasks such as communications, finance, or military affairs.[21] Their area of operations is divided administratively into four regions: central, east, west, and south. In theory, a regional *emir*, reporting to Droukdal, oversees the *katibas* of the region, although politics can sometimes blur strict organizational lines. Smaller *katibas* are sometimes referred to as *saraya* (sing. *sariya*).

The central and southern regions are by far the most important. The central region covers Algiers and the leadership's safe haven in the Kabylie mountains to the east, and the southern region includes the whole of southern Algeria and the Sahara. The central region has had as many as eight *katiba* in operation at any one time, while the southern region has had as many as four.

The *katiba* themselves are made up of several small units organized around individual vehicles, usually pickup trucks with guns mounted on the back. These vehicles, normally called "technicals," serve as the military unit of choice in conflicts across Africa. A typical *katiba* might include six or more technicals and as many as 100 fighters, with the emir's vehicle bearing a prestige weapon, such as a rocket launcher.[22]

In the years following the attacks on the World Trade Towers and Pentagon, U.S. and allied counterterrorism pressure on jihadist groups increased in the region. In Algeria, the extremely aggressive and capable Algerian military and security services, in cooperation with the United States and other countries, intensified counterterrorist operations. This forced Droukdal to look beyond Algeria proper into the thinly populated Sahara Desert, which sprawls across no less than eight predominantly Muslim states. There, the Algerian jihadists could move with less concern of being tracked or captured by regional powers, most of which lacked the resources and often interest in patrolling this vast expanse and its borders. For years, jihadists troops buried food, medicine, weapons, and other supplies across the desert, creating a logistical network that could support their activities in this most inhospitable land.

Al Qa'ida in the Islamic Maghreb's expansion into the Sahel also promised new sources of revenue. The region is a major conduit for illegal trafficking of all sorts, within the region and from other parts of the world to Europe. Regional drug smuggling along the ancient, sinuous routes of the Sahara increased significantly since the 1990s, as South American smuggling operations in the Caribbean came under pressure from U.S. law enforcement operations. Air, land, and sea routes via Guinea Bissau, Nigeria, Senegal, Mali, Algeria, Libya, and Morocco were estimated to be bringing as much as fifty tons of cocaine onto the European market annually by the mid-2000s.[23] Large quantities of heroin were also smuggled through the region, and seizures of cannabis headed for the Gulf and Asia more than doubled in Mali and Algeria between 2007 and 2011.[24] Cigarette smuggling was even more rampant, and human trafficking was a serious problem in Algeria, Libya, Tunisia, Mali, and Mauritania, according to the U.S. State Department.[25]

Many jihadists were unwilling to engage directly in the drug trade, so to think of them simply as drug smugglers would be a mistake.[26] Still, the control of cigarette and other trafficking routes offered ample opportunities to fill Al Qa'ida in the Islamic Maghreb's war chest, while also ensnaring many regional leaders – including Mali's – in the same web of illegal activities that made the local authorities disinclined to expend much effort rooting al Qa'ida out.

Some of the profits from the smuggling trade were sent back to Droukdal, from where portions likely made their way back to core al Qa'ida. At the time, Bin Laden and his lieutenants were seeing many of their traditional lines of financing dry up as a result of sanctions and other forms of global pressure. In contrast, the financial fortunes of their affiliate in the Maghreb were growing by the day. Cash from the Sahel became part of the glue that bound the organization to core al Qa'ida, as evidenced anecdotally by Bin Laden's later suggestion that an emissary "hint to the brothers in the Islamic Maghreb that they provide [senior al Qa'ida leader Yunis al Mauritani] with the financial support that he might need in the next six months, to the tune of approximately 200,000 euros."[27]

Not all the money, however, was making its way back to the Kabylie, much less to core al Qa'ida in Pakistan. Cooperation between Droukdal and his southern leaders was strained. Many of North Africa's jihadists, both within al Qa'ida in the Islamic Maghreb and in groups associated with it – for example in Libya – once fought together in Afghanistan against the Soviet Union. Droukdal fought with Bin Laden and other al Qa'ida leaders against the Soviet Union in Afghanistan in the late 1980s and early 1990s. So did Belmokhtar. So did the man believed to be behind the 2012 Benghazi attacks, Abu Khatalla. Experience as *mujahideen* provides both a frame of reference for their approach to jihad in Africa and serves as a foundation for their cooperation, which itself strengthens them overall. It does not, however, mean that the jihadist groups of North and West Africa march in lockstep under Droukdal's banner. Indeed, significant divisions within al Qa'ida in the

Islamic Maghreb developed in the years after its inception that made it increasingly difficult for Droukdal to maintain control of some of the more prominent *katibas* in his own organization.

At the time of the alliance with al Qa'ida, the most powerful and well known of the group's southern leaders was Mokhtar Belmokhtar. Belmokhtar had been in command of the GSPC's southern operations since the 1990s, a position he used to intermarry and bind himself to the Arab Berabiche and Tuareg Idnan tribes of the region, especially around Timbuktu.[28] He became a well-known smuggler, especially of cigarettes, and earned himself the moniker "Marlboro Man."

Belmokhtar's success with smuggling made him increasingly independent of Droukdal. Eventually it was unclear whether or not Belmokhtar's *katiba* could actually be considered part of Droukdal's organization (it would eventually split off and form another group, al Mulathamin). This created a core tension within and around these terrorist groups that would manifest itself in open fissure just before the French intervened.[29]

In part as a counter to Belmokhtar's growing independence, Droukdal appointed another former member of the Armed Islamic Group, Abdelhamid Abu Zeid, to command a second, and hopefully more loyal, southern battalion. Abu Zeid smuggled and engaged in other criminal activities just like Belmokhtar. His reputation for cold-bloodedness, even among the jihadists, was widespread. The few hostages who did meet him and live to talk about it described a calculating, cerebral man, respected by his troops, and devoted to the cause. The Frenchmen Pierre Cammette, who Abu Zeid held for three months in northern Mali, said that Abu Zeid "always spoke to me in a neutral tone, without aggression. His questions were almost technical."[30]

KIDNAPPING AS TERRORISM

In addition to the proceeds of smuggling operations, al Qa'ida in the Islamic Maghreb also made money from its kidnapping operations, which were both a lucrative and effective terrorist complement to murdering European civilians in the region.

El-Para had managed a dramatic kidnapping of thirty-two European tourists in 2003, but kidnapping of European citizens did not become a mainstay of their operations until 2009. Al Qa'ida in the Islamic Maghreb's kidnapping spree began with the capture of several European citizens in Niger early that year. Some were released, but a British citizen named Edwin Dyer was executed in June. In November the Frenchmen Pierre Camatte was captured and held for three months before his release, likely in exchange for the release of al Qa'ida prisoners.

The following spring, an aging French relief worker named Michel Germaneau was abducted in Niger and held for several months. Germaneau was sick and needed medication, but his kidnappers refused to accept its delivery. Pressure built to take action, and a joint Franco-Mauritanian operation was launched along the border between Mali and Mauritania at a site where Germaneau was believed to be held. Although several jihadists were killed in the assault, Germaneau was not found. His death – either by execution or physical exertion as the jihadists dragged him with them as they fled – was reported a few days later.

In September 2010, five French citizens and two others who worked for the French conglomerate Areva and its affiliate Satom were abducted by Abu Zeid and his henchmen from their houses in the remote Nigerian town of Arlit. Unlike the kidnapping of Dyer, which by all appearances was opportunistic, the Arlit operation was well planned and involved multiple teams tracking and then capturing the foreigners. Droukdal announced that any "negotiations over the release of the hostages should be carried out directly with the Lion of Islam, our leader Usama bin Ladin."[31] Observers speculated that the kidnappings were intended as a revenge for losses incurred in the effort to free Germaneau. In February 2011, three of the hostages were released – a French woman, Françoise Larribe, and the two non-French citizens. A generous ransom of 10–15 million euros was rumored to have clinched the deal.[32]

Meanwhile, a separate rescue effort had gone seriously wrong. On January 7, 2011, two young Frenchmen, Vincent Delory and Antoine de Léocour, were kidnapped at gunpoint from a restaurant in Niamey, the capital of Niger. The audaciousness of this particular attempt was something new. Nigerian forces, backed by French special forces teams, took quick pursuit, but failed to save the captives – Delory was burned alive when the car carrying him burst aflame from the gunfire of his would-be rescuers. Léocour was executed shortly thereafter. For the French, the tragic loss was evidence of the serious risks involved in such operations – and for some, no doubt, worked in favor of a policy favoring ransom payments over military operations to free hostages.

The kidnappings continued in November 2011, with multiple abductions within a few days of each other in Timbuktu and Hombori. Even if these kidnappings did not normally meet the gruesome "kidnapping-to-beheading" standard that would later distinguish ISIS, they deeply troubled the French public and worried many counter-terrorism experts. No less of a concern was the fact that al Qa'ida in the Islamic Maghreb appeared to be acting as a catalyst for regional terrorism, even beyond its expanding area of operations. Groups that were otherwise somewhat isolated, including Boko Haram, established ties with the Algerians. These ties promised to facilitate the spread of funding and knowledge about terrorist tactics across the continent.

The threat posed by AQIM was thus real. But, as of 2011, five years after it joined with al Qa'ida, the overall magnitude of the threat remained uncertain. After an initial burst in 2007, Droukdal had difficulty sustaining the violence, as shown in Figure 4. They clearly wanted to establish *shari'a* across the region and frequently repeated the call for France and the United States to withdraw from Afghanistan, yet it was unclear how important they thought terrorist attacks on the West were to achieving their objectives. In 2007, Droukdal's group had managed several high-visibility attacks against civilian targets. These attacks were clearly intended to make a statement and demonstrate their bona fides as an important force in al Qa'ida's growing global franchise operation. Yet, like the overall levels of violence, these types of classic terrorist attacks against civilian institutions and symbols of state power diminished subsequently as they focused more and more on kidnapping French and European citizens. In principle at least, the kidnappings could serve the purpose of putting pressure on the French to withdraw from Afghanistan, and hence served al Qa'ida's global

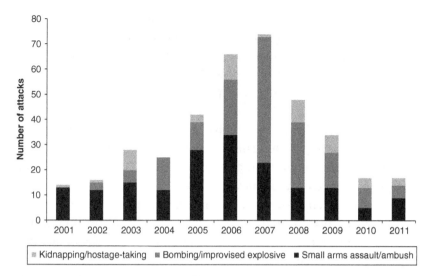

Figure 4. Evolution of AQIM and GSPC Attacks by Type, 2001–2011.
Source: START Global Terrorism Database (GTD); RAND calculations.

objectives. But it seems unlikely that Afghanistan could have been the primary concern of the North Africans. More likely, the kidnappings were intended to reduce French influence in the region, demonstrate commitment to core al Qa'ida for more self-interested reasons, and, above all, fill the group's coffers with the lucre of ransoms.

Most attacks moreover focused on military targets, often using guerilla tactics. These attacks included suicide bombings and car bombings, but they were not, strictly speaking, terrorist attacks, in that they did not target civilians. They were instead run of the mill insurgent attacks, carried out by a Salafist jihadi group that had also proven itself capable of terrorist acts. This is an important distinction that can often become obscured in public discussions about these types of threats. Much of the military gains that ISIS would later make in Iraq, Syria, and Libya fell into this same category – classic guerrilla warfare carried out by an insurgent group that also espoused a virulent anti-Western, anti-modern ideology and glorified terrorism and violence in general.

Few of the attacks in this period, moreover, appear to have been very discriminating – that is, carefully chosen to provoke a particular political or military response. This lack of discrimination parallels the loose-knit structure of the organization, although it is hard to see which drove which – in other words whether or not Droukdal would have been more discriminating if he could have kept a tighter leash on his deputies, or whether he was satisfied with the relatively diffuse set of targets chosen by his deputies, provided there was congruency with the organization's broad goals.[33] The letters discovered in Timbuktu after the French chased Belmotkhar out (see Chapter 4) suggest the former, although the latter cannot be entirely ruled out.

The tendency is to think of a group like al Qa'ida in the Islamic Maghreb as a terrorist organization, and on a certain level it clearly is. However, between 2007 and 2011, it was increasingly moving toward what more accurately might be described as a local insurgency carried out by Salafist extremists capable of terrorist acts – again, like ISIS later. Nevertheless, even if this was a loose organization with uncertain commitment to Bin Laden's global strategy of attacking the West and a declining number of overall attacks, the threat it posed to Europe was still significant in a different way: Droukdal, Belmokhtar, and their local allies were about to build what would become, in 2012, one of the world's most threatening terrorist safe havens.

3 HOSTAGES, RANSOMS, AND FRENCH SECURITY POLICY

As al Qa'ida in the Islamic Maghreb expanded its reach after 2007, France was largely focused elsewhere in the world, pulled in multiple directions between dwindling resources for defense and security and waning public support for French operations in Afghanistan. The key French national security document of the period, the 2008 White Paper on Defense and Security, depicted an "Arc of Instability" stretching from the Atlantic, across Africa, through the Middle East and into South Asia as a primary geographical zone of trouble. It deemed a major terrorist attack in France or Europe as the single biggest threat the nation faced, especially if a terrorist group managed to get its hands on a chemical, biological, or nuclear weapon of some kind. Yet, in keeping with the 2006 White Paper on Counter-Terrorism, produced by the Ministry of Interior, the 2008 paper pointed toward a counterterrorism strategy that focused primarily on national police, detection, and domestic response. Specialized military units were to intervene outside France "when needed," yet such operations fell under the least important of four possible overseas operations ("special," "medium," "significant," and "major").

Between 2008 and 2012, the French thus eschewed large-scale military intervention to counter the jihadists in the Sahel, relying instead on indirect negotiations with the jihadists and small-scale, special-operations raids undertaken jointly with West African partners. For years, indeed, up until the intervention itself, the mantra in France, as in the United States, was that Africans themselves had to take the lead against the terrorist groups. Additional French "boots on the ground" were out of the question. French leaders were looking to shrink the French military footprint in Africa, not expand it.

THE IRAQ WAR AND FRENCH VIEWS ON MILITARY INTERVENTION

History, after all, taught that there were good reasons not to rush into a military intervention. The most significant foreign policy development in transatlantic relations after the 9/11 attacks was French-led European opposition to the 2003 U.S. invasion of Iraq.[1] French opposition had been as adamant as it was vociferous. Here is French foreign minister Dominique de Villepin at the United Nations on February 14, 2003, in a sadly clairvoyant speech, delivered at the height of the fury over the imminent U.S.-led operations that would overthrow Saddam Hussein:

> [T]he option of war might seem a priori to be the swiftest. But let us not forget that after winning the war, one has to build peace. Let us not delude ourselves; this will be long and difficult because it will be necessary to preserve Iraq's unity and restore stability in a lasting way in a country and region harshly affected by the intrusion of force.... No one can assert today that the path of war will be shorter than that of the [ongoing UN] inspections. No one can claim either that it might lead to a safer, more just and more stable world. For war is always the sanction of failure.... Such intervention could have incalculable consequences for the stability of this scarred and fragile region. It would compound the sense of injustice, increase tensions and risk paving the way to other conflicts.[2]

Villepin and President Chirac's opposition to the Iraq war generated enormous support domestically and in the many parts of the world eager to vilify the Bush administration and its policies. It also caused the deepest rift in Franco-American relations since de Gaulle withdrew from NATO's military command in 1966. With his opposition to the Iraq war, Chirac aligned France not only with Germany, but also with Russia, China, and other countries that were far from American allies. The haughty views of the French leaders were matched by the populist anti-French uproar in the United States in the halcyon days of "freedom fries" and the enthusiastic resurrection of many older anti-French epithets that followed. France would subsequently stay out of the Middle Eastern war that most defined the post–9/11 decade for France's American and British allies.[3]

When interpreting the significance of the Franco-American rift over the Iraq war, it would be too easy, however, to misconstrue the nature of the French government's opposition and draw the wrong conclusions about French foreign policy today. French opposition to the war had fairly little to do with timidity regarding military intervention or uneasiness with the use of force against terrorist or other threats. Instead their opposition sprang from concern about the rules and norms that would shape the post–9/11 world, Chirac's pro-Arab inclinations, and, of course, his judgment that the invasion would end badly.

To be sure, Chirac and de Villepin benefitted politically from their stance against the Bush administration's push to invade Iraq, but behind the French policy lay a deeper concern with U.S. readiness to circumvent international law in the name of fighting terrorism, a phenomenon that many French elites viewed as criminal in nature and thus best tackled through the application of law rather than its circumlocution. Especially against the backdrop of the U.S. rejection of the Kyoto Protocol on global warming, the push for war in Iraq was perceived by the French as raw American will to power, coupled with cocksure righteousness and lack of historical perspective. In short, French leaders thought the U.S. was threatening the rules-based order on which France – and to a degree, the United States – depended in the age of globalization.

French opposition to the Iraq war was also rooted in a belief that the U.S. "war on terror" was a dangerous misnomer bound to lead the United States toward a strategic dead end that risked exacerbating the global terrorist scourge. France had no shortage of experience with terrorism, whether Algerian, Basque, or Corsican. But notwithstanding an outpouring of French sympathy for the United States on September 12, 2001, the French feared that the U.S. approach to al Qa'ida displayed in the run-up to the Iraq war would legitimize and strengthen the enemy by affording it an importance that it did not warrant. The Manichean terms in which the war on terror was cast by the Bush administration, combined with the call for a prolonged military action against terrorism on all fronts simply did not sit well with French foreign policy elites, more inclined to focus on the "root causes" of terrorism.[4] As one French writer and former official put it, for the French, "a 'war on terror' was such a broad undertaking that it could only be lost."[5]

"UN PARFUM D'INDOCHINE"

That French leaders opposed the Iraq war and were skeptical about the "war on terror" did not mean that they were squeamish about the use of force in general, however after all, by the time that French citizens were being kidnapped in the Sahel by Droukdal's henchmen, French troops had been deployed in Afghanistan for several years. Throughout the 1990s, France, like many Western countries, had debated the pros and cons of military intervention (l'ingérence) as crises in Africa and especially the Balkans flared. In the early days of his tenure, Chirac himself was a powerful voice for intervention in Bosnia, and helped turn President Clinton's own initial reluctance to intervene into support for coercive diplomacy against Serbia. France had similarly participated in Operation Allied Force over Kosovo; while French leaders had been the most prone to what U.S. military leaders considered "meddling" in target selection and other aspects of military operations, French warplanes also flew the second most strike missions after the United States.[6]

France supported U.S. and later NATO operations in Afghanistan from the outset, largely because of a sense of solidarity after the 9/11 attacks, but also out of genuine concern about the al Qa'ida threat. France fully backed UN Security Council Resolution 1368, which made military action against the perpetrators of the 9/11 attacks legitimate self-defense; they also supported NATO's invocation of Article 5 defense after those same attacks. On September 18, 2001, President Chirac was in Washington, pledging French cooperation against al Qa'ida to President Bush. Little more than a month later, French aircraft and soon French troops were participating in the initial stages of Operation Enduring Freedom in Afghanistan.[7] A year and a half later, even as French leaders pilloried the Bush administration for invading Iraq, France was pledging its support for NATO's takeover of the International Security Assistance Force (ISAF) in Afghanistan. (Unlike the Iraq mission, ISAF had sanction from the United Nations and was clearly directed against al Qa'ida.) French support for U.S. objectives in Afghanistan was intended to underscore that despite France's pique over Iraq, France had no qualms about using military force against terrorists, provided the proper international legal norms were obeyed and the threat clearly identified.

As time wore on, however, Chirac grew skeptical of the U.S. approach to the Afghanistan war. They began to believe the U.S. goals were becoming unrealistic, especially after the 2006 move into the southern Pashtun provinces. Chirac was also wary of backlash from a widening war. The Afghanistan deployment had been inaccurately portrayed in France (as in many European countries) as largely a peacekeeping operation and hence different in character from U.S. operations in Iraq, which were still strongly opposed by the majority of the French.

At 1,200 troops the French contribution to operations in Afghanistan under Chirac was much lower than the German or British contributions, but Chirac kept it there. French forces moreover operated only in Kabul, reducing the chances they would incur casualties or end up responsible for the war's growing number of civilian deaths. The deep wounds created by the Franco-American rift over Iraq, however, deterred the Chirac government from criticizing the war too much or reducing the French role in Afghanistan beyond this level.[8]

When Sarkozy came to power, French policy on Afghanistan changed. After his 2007 election, Sarkozy couched the war in broader terms as a war on fundamentalism and for the freedom of the Afghan people. Increasing French participation in Afghanistan also fit Sarkozy's policy of normalizing France's relationship with NATO and the United States.[9] Early in his tenure he announced that French strike-fighters would be redeployed to Kandahar and that France would also send 150 much-needed trainers to embed with Afghan militaries. At the NATO Bucharest summit in 2008, eager to demonstrate his bona fides at the time the Alliance was in the process of revising its Afghanistan strategy, Sarkozy committed to deploy French forces in regional command east, one of the most treacherous in the country. France soon took responsibility for the province of Kapisa with 1,000 additional troops. The French effort would peak at nearly 4,000 troops, a significant number for a military the size of the French, especially factoring in a 4:1 troop rotation ratio. Over time 30,000 French soldiers would serve in French operations in Afghanistan with more than 23,000 in Afghanistan itself.[10]

France thus entered the fray in a much more significant way than in the first seven years of the Afghan war. The French military paid for the show of solidarity almost immediately when an ambush in the valley of Uzbin in 2008 killed ten French soldiers. Uzbin was the largest loss of life the French military had suffered in a single incident since the 1983 terrorist attacks on French and U.S. forces in Beirut.[11] The attack exploded the myth that France was involved in a nonlethal and benevolent peacekeeping operation akin to those it had known in the Balkans in the 1990s. Further attacks followed, and France's operations, so far largely conducted out of the public eye, gradually became a subject of debate. Public opinion against the war effort grew. As one French writer put it, *Il flotte sur cette guerre un parfum d'Indochine*, a reference to France's ill-fated attempt to hold onto its colonial empire in Indochina.[12]

Before long, facing plunging approval ratings Sarkozy started to rethink his approach.[13] When an Afghan soldier turned his gun on his French allies, killing three of them in early 2012, Sarkozy, now amidst a tough reelection campaign, openly began to reconsider France's commitment to the mission, soon moving to withdraw French forces.

As the French public looked to the problem posed by terrorist groups in Africa, there was much from the French experience in Afghanistan that did not invite replication elsewhere. At the same time, however, the French military effort in Afghanistan provided a reservoir of experience with counter-terrorism combat operations that would serve them well in Mali.

A GROWING FRENCH RESPONSIBILITY

Operations in Afghanistan were moreover only one part of France's cooperation with U.S. global counterterrorism efforts. France cooperated increasingly with the United States on counter-terrorism following the 9/11 attacks, including by sharing one of the most critical element of successful counterterrorism operations – intelligence.[14] In the later years of the Sarkozy government, French and U.S. special operations forces in Afghanistan and Africa also developed close links – in large part as they fought together against al Qa'ida.[15]

By 2011, with Iraq and Afghanistan wars dragging on far longer than initially projected, America had grown demonstrably less eager to expend blood and treasure on international problems that had frustrated a growing number of Americans. The U.S. decision to restrict its participation in *Operation Unified Protector* in Libya to those military capabilities that the United States "uniquely" possessed signaled to the French that, after a decade of foreign wars, the United States had tired and would not play the same omnipresent role that it once had in combatting global threats. The United States was simultaneously beating a retreat from Iraq and planning to "pivot" many remaining U.S. military assets in Europe to Asia. French leaders believed they would need to take on more responsibility for counter-terrorism and other challenges in the face of declining U.S. and European will. As President Sarkozy put it a few days after the fall of Tripoli in August, 2011, "President Obama has presented a new vision of American military involvement whose implication is that the Europeans must assume more of their responsibilities."[16] Indeed, there was much water under the bridge since 1999, when French foreign minister Hubert Vedrine had referred the United States as an *hyperpuissance*. As one French scholar put it, if the Obama administration had chosen to "lead from behind" on Libya, French officials increasingly saw themselves as "leading by default" – at least on a few critical issues.[17]

American decline had figured in French thinking about international affairs for many years. When decline appeared to manifest itself in Iraq and Libya, French leaders naturally concluded they would need to do more to address problems on their own. Disillusionment with the European Union as a vehicle for military action, after Germany's resistance to the Libya intervention, and concern about the strains placed on Great Britain by the Iraq and Afghanistan wars, further reinforced this view.

A COMPLICATED RELATIONSHIP WITH AFRICA

If these trends suggested France would need to take the lead in any operation in Africa, other factors augured against such a lead, creating inherent tension. Among these factors, France's colonial and post-colonial history in the region loomed large. The legacies of France's nineteenth-century conquest and their twentieth-century aftermath generated repulsing and attracting forces. Francophone West Africa was familiar territory, a part of the world the French still felt they understood better than anyone else – including the United States. But France's long and often bloody history with the peoples of the region also greatly complicated matters, as evidenced, for example, by Algeria's adamant and frequent resistance to French military operations there.

Despite the frequent promises to distance themselves from Africa, especially militarily, after the Cold War France was been drawn again and again into a leading role in African affairs. During the Cold War, France retained a close network of relationships with its former colonial sphere in Africa – far more than did its one-time British competitors for colonial influence. Although French colonies, including Mali, gained independence in the 1950s and 1960s, most maintained special relationships with France. France continued to serve as a protector – for better or worse – of the fledging states. French power and influence thus remained strong across West Africa and so did the pull of the postcolonial societies within France itself. France intervened militarily on many occasions to prop up failing governments, prevent revolutions, and sustain pro-French, anticommunist political allies. French troops were sent in to prevent ruptures in Chad, Djibouti, the Central African Republic, Mauritania, Zaire, Gabon, Togo, and Comoros – in some cases repeatedly. Although personal financial and political interests played a major role in sustaining the apparatus of the postcolonial French system, dubbed *francafrique* in the later 1990s, at the national level, economics was not the primary reason for France's continued close relationship with the continent.[18] Social, political, and personal relationships also mattered.

Africa was, after all, still one of the few, if not the only, corner of the world where France was unquestionably a great power. Limited U.S. interest in African issues, coupled with French military presence and proximity to Europe made West Africa, including Mali, a part of the world where France retained great power influence and played a deciding role in many important regional issues. The simple fact of French power created a sense of responsibility and propeled France toward a sustained regional commitment.

The end of the Cold War, however, meant that the French could no longer lean on anticommunism as a rationale for intervening to protect their regional allies, whose sometimes abysmal human rights records were meanwhile more and more in the spotlight. The end of the Cold War also meant changes in French defense policy (see below), an overall reduction in the number of troops in the French Army, and a concomitant reduction in the number of French forces deployed permanently in Africa. Diminishing numbers of French forces on the ground were coupled with declining French foreign assistance, making it more difficult to maintain neocolonial webs of influence. The nature of conflict in Africa was also changing, as social, demographic, and economic trends often rendered cleavages more difficult to manage with traditional French military strategies. The clientelistic relationships that France sustained across the continent led France into a humiliating, abject failure in Rwanda, in which France was widely censured for abetting Rwandan *genocidaires*. The public outcry that followed the Rwanda massacres further accelerated the process of disentanglement that was already underway since collapse of the Communist Bloc a few years earlier.

When the socialist Lionel Jospin became Prime Minister in 1997, this policy shift further quickened. Military power was downplayed as a tool of foreign policy on the continent. Wherever possible, French troops were deployed under a European rather than a French flag. In theory, this strategy would be less costly for France, offer greater legitimacy, and reduce the pressure from the anti-neocolonialists at home. The Jospin government and its successors invested in building Africa's own capabilities for peacekeeping operations, especially through regional organizations such as the African Union and Economic Community of West African States (ECOWAS). French forces were meanwhile reduced, and in 2008, President Sarkozy's White Paper on Defense and National Security called for a reduction in the number of permanently deployed French forces in Africa to two lonely outposts on opposite shoulders of the great continent, in Dakar and Djibouti.

Here, however, lofty political ambition met with the reality of France's connections to this crisis-prone region. The ongoing pressure of operations on the continent made Sarkozy's proposed reduction difficult to achieve, and by 2012, France still had not consolidated to two bases. In Senegal, Djibouti, and Gabon there were permanent bases. In several other countries, including Chad and Côte d'Ivoire, there were significant numbers of troops deployed in long-term operations. A large number of French troops thus remained on African soil. Even if the number had declined greatly since the 1990s, military forces deployed in Africa were still a big part of France's overall overseas troop deployments. Moreover, despite its best intentions of turning responsibility for intervention in Africa over to the European Union and other multinationals, France had intervened unilaterally in Côte d'Ivoire in 2002 and been forced to remain with several thousand troops. It was also continuing its long-standing yet theoretically temporary intervention in Chad, for fear that the departure of French forces would open the door to state collapse and all its consequent woes. As a result, the French still had a significant number of forces deployed in Africa in 2012.

The fact was that France was torn over its relationship with its former colonies, drawn on the one hand toward continued engagement, repulsed on the other by charges of neocolonialism and continued pressure on French defense budgets.

U.S. AND FRENCH POLICY IN THE SAHEL, 2008–2012

French security cooperation with the states of the Sahel since 1997 had focused on military training through the multiple French-funded training academies. As of 2012, there were sixteen such establishments spread out in ten West and sub-Saharan African states.[19] More than 15,000 students passed through these schools between 1997 and 2012. Their purpose goes far beyond counterterrorism, and aims primarily as improving professionalism and generally strengthening the militaries of the region.[20]

In addition, French troops worked regularly on a bilateral basis to strengthen regional security forces, alongside the United States. France spent 1,080,000 euros on aid to Niger in 2011, a large part of which aimed at developing antiterrorist judicial institutions. The same year, France provided 166,000 euros in support of Mali's National Guard and gendarmerie. Mauritania received 531,000 euros for internal security, most of which went to training efforts.[21] Between 2009 and 2012, the French Army trained a thousand soldiers for intervention units, whose primary function was to combat the jihadists, for example in the Wagadou Forest along the border with Mali. The French Air Force meanwhile trained Mauritanian pilots to use their three Embraer 312 Tucanos in surveillance operations. The French made a similar effort in Niger and also trained some 800 soldiers in Mali.[22]

These French efforts included nothing on the scale of the U.S. Flintlock exercises, which since 2005 had brought multiple countries from Europe and the region together for joint training with a strong counterterrorism focus. French regional training work did, however, allow French troops to operate sometimes alongside their regional counterparts. Such was the case in 2010 during the joint raid conducted with Mauritania against the al Qa'ida stronghold in Mali where Michel Germaneau was believed to have been held. It was also the case in the ill-fated attempt to rescue Vincent Delory and Antoine de Léocour after their kidnapping in Niger in January 2011.

The relationships the French established with the regional powers also facilitated their insertion of a small special operations force of approximately 100 strong into Burkina Faso in 2009. This operation, code named *Sabre* (and intermittently acknowledged and denied by French authorities) was centered in Ougadougou, with nodes in Niger, Mauritania, and Mali.[23] It would become the first line of defense in 2013 when al Qa'ida and its allies made their charge on Bamako.

Finally, in 2009, the French government announced a "Plan Sahel" that combined economic and military assistance to strengthen internal security in the countries of the region and help them combat Salafi jihadist groups. This one million euro program was put in place for a three-year period, specifically to help battle al Qa'ida in the Islamic Maghreb and the smuggling off of which it fed. Plan Sahel aimed at strengthening the interior security forces of nine partner countries and sought to build a cadre of local experts capable of training African police and gendarmes in several related fields.[24] This was obviously a limited program, however, the kind helpless bureaucracies around the world produce to prove they are taking action on a particularly intractable issue for which they lack resources or reliable solutions.

Although France was the historical great power in the region, U.S. efforts were also significant. Despite the U.S. focus on fighting al Qa'ida in South Asia and the Middle East, some offices in the United States and especially the French government recognized that the social, economic, and historical conditions in the Sahel were dangerously ripe for the spread of violent extremist groups. In both countries, concern about the region went back several years, even if funding and programs targeted at the region's problems never reached anywhere near the level of counterterrorism efforts in other parts of the world. Like France, the United States was also engaged along with a panoply of international organizations in combatting the root causes of terrorism.

The U.S. counterpart to the French "Plan Sahel" was a plan called the Trans-Sahel Counter-Terrorism Partnership, which dated back in one form or another to 2003, and eventually came to include Chad, Niger, Mali, Mauritania, Algeria, Morocco, Burkina Faso, Senegal, and Cameroon. Although conceived as a regional approach, the effort was carried out in a largely bilateral capacity.[25] Mali received significant resources and attention (by regional standards, at least) for deradicalization, promoting moderate Islam, and generally reducing north-south tensions.

Like France, the United States invested in military training programs region-wide. Among the countries the United States engaged in its regional strategy, however, Mali received much of the training, due both to the growing presence of al Qa'ida's affiliate there and because coups in several neighboring countries precluded much U.S. engagement elsewhere. U.S. special operations forces from the U.S. Army special operations Europe under U.S. Africa Command, conducted intermittent training of Malian troops deployed in the North. As recently as February 2011, U.S. special forces had run a joint combined exchange training (JCET) operation with Mali's 33rd Parachutist regiment.[26] Training largely involved basic skills such as driving, shooting, and tracking.[27] Even these, within the standards of the Malian army – where literacy, driving, and other skills were limited – could be a challenge. Depending on the estimates, the United States spent some $25–$50 million over the course of the decade prior to the revolt on training the Malian military.[28]

These efforts were sporadic, however, and did not always get full cooperation from Bamako. President Amadou Toumani Touré was more than willing to work with the United States and France on counterterrorism in theory, but proved reluctant when it came to the tough measures that would have enabled U.S. training to have a lasting effect. This was in no small part due to the fact that the patronage networks on which his power was built were inextricably intertwined with the smuggling operations the Tuareg separatists and jihadist radicals controlled in the North. Mali's leaders had little incentive to see these networks disrupted permanently, and so played along with U.S. training efforts, but did little to ensure that they became a lasting success.[29]

Some officers later even accused the President of raking in cash as a middle-man for Belmokthar's kidnapping operations. "We knew for months, thanks to satellite imagery that there was an al Qa'ida base within fifteen kilometers of our positions," said one Malian officer, "but the political powers did nothing, preferring to discuss the liberation of the western hostages with them and then take a percentage of the ransom."[30] At a minimum, the Bamako government was willing to tolerate the jihadists in the vain hope that the funds garnered thereby might bring a modicum of stability to the North.

French efforts to strengthen regional military and counter-terrorism services often ran into similar obstacles of limited resources, complex local political dynamics, and resultant lukewarm cooperation. Consequently, at the outbreak of the 2012 conflict, Mali's security services proved even weaker than they looked on the surface. Malian units like the 33rd Paras had gained some rudimentary tactical proficiency from their training with the United States, but the supporting structures and institutions that they needed to operate effectively, especially in the remote regions of the Sahara, were basically nonexistent. U.S. military leaders would later argue that the State Department had not given them the leeway they needed to do the kind of persistent training that Mali's military so badly needed.[31] This may have been true, but the fact was that Mali's institutions, both military and civilian, had been hobbled by years of corruption and economic fragility. Mali was a democracy, but its state was collapsing from within. With such hollowed out military institutions, it is hardly surprising that the state collapsed when it was attacked by jihadist groups as dedicated, ruthless, and violent as al Qa'ida in the Islamic Maghreb.

4 MERAH AND MALISTAN

In the years following the 2004 Madrid and 2005 London bombings, the nature of the challenge al Qa'ida and its affiliates posed began to change. The threat of large-scale 9/11–type attacks declined, but terrorist and guerilla attacks by Salafist groups against local targets around the world increased. Al Qa'ida in Iraq led this trend with its campaign of suicide and other attacks on U.S. forces and Iraqi civilians, but violence by al Qa'ida in the Arabian Peninsula, the Islamic Courts Union (al Shabab's predecessor), and al Qa'ida in the Islamic Maghreb also contributed to the global tally. If the trend was toward smaller scale, localized attacks, therefore, the problem had also become more diverse, as al Qa'ida's affiliates offered new, broader opportunities for would-be terrorists from the West to draw inspiration, train, and attack. By 2011, an established part of this trend was the growth of attempts at terrorism by permanent residents of the West, inspired by al Qa'ida's message and trained in camps of al Qa'ida or its affiliates – such as in the cases, for example, of U.S. residents Najibullah Zazi[1] and Faisal Shahzad.[2] In 2015, France would suffer a direct hit even more indicative of this trend with the murders of twelve staff of the satirical magazine *Charlie Hebdo* by Chérif and Saïd Kouachi, at least one of whom had trained in an al Qa'ida in the Arabian Peninsula run camp in Yemen.

The *Charlie Hebdo* attacks were not the first of this kind in France. In March 2012, France was already shaken by a series of equally gruesome attacks that underscored the risk posed by the proliferation of al Qa'ida affiliates, their safe havens, and training camps. The attacker was Mohammed Merah, a second-generation French Muslim from Toulouse. On March 11, Merah answered an advertisement for a used motor scooter posted on the Internet by a French Muslim soldier named Imad Ibn-Ziaten. After meeting Ibn-Ziaten and confirming that he was a soldier, Merah shot him in the head at point blank range.

Three days later, Merah videotaped another shooting of three more soldiers outside an ATM near their base in the nearby town of Montauban. Two of the three, Mohamed Legouad and Abel Chennouf, were killed, while the third, Loïc Liber was gravely wounded.[3] The video showed Merah shouting, "You kill my brothers, I kill you" and "Allah au Akbar" as he fired and then rode off.[4]

The most revolting of Merah's attacks, however, was still to come. On March 19, after having failed in a rendezvous for what was likely to be a third attempt on a French officer, Merah rode his scooter up to the Ozar Hatorah Jewish school, and shot and killed Gabriel Sandler (age 4) and Arieh Sandler (age 5) as they stood waiting for the school bus with their father. When a third child, Miriam Monsonego (age 7), tried to run, Merah caught her by the hair and shot her in the head.

As fears of a broader wave of terrorist or retaliatory violence grew, the French terrorism alert system, *Vigipirate*, was put on the highest level of alert, a first in French history. On March 20, however, Merah was found in his apartment. The nation watched, transfixed, as a massive standoff ensued. Finally, after thirty-two hours, police blasted their way through the walls. He met them with guns blazing and was shot dead when he tried to jump from the window.[5]

MOHAMMED MERAH

Merah was the twenty-three-year-old son of an Algerian immigrant. A petty criminal, he had spent twenty-one months in prison between 2007 and 2009, during which time he claimed to have radicalized himself by reading the Koran.[6] He cited the plight of the Palestinians, France's role in Afghanistan, and the banning of the veil in France among his major grievances.[7]

Immediately after the murders, French investigators claimed that Merah had exaggerated his al Qa'ida training and did not appear to have the support of any local terrorist cell. By many appearances he was a "lone wolf."[8] The director of the *Direction Centrale du Renseignment*

Intérieur (DCRI), Bernard Squarcini, called Merah "a Janus, someone with two faces," and downplayed possible links to Salafi jihadists. "He appears to be part of the new generation of Islamic terrorists who act alone, abetted by jihadi web sites and their own anger," said Jean-Louis Bruguière, France's most well-known counterterrorism judge.[9] Beardless in his jeans, sneakers, and Lacoste shirts, Merah certainly did not look the part of the radical Salafist. The appearance of normalcy only made his actions seem all the more sinister and confusing.

Yet, at a minimum, it was clear that Merah – like the Kouachi brothers – had sought to develop links with jihadist groups overseas. In 2010, he traveled to several Middle Eastern and Muslim countries, including Israel, Jordan, Lebanon, Syria, Iraq, and possibly Iran.[10] He also visited Afghanistan via Tajikistan in 2010 and was detained for questioning in Kandahar. After being returned to France and put on the "no-fly" list, he again traveled to Pakistan in October, 2011, where he later told the police he had received training in Waziristan.[11]

There were also some indications that Merah may have had help, at a minimum, in distributing the video footage of his carnage. One possible source of assistance was his brother, Abdelkader Merah, known to be in contact with Salafist groups in Egypt.[12] French authorities investigated both of their links to the "Toulouse group," which was created in 2006 and aimed to recruit al Qa'ida foot soldiers in France to attack U.S. interests there and in Iraq.[13] The possibility that Merah may have had help raised the specter of a broader terrorist network and hence further attacks on French soil.

It also resurfaced the question of whether the social and economic alienation of French Muslims and especially North African Muslims was creating a culture in which jihadist ideas were taking root. Millions of Algerians, Moroccans, Tunisians, Malians, and other North Africans live in France, often in the turbulent *banlieux* that ring France's major cities. The Parisian suburb of Montreuil, for example, is home to the world's second largest population of Malians outside of Bamako. Overall, there were 2,362,099 African immigrants in France in 2010.[14] This was roughly half of France's total immigrant population and a little less than four percent of the overall population of the country. This does not, however, include the sons and daughters of the immigrants, who are often those most at risk of radicalization. The French scholar

Olivier Roy, a leading global expert on jihad, wrote that Merah "was a loner and a loser. Far from embodying a growing radicalization among the youth, he stood at the margins not only of French society but also of the Muslim community."[15]

Though not inaccurate, such observations were unlikely to comfort a public traumatized by Merah's rampage.[16] The murders had spawned fears that jihadists could be hidden behind every door. In the wake of the tragedy, French officials raided several sites, arrested nineteen people and seized many weapons. President Sarkozy, clearly working to project his authority in the face of the disaster, promised the raids would continue.[17]

The murders pushed France toward a more aggressive strategy against the Salafi jihadist threat in Africa. France had been the victim of terrorist attacks in the past, of course – in 1995, al Qa'ida in the Islamic Maghreb's predecessor, the Armed Islamic Group of Algeria, had launched multiple attacks in the Parisian Metro, one of which had killed eight people and wounded 150 more. The Merah attacks were the first major attack, however, since 9/11, 2001. There was a distinct possibility that Merah had received training in camps abroad. His case demonstrated that France was far from immune to the threat of self-radicalization and thus needed to pay closer attention to al Qa'ida's new franchises and especially the safe havens and training opportunities they offered willing young French recruits. Concern about what a tiny cell of disaffected youth might do – especially if they managed to get the right training from one of al Qa'ida's African franchises – ran high. There was evidence that would-be French jihadists were seeking training from African sources. At least two individuals were later caught trying to join African jihad – one named Ibrahim Aziz Ouattara, the other simply called Djamel.[18]

MALI'S COLLAPSE

The Merah attacks came at exactly the moment when a terrorist safe haven was materializing in North Africa, under the control of the al

Qa'ida franchise that for years had singled France out as Western enemy number one. In 2011, the shock of the Arab Spring, for all the high hopes of democratic change, actually opened the door to the expansion of already growing Salafi jihadist movements across North Africa. As turbulence from Qaddafi's overthrow and the broader regional political turmoil spread westward from Egypt, it revived old ethnic and tribal cleavages and increased an already burgeoning regional supply of small arms, ultimately facilitating and encouraging the spread of jihadist forces. When these forces hit, Mali, large, poor, and landlocked, was already weak by the compounding maladies of corruption, northern separatism, and smuggling.

French explorers first came to the region in the early nineteenth century. As French holdings in West Africa expanded inland from Senegal and southward from Algeria under the Second Empire and over the course of the later nineteenth century, Mali was incorporated into French West Africa as the French Sudan. Mali gained independence in 1960 in a complicated and strained, but ultimately peaceful, process that involved a failed effort at union with neighboring Senegal. Like so many other states that decolonized in those years, Mali soon fell to authoritarian ruler Moussa Traoré, who overthrew a communist government led by Modibo Keita in 1968. Traoré ruled until 1991, when the combination of the end of the Cold War and a bout of conflict with the Tuaregs combined to weaken his grip on power and usher in the nation's first experience with democracy.[19]

The prospects that democracy would take hold in Mali were inherently low, given Mali's poverty.[20] The apparent success of Mali's democratic record in the next two decades thus came as a welcome surprise, a bright spot in a part of the world where such prospects were too often bleak. In the broader region, Côte d'Ivoire descended into a brutal civil war, Nigeria experienced frequent violence, and Niger saw repeated coup attempts. Algeria and Libya were meanwhile under the rule of strongmen. In Mali, however, there was peace and elections were held regularly, without interference. More important, Malian political elites – military and civilian alike – embraced key democratic norms, including the principle of alternation of power. Alpha Oumar Konaré, who was elected president in 1992 and 1997 in elections that were generally agreed to be free and fair, gave up power peacefully when he was defeated at the polls by Amadou Toumani Touré (known widely as "ATT"). The new president, a military hero of the 1991 revolution, would rule until the 2012 crisis.

During Mali's two decades of democratic rule, there was some progress on social and economic fronts. But Mali has nevertheless remained one of the poorest countries on earth. Per capita gross domestic product grew from $720 in 1990 to $1046 in 2012 (see Figure 6), but on the UN human development index, Mali was still ranked 182 of 187. Almost half the population (47 percent) live below the poverty line. As in many neighboring countries, malaria is widespread, and far too many people live in threat of recurrent food crises. According to the most recent assessment, which was taken in 2006, the mortality rate for children under five years old was 215 per 1,000. In other words, more than one in five Malian children did not live to see their fifth birthday.[21]

Scholars have debated the underlying factors that cause state collapse or contribute to the relapse of civil wars. For illustrative purposes, Figure 5 shows some of the indicators that have been found to correlate with peace-building success.[22] These indicators are also relevant when it comes to the outbreak of civil war. (These are correlative, not necessarily causal). Of five examined, two augured in Mali's favor: It was not a primary commodity exporter and not dependent on energy resources for income. Three others, however, were highly unfavorable for stability: Mali's extremely low per capita electricity consumption, low per capita income, and especially its negative rate of economic growth on the eve of the war.

Moreover, although Mali had all the trappings of democracy, there were evident problems. Voter registration and participation in the elections, for example, was very low, with only slightly more than one-third of Malians voting in the 2007 presidential elections.[23] This level of interest in and demand for democratic institutions was perhaps to be expected in a country where income was so low. "We care about food, not democracy," said one Malian elite bluntly in Bamako.[24] The state was also weak and probably growing weaker, as the government and bureaucracy became increasingly complicit in the growing illicit trafficking in the north. Funds from trafficking supported patronage

Local Capacity Proxy	Value
Electricity Consumption (kWh per capita)	34.6 kWh/person (2010 est.)
Primary Commodity Exports as % of GDP	13.1% (early 1990s est.)
Oil Exports Greater Than 30% of GDP	No
Real GDP Per Capita	$699.34/person (current 2012 USD)
Annual Rate of Growth of Real Per Capita GDP	–3.3% (2011 to 2012, constant 2005 US$)

Figure 5. Select Proxy Indicators for Malian Local Capacity. *Sources*: *World Development Indicators, 2014; CIA World Factbook, 2014;* Doyle and Sambanis, *Making War and Building Peace;* RAND internal calculations.

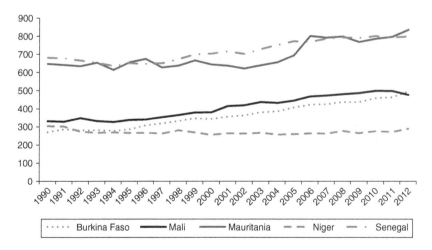

Figure 6. GDP Per Capita in Mali and Selected Neighboring States (Constant 2005 USD). *Source*: World Bank, *World Development Indicators (WDI)*, 2014.

networks nationwide. Reflecting on the collapse later, some observers saw ATT's consensual leadership style and unwillingness to confront corruption as a root of the problem.[25] His consensual governing style sought to bring all the parties in the parliament under a single governing coalition, creating thereby an unwieldy government that effectively became a vehicle for the distribution of patronage – and gradual weakening of the state.[26]

Neither France, the United States, nor any other major international player, however, recognized how weak Mali really was beneath the surface. Mali's 2012 implosion would prove especially awkward for the United States and France, both of which had worked for years to strengthen this nascent democracy, often holding it up as a rare success story in Francophone Africa, one of the most impoverished regions of the world. "I was really surprised at how shallow the Malian state was and how weak the democratic institutions [were]," said one senior official who witnessed the collapse from inside the U.S. State Department.[27] This official was not the only one. Many others were caught off guard when al Qa'ida easily grabbed Mali's vast northern reaches and its political institutions crumbled. The *New York Times* later reported that a confidential internal review at U.S. Africa Command concluded the collapse had come too fast for U.S. commanders or intelligence analysts to detect any clear warning signs. Others, however, were less confident and blamed Mali's foreign sponsors for being blind to the depth of Mali's weakness – and with that, the impending storm.[28]

TAUREG SEPARATISM

The weakness of the Malian state can at least in part be attributed to geography, which has left the country with a very plural and sometimes incohesive social landscape. Malians are proud of the role that towns like Djenné, Gao, and Timbuktu once played as power centers of the ancient empires of Songhai, Ghana, and Mali. These once stretched well across west Africa, and served as hubs of a broader civilization that reached as far as Morocco and had extensive contact with the Middle East through trans-Saharan trade routes. Mali's ancient empires, like the social and political groups that inhabit the country today, had only a vague relationship with Mali's current borders.

All it takes is a superficial glance at a map of west Africa to grasp the basic artificiality of today's boundaries (Figure 2). The northwestern frontier with Mauritania cuts a straight edge south from Algeria to make an almost perfectly square corner in Mauritania's southeast. Much of Mali's border with Algeria is also as straight as a razor. As is so often the case in Africa, borders like these result from administrative decisions or other agreements made far away in colonial times or during decolonization itself, decisions that bear little relationship with organic social and political realities on the ground.

Most of all, Mali's borders encompass a vast expanse of the Sahara Desert that stretches south to the sixteenth parallel, from which extends the semi-arid Sahel to approximately the fourteenth parallel, after which the tropics begin. The peoples that inhabit these different climates are widely varied. Mali is home to a range of ethnic groups including Bambara, Bobo, Bozo, Dogon, Malinké, Maure, Minianka, Peul, Sarakolé, Sénoufo, Songhai, and Tuareg. Although they have coexisted for centuries, some of them also have histories of violent conflict. Different modes of existence – nomadic in the harsher northern territories and sedentary and pastoral in the more southern – have also created conflicts. Combined with poverty and the institutional weakness that comes with it, these conditions make Mali inherently very difficult to govern.

Although many of Mali's ethnic groups have coexisted peaceably in the post-independence era, the nomadic Tuareg tribes of the north have been a source of tension and violence. "The 'Tuareg problem' in the north is the one ethnic divide in contemporary Mali with political salience, and groups on both sides of this divide consider themselves the historical victims," explains a leading ethnographer of contemporary Mali.[29]

As shown in Figure 7, the Tuaregs are a nomadic people that inhabit a wide expanse of the Sahara desert stretching from Mauritania, though Mali, Algeria, Nigeria, and Libya. In Mali, there are some 300,000–400,000.[30] Seven major tribal confederations, or "drum groups" – a term that comes from the placement of a drum outside the

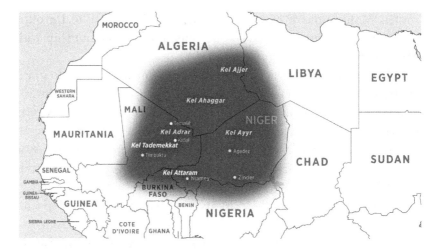

Figure 7. Tuareg Areas in the Sahel.
Source: http://www.dorsum.org/africa/the-tuareg-a-people-without-an-own-country/

tribal leader's dwelling – include the Kel Tademaket in Timbuktu and to the west around Lake Faguibine; the Iwellemmeden Kel Ataram; the clans of the Ifoghas Mountains, who would become a key center of revolutionary discontent.[31] Historically the Tuaregs abjured agriculture, preferring stockbreeding, caravan trading, and raiding for their livelihood. Raiding, which was common until the early twentieth century, was both an accepted livelihood as well as a political tool.[32] Once an important occupation, caravan trading has been dwindling for decades, as shifts in demand and more modern modes of transport replaced the camel trade.[33] Tens of thousands of camels once crossed the Sahara laden with salt from Niger, but by the 1970s that number had shrunk to only a few thousand.[34]

For centuries, the Tuareg eeked out an existence in the extraordinarily harsh environment of the Sahara. The Tuareg's natural nobility was a common theme in much popular nineteenth and twentieth-century European writing on Tuareg culture. European versions (mostly likely wrong) of the history of the Tuaregs often linked them to medieval crusaders or other European knights of time long past. Their nomadic life was widely romanticized. A popular nineteenth-century account written by the Frenchman Henri Duveyrier, *The Tuareg of the North*, depicted "great serried squadrons of tall, blue-veiled men, mounted on fast white camels, crashing forward like a vast roller … one of the most stunning spectacles to be seen on any battlefield."[35]

But Taureg viciousness was equally legendary. The first European explorer to reach Timbuktu was an unlucky, insouciant thirty-two-year-old Scotsman, named Gordon Laing, who was brutally murdered by the local chief. The impression left by this encounter was reinforced by later encounters in which Tuareg tribes murdered the increasingly invasive Europeans who came to explore and colonize their lands. Jules Vernes's last novel, *Invasion of the Sea*, published in 1905, describes the Tuareg in this light: "[A]ny individual Targui might work, ostensibly at least, as a caravan guide and even as its guard, he was nevertheless a thief by instinct and pirate by nature, and his reputation was too well established not to inspire profound distrust."[36] The protagonist of Verne's novel dreams of turning the Sahara into a great inland lake – to help the region develop while conveniently ridding it of its fearsome Taureg tribes.

The reality was that the Tuaregs lived under some of the most extreme and difficult geographical and climatic conditions in the world. Survival in these conditions has clearly often required a ruthlessness that other, especially modern, societies do not. One later twentieth-century Danish ethnographer's account of the Tuaregs from the later twentieth-century records, for example, describes the practice of making small leather medicine sacks from kid (i.e. of a goat) scrotums.[37] Within the boundaries of contemporary Mali, Tuareg populations had thus long lived at least in part by raids on the more sedentary peoples to their south. Tuareg raiders would carry off livestock, slaves, and other loot from the southerners. The advent of independence, however, shifted the balance of power against the nomads. With a capital in Bamako, and far more black Africans than Tuaregs in the new nation, democratic power fell almost entirely into the hands of non-Tuareg groups. These continued to harbor ill will toward the northern nomads who had plundered and threatened them for so many years.

Given these historical north-south tensions, it is hardly surprising that after independence, the scarce resources of the Malian state were not invested in improving the livelihoods of the Tuareg tribes. Mali's

Tuaregs were largely excluded from the reigning narrative of modern Malian nationalism.[38] Some Tuaregs even sought incorporation into France as a solution to their exclusion from Mali. Simultaneously, droughts of the late 1960s and early 1970s decimated Tuareg livestock, while population growth generated additional pressure.[39] As a result, many younger Tuaregs fled the country, often to Libya, where Qaddafi offered them employment as mercenaries in his army.

The consequence of these tensions was repeated Tuareg insurrection. From 1963 to 1964 Malian Tuareg groups revolted and were put down. They would do so twice again before the 2012 crisis, in 1990 and in 2006. During these revolts, the Tuaregs were frequently depicted as "white slavers" and "Qaddafi's Arab mercenaries" – outsiders who aimed to dominate the south, leaving malign sentiment behind on all sides even after the conflicts were over.[40]

The failure of Traoré's authoritarian government to effectively address the 1990 Tuareg revolt had helped bring him down and usher in democracy. (The protagonist of that revolt was a Tuareg named Iyad Ag Ghali, who twenty years later would become a key provocateur in the national crisis that led to the French intervention. Ghali had spent much of the 1980s fighting for the Palestine Liberation Organization and Qaddafi, like other key leaders of the 2012 revolt.) In January 1991, after a violent six-month struggle between the government forces and Ghalis's Tuareg rebels, a negotiated settlement was reached at Tamanrasset, Algeria. Although the Tuareg problem was subdued for fifteen years, the insurrection strained the already weak government in Bamako to the point of collapse. The military hero of the anti-Tuareg forces, ATT, took over as the head of a caretaker government and organized the country's first democratic elections later that year.

Initial hope that Mali's economic prospects would improve under democratic rule, alleviating the problems with the north, were disappointed.[41] Mali remained extremely poor, and conditions in Tuareg areas stagnated. In addition, many Tuareg separatist fighters, who, according to the terms of the Tamanrasset accords, were to have been integrated into Mali's regular army, were not. In 2006 there was thus yet another revolt, which continued sporadically until a new peace accord was signed in 2009. By then, however, the challenge of Tuareg separatism had been rendered immensely more difficult by al Qa'ida in the Islamic Maghreb's infiltration of the north and its Tuareg tribes.

"MALISTAN"

Again and again in its history, whether in Afghanistan, Iraq, Yemen, or elsewhere, al Qa'ida and its allies have sought to graft onto local conflicts, taking advantage of poor, isolated groups with grievances that are eking out an existence on the margins. Radical Salafi jihadists have used such cleavages to establish operating bases for planning attacks against their enemies and as a springboard for regional political ambition. Over the course of 2012, this pattern played out again in Northern Mali, as al Qa'ida in the Islamic Maghreb took advantage of the Tuareg revolt to extend its control over a territory, which, while thinly populated and inhospitable to most, was as large as France.

Too many pundits have pointed to NATO's 2011 intervention in Libya as the reason for Mali's collapse.[42] As the foregoing discussions should make clear, this is a grossly oversimplified account of Mali's history. Mali was a weak state with a long-standing separatist problem and had been an al Qa'ida hub for several years. ATT had pursued a live-and-let-live relationship with al Qa'ida in the Islamic Maghreb for a long time. One U.S. senior official said they had something of an "unspoken agreement not to bother each other."[43] This arrangement would now come back to bite Bamako.

Nevertheless, the civil war in Libya did have a catalyzing effect that accelerated Mali's slide off the precipice, creating an environment that French and other terrorism experts began to liken to Afghanistan in the 1990s – "Malistan," as some dubbed it, a remote safe haven where terrorists could muster their forces, attract and train recruits, and plan attacks on targets far and near.

Many of the Tuaregs who had left Mali in the early 1970s to fight for Qaddafi as mercenaries were the idealists, the "irreconcilables" of the movement, as one Mali expert on the ground dubbed them.[44] When Qaddafi's fortunes turned, they returned to Mali ready to take up arms for their old cause. Estimates of the number of returning Tuareg mercenaries ran as high as 4,000, although the numbers may well have been fewer. This is certainly the case when it comes to returnees who would eventually join the revolt, which was likely closer to 1,000.[45] Nevertheless, these fighters brought arms and military experience with them and by late 2011 had reignited the Tuareg separatist movement, turning it again toward violence against the state. "With our new arms and our new equipment, we have a military capacity that is superior to the Malian army's," boasted the rebel's spokesman, Hama Ag Sid Ahmed, in Paris in December 2011.[46]

A leading figure in the Tuareg revolt, Mohammed Ag Najim is a prime example of the link between Libya's collapse and northern Mali's relapse into war. Born in the Kel Adagh drum group at the end of the colonial era, Najim's father was killed by Malian military during the 1963 Taureg uprising. As a young man Najim fled the drought-ridden north to join Qaddafi's army, where he served for many years before returning to fight for the Tuareg cause during Ghali's 1990 revolt. Evidently disappointed in the Tamanrasset compromise, however, Najim headed back to Libya, where he became a commanding officer in the southern Saharan region of Sebha. He remained a Qaddafi henchman until he recognized that the Libyan dictator's days were numbered in July 2011. He then fled back to Mali, bringing with him a large cache of weapons and years of military experience, including in the harsh desert environment.

Upon his return, Najim's desire for Tuareg independence had not dwindled. He quickly set up training camps for Tuareg rebels along the Algerian border at Tigharghar and Zakak in the Tin-Assalak hills, the same area where Tuareg rebels had established themselves in earlier revolts.[47] Soon, Najim was elected the military leader of a rekindled Tuareg independence movement rooted in local Imghad and Ifoghas clans and now called the Mouvement Nationale pour la Libération de l'Azawad (MNLA).[48]

Meanwhile, Ghali, the protagonist of the 1990 revolt, was preparing his own comeback. During the last revolt, ATT had sought to use Ghali as an interlocutor in the negotiations that ended the conflict, giving him a government position in Bamako. In 2008, however, ATT decided it was better to have Ghali out of the picture and sent him to serve as Mali's consul in Jeddah, Saudi Arabia. Ghali had been a less than pious Muslim for most of his life, but in Jeddah he underwent a rather abrupt conversion to Wahabbist orthodoxy. Returning to Mali in late 2011, he had high hopes that he could lead the next Tuareg uprising. But he lost his bid for leadership to Najim.

A rift thus emerged among the rebels that would be difficult to repair. Ghali formed a new group grounded in jihadist rather than Tuareg ideology, Ansar al Din – "partisans of the religion of the prophet." Ansar al Din drew largely on forces from Ghali's home-town, the Tuareg stronghold of Kidal, and relied at least in part on links to a smaller faction. Ghali's jihadist turn may have stemmed from newfound convictions, but it was also politically expedient. One of Ghali's cousins, 'Abd al Karim al Targui commanded a smaller al Qa'ida *katiba* in the region.[49] Moreover, the link to al Qa'ida and jihadism in general gave Ghali a means of broadening his recruitment and financing base beyond his tribe and even beyond the Tuareg cause itself. In other words, Salafism was a new source of legitimacy and made his movement about something bigger and more univer-sal than just Tuareg discontent. Indeed, given his secular past, not a few outside observers questioned the strength of Ghali's allegiance to jihadism – and the durability of his ties to al Qa'ida in the Islamic Maghreb. In the early days of the revolt especially, Algeria and other countries continued to downplay his jihadist credentials and portray him as a potentially useful interlocutor in the conflict. It would be a surprise then, when Ghali later pushed for an attack on Bamako.

Two Tuareg insurgent groups thus formed – the secular Mouve-ment Nationale pour la Libération de l'Azawad and the Salafist Ansar al Din. By the time these groups had formed, Droukdal's Arab deputies, Abu Zeid and an increasingly independent Belmokthar, had already been operating their jihadist *katibas* in the region for years. To fur-ther complicate the regional jihadist picture, yet another Salafist group emerged, the West African Movement for Unity and Jihad. Known by its French acronym, Mujao, this group was led by a Mauritanian, but composed in large part of radicalized black Malians, especially from Gao, long a hub in the regional drug trade.[50] Mujao thus had a far more local flavor than Abu Zeid or Droukdal's groups. It would prove one of the more tenacious, creating problems for French forces as they tried to secure Gao and its environs.

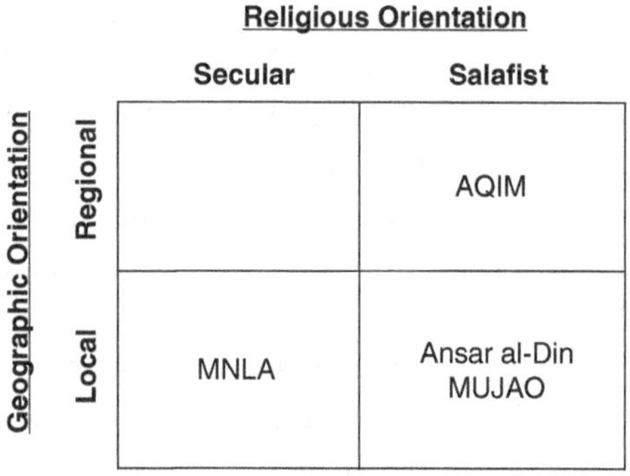

Religious Orientation

		Secular	Salafist
Geographic Orientation	Regional		AQIM
	Local	MNLA	Ansar al-Din MUJAO

Figure 8. Orientations of Armed Rebel and Jihadi Groups in Mali.

While the groups that participated in the revolt would frequently be lumped together during the conflict and after, they were in fact a diverse bunch, with complex and often fluid relations of their own to manage. The competition between Najim's secular Tuareg separatism, Ghali's Salafist Tuareg separatism, Abu Zeid and Belmokhtar's al Qa'ida brigades, and Mujao could be significant. (The differences are depicted graphically in Figure 8.) The Tuaregs are Muslims, but their ideological affinity with al Qa'ida is not inherently strong. The French explorer Réné Caillie, one of the first modern Europeans to travel extensively in Tuareg areas, reported that "Many of them do not know the first prayers of the Koran."[51] Women play a significant role in Tuareg society and are expected not only to go to school, but even to go to mixed schools. Thus, although Wahhabbism had been making some inroads in recent years in the North – some of the villages around Gao had begun to practice *shari'a,* for example – the Tuaregs in general were not Afghanistan's Pushtun people.[52] Much less were they its Taliban rebels, who had harbored core al Qa'ida in part due to religious affinity. In contrast, the alliance between the jihadists and the Tuaregs was based less on ideological or religious affinity than on mutual interest. This was especially true in the case of Najim's fighters, who were secular in their objectives and outlook.

Certainly the jihadists would have found it difficult if not impossible to make inroads into northern Mali if the Tuareg had not been Muslim, but this was not the primary basis for their cooperation. Indeed, some Tuareg rebels would soon regret this alliance of convenience when al

Qa'ida began to sideline them only a few weeks into their occupation of the north. Even as al Qa'ida expanded its influence across the north, however, southern political elites, including ATT, would still see the Tuaregs as the real villains. More often than not, these southern elites regarded al Qa'ida's grip on the north as either a secondary or the same issue as the Tuareg revolt.[53] This greatly complicated relations with the French, who were much more willing to work with the secular Tuaregs, especially if it helped in defeating al Qa'ida.

THE AGUELHOK MASSACRE AND SANOGO COUP

The crisis in Mali began when Najim's and Ghali's fighters fanned out across northern Mali in January 2012 and, with help from al Qa'ida in the Islamic Maghreb, conducted multiple attacks on government outposts in Kidal and neighboring towns (Figure 9). Najim mounted an attack on an outpost at Menaka on January 17, and fighting between the Malian army and the rebel groups ensued, spreading to Tessalit and Aguelhok. Some twenty rebel vehicles, armed with small arms and a few heavy weapons, attacked the Malian military barracks.[54] On January 20 the Malian army reported retaking all three towns and killing forty-five rebels and losing two soldiers, but spokesmen for the Tuareg separatists in Manchester, England, claimed the towns were in rebel control and that the military had killed several civilians.[55] Fighting intensified over the course of the next week, spreading first to Anderamboukane on the border with Niger and then to Léré on the Mauritanian border, where Belmoktar's katiba attacked.

Meanwhile, there was a fierce back and forth at Aguelhok. Ghali's fighters surrounded the Malian base and cut off the army's efforts to resupply their troops. Running low on ammunition, Malian troops soon retreated to Kidal. Malian military then returned and hit the rebels in Aguelhok in an effort to dislodge them, destroying several rebel vehicles and allowing government forces to retake the base. Ghali's fighters then again riposted, this time inflicting a humiliating defeat for the Malian Army and killing more than fifty soldiers.[56]

Bamako was caught off guard by the renewed outbreak of the Tuareg revolt and the failure of its own forces – many of whom had

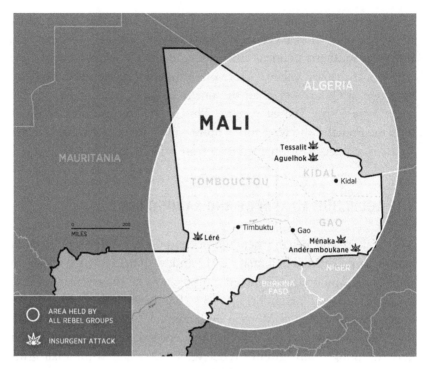

Figure 9. Initial Insurgent Advances in January 2012.
Source: "Northern Mali conflict" by Orionist – own work. This vec-
tor image includes elements that have been taken or adapted from:
Mali relief location map.jpg (by Carport); Mali2 location map.svg (by
NordNordWest). Licensed under Creative Commons Attribution-Share
Alike 3.0 via Wikimedia Commons – http://commons.wikimedia.org/
wiki/File:Northern_Mali_conflict.svg#mediaviewer/File:Northern_Mali
_conflict.svg

received U.S. training – to get it back in the box. "All of a sudden we
found ourselves face to face with a thousand men, heavily armed,"
reported Mali's foreign minister, Soumeylou Boubèye Maiga, warning
that "the stability of the entire region could be under threat."[57] The
reality, however, was that the government had failed to provide the
forces with the ammunition and other logistical support they needed
to operate effectively in the north. The training the Malian forces had
received from the United States may have given ATT a false sense
of confidence and made him too optimistic about the prospects for

retaking the north from what was a well-armed and committed rebel group.[58]

The consequences of this overconfidence were disastrous. Soon, rumors of a massacre trickled into Bamako, and in early February it emerged that nearly 100 civilians and soldiers had been killed by Ghali's men, many in cold blood, hands tied behind the back, throats slit, by the rebels.[59] The French, cognizant of the risks for its hostages in the region, pushed for negotiations. But this proved difficult given the divisions within the rebels and the fact that ATT was weak on account of the combination of an upcoming presidential election in April and the very fact of the renewed revolt. Many editorialists in Bamako moreover equated negotiating with the rebels under these circumstances to treason.[60] Hence, Bamako did little and the revolt continued to grow.

At first, the revolt seemed (and was) far, far away from Bamako. But as in 1991, the reverberations of the violence eventually began to be felt in the capital. In early February, the wives of soldiers slaughtered in Aguelhok stormed the presidential palace, demanding retribution from the government. Troops camped in Bamako meanwhile grew restive as rebel forces made headway against them in the north and the government struggled to get them the logistical support that they needed to repel the attack.

These tensions boiled over in mid-March. Mutinous soldiers took control of the national broadcasting station in Bamako and protested at a military training camp called Kati a few miles outside town. When the defense minister bungled a talk intended to calm the mutinous troops, a full-on coup ensued. Soldiers stormed the presidential palace on March 22, setting it afire and chasing the aged ATT out. They announced an end of the "incompetent" regime, called for the dissolution of all the institutions of government, and suspended the constitution. Mali's twenty-one years of democracy was imperiled.

Thrust into the role of head mutineer was a man named Colonel Amadou Sanogo. Sanogo had been the beneficiary of several training trips to the United States – many for English language, which he eventually learned to speak with extraordinary fluency and a nearly perfect

American accent, to the astonishment of at least one U.S. diplomat who spoke with him on the phone.[61] He had also received U.S. intelligence and infantry training, a fact that did not please officials in Washington. Nor did his subsequent appearance on television with a U.S. Marine Corps pin on his uniform.[62] Sanogo promised a government of national unity and return to democracy as soon as possible, but few outside observers were ready to believe him. Mali's democracy seemed to have finally succumbed to the fate of so many of its troubled neighbors.

As Sanogo and his comrades struggled over the course of the next few days to put a gloss of respectability on their coup, it became increasingly clear that they had little to no idea what they were doing. Although the overthrow of one of west Africa's longest-standing democracies by a military junta played in the international media as a sinister act, it was hardly a well-planned plot against the government. Sanogo's ascension was more like a haphazard fluke springing from the army's desperation.[63] Some observers even speculated that the captain had been thrust in front of the cameras primarily because the real mutineers, who were rank and file, needed someone of sufficient authority to represent them – or maybe just someone who spoke decent English. It was even rumored that the coup impresarios had pulled the miserable colonel out of a bar and thrust him in front of the camera. In another rumor, Sanogo's mother is said to have fainted when she saw him on television at the head of the coup.[64]

In any event, high-level Malian military leaders did little to stop or reverse the coup once it was underway.[65] Condemnation from abroad was swift. Several important African leaders, along with the United States, France, the European Union, the African Union, and the United Nations all censured the junta. The U.S. State Department was unyielding in its insistence that the United States would not truck with these antidemocratic forces and demanded the strictest possible interpretation of U.S. law, which required the U.S. government to cease all assistance to a country where a coup has taken place. This meant shutting down operations in a wide range of areas from humanitarian assistance to political and diplomatic relations. Despite some resistance from the U.S. Agency for International Development, which feared that cutting off certain core programs might threaten lives in fragile regions, the United States ultimately shut down nearly all its activities in Mali and drew its personnel down to a bare minimum.[66] France also had restrictions, but fewer, and the French remained more deeply involved on the ground, with an even greater share of the burden for managing the tumult.

It was Mali's neighbors, however, who took the lead in trying to restore democratic rule. Under the auspices of the Economic Community for West African States (ECOWAS) representatives from the Côte d'Ivoire, Burkina Faso, Liberia, Benin, and Niger took off in a plane from Abidjan for Mali on March 29. Protests on the tarmac in Bamako forced them to turn back mid-flight. The next day they threatened to close Mali's borders and cut off its access to the regional central bank, on which Mali relied for currency, if the coup leaders refused to back down. They also threatened to deploy a military "standby" force to restore order if the junta would not yield.

But Sanogo stood his ground. So on April 3, regional leaders acted on their sanctions threat, effectively cutting off Mali's fuel, cash supplies, and much of its food – a difficult and contentious decision given that it would imperil Mali's many fragile populations. Sanogo then capitulated, agreeing to a power-sharing deal late on April 6. He would share power with Mali's parliamentary leader, Dioncounda Traoré, who became the interim president. Elections within forty days were proposed, and sanctions were lifted.

This agreement was far from perfect. It gave the country a divided government in which the civilian leadership was weak and operating at constant personal risk. But at least it was a government. The hope was that Sanogo and his allies could gradually be sidelined.[67] This turned out to be much harder to orchestrate than originally thought, however. Without any foreign forces on the ground, Sanogo and his fellow mutineers continued to wield significant power in Bamako. Soon, they started a campaign of arrests and intimidation, creating the impression that the Traoré government was simply a façade.[68] A subsequent meeting of regional leaders extended the transitional period to a year and called for a regional standby force. Both of these moves were unpopular with Sanogo supporters, who wanted to vote on a new president as soon as possible, and preferably while the Kati group was still dominant militarily, in other words, without foreign troops around. More clashes in Bamako followed, and ECOWAS backed down from its threat to deploy the standby force.

Political uncertainty continued until May 20, when under continued pressure from regional leaders, Sanogo finally agreed to stay out of politics and accept Traoré as the interim president for a year. In exchange he was given status as a former head of state, standing that brought with it certain protections. Two days later, however, was assaulted by a group of coup supporters he had agreed to see at the presidential palace. The mob beat the seventy-year-old Traoré within inches of his life, leaving him for dead on the floor of the presidential palace. He was rushed to Paris for treatment, and the political situation in Bamako slipped back toward precarity again.

Traoré's beating, however, caused the junta and its supporters to begin to lose support. Public mood swung away from them in favor of the battered civilian leadership. But the crisis was hardly over. Sanogo's group had its wings clipped, but they were still influential, with several important ministers in their camp. "The situation in Bamako has become as disquieting as the situation in the north," lamented one west African leader, who complained of "a three headed hydra where each plays his part. As soon as one has the agreement of one party, the other two immediately contest it."[69]

AL QA'IDA SPREADS ACROSS THE "AZAWAD"

The turmoil in Bamako only made matters worse in the north, facilitating and encouraging rebel advances. In late March, the secular and the Salafist Tuareg groups easily captured Kidal and Gao. On April 2, Timbuktu also fell. Najim's secular troops appear to have entered the town first, but within forty-eight hours, the al Qa'ida–linked Arab Salafists had also encamped there. Belmokhtar himself was reported among them.[70] The better-funded Salafi jihadists quickly pushed the Tuareg secularists out and raised the black flag of jihadist cause over the ancient town. "Everyone who is not on the path of Allah are miscreants," proclaimed Ghali on the local radio.[71] "Our war is a holy war," shouted another Ansar al Din leader upon entering Timbuktu, "America and France are the cause of the suffering in the world today. They came to dominate us, and leave the path of Allah."[72] On April 6, the Mouvement Nationale pour la Libération de l'Azawad declared the north independent, thus realizing their dream of reestablishing the mythical (and largely fictional) Azawad, a land that they claimed to include the regions of Gao, Timbuktu, and Kidal, thus encompassing 10 percent of Mali's population, and stretching 800,000 square kilometers across two-thirds of the country.[73]

By May, a growing number of Western observers were voicing concerns about the events that had transpired and drawing comparisons between the situation in Mali and Afghanistan in the late 1990s. "What's going on reminds me of what happened in Afghanistan and the Northwest Frontier Province of Pakistan," said a Western diplomat, describing the situation not inaccurately as "a Somalia situation with different groups competing and no one has control."[74] Indications were that Salafi militants from outside the region were heading to northern Mali, just as foreign fighters had once flocked to support al Qa'ida in Iraq and Afghanistan and would later flock to join ISIS and al Nusrah in Syria, Iraq and Libya.[75] These enthusiasts for jihad included some European and French citizens, alongside the recruits from elsewhere in Africa who wanted training from a real al Qa'ida's affiliate. Members of Boko Haram, a Nigerian jihadist group, had been in northern Mali for training and were also suspected of having received financing from al Qa'ida there.

In June, things only got worse as Ansar al Din and al Qa'ida began to institute a harsh form of *shari'a* in Timbuktu and other areas they controlled. Women were forced to cover up. Men were ordered to wear their pants above the ankle. Smoking, drinking, television, music, and football were all banned. Lashings were doled out as punishment for transgressions. Ansar al Din militants meanwhile set about destroying mausoleums of Muslim saints that were an irreplaceable part of the city's ancient heritage. In an act of defiance, they destroyed the doors on the Sidi Yeyia mosque, whose opening was held by locals to lead to the end of the world.

Increasingly the Mouvement Nationale pour la Libération de l'Azawad was sidelined from management of the towns it had originally captured, and clashes between it, Ansar al Din, and Mujao became frequent. In July, Muajo successfully chased Najim's forces from Gao, and imposed *shari'a*. In August, in a small town called Ansogo, near Gao, Mujao publicly amputated a man's hand with a crude knife and no anesthesia. They had earlier stoned a young couple to death for allegedly having children out of wedlock.

Most locals do not appear to have been very fond of *shari'a*. Most Tauregs did not share the extremist vision of the Salafist groups – Tuareg or Arab. "We are a country of religious tolerance" said Imam Mahamous Dicko, the head of the High Islamic Council of Mali. "Coming to any place with weapons to close bars – that's not how it's done. Stopping people playing football? That's archaic."[76] The public even staged protests against *shari'a* in towns of the north.

Watching the situation develop from far away in the Kabylie, Droukdal grew concerned that the imposition of *shari'a* would potentially undercut his underlings' startling gains. He sent orders to his commanders in the region to take it easy on the population. Letters discovered in Timbuktu later by the journalist Rukmini Callimachi as Belmokhtar and Abu Zeid's forces retreated showed considerable discord between Droukdal and his deputies. While the long-term objective was the imposition of *shari'a*, Droukdal argued, it was important not to turn the people against them. Going too swiftly toward *shari'a* also risked encouraging the international community to intervene. "The current baby is in its first days, crawling on its knees, and has not yet stood on its two legs," Droukdal wrote, anthropomorphizing Mali. "If we really want it to stand on its own two feet in this world full of enemies waiting to pounce, we must ease its burden, take it by the hand, help it and support it until its stands."[77]

Perhaps because the groups in the north needed to demonstrate their fearsomeness in order to control a much larger population, the Emir's warnings were not closely heeded. *Shari'a* was not the only thing the jihadists brought to the northern towns, however. As elsewhere in the world, al Qa'ida operations in the north were well organized and businesslike, with fighters assiduously collecting receipts for their expenses and holding regular meetings and even "workshops" that addressed a range of practical and theological issues. In Timbuktu they paid thousands of dollars for fuel to keep the town generator running, and spent considerable sums on charitable works aimed at wooing the population.[78] Although far from a Western army, this was not the rag-tag bunch that some press reports made them appear. They were working carefully to realize their dream of a regional caliphate. And by the summer of 2012, they were making progress.

Half a year after the initial outbreak of the revolt, the Salafi jihadist groups controlled the main cities of the north. Gao was now largely under Mujao's control, with growing cooperation from Belmokthar. Kidal, Timbuktu, and Léré were under the control of Ansar al Din. The northernmost towns along the Algerian border were controlled by Abu Zeid. The French estimated that each group was roughly 300 to 500 strong, such that the total number of jihadists was a little over 1,000.[79]

The towns the jihadists controlled drew more and more international attention over the course of the summer and fall of 2012. "As each day goes by, al Qa'ida and other organizations are strengthening their hold in northern Mali," General Carter Ham, commander of U.S. forces in Africa, said in Washington in December.[80] UN secretary general Ban Ki Moon issued a report on the situation, which found that northern Mali was "at risk of becoming a permanent haven for terrorists and organized criminal networks where people are subjected to a very strict interpretation of *shari'a* law and human rights are abused on a systematic basis."[81] As one French diplomat put it, "The danger that we will see the emergence of an Afghanistan in the heart of the Sahel, with risks that will weigh on the neighboring countries as well as France, are too great."[82] Another pointed to the Sahel more broadly, expressing concern that "tomorrow France could be the target of a new September 11" attack.[83]

As the jihadists entrenched themselves across the north and Bamako remained mired in the effects of the coup, there was a growing consensus in Paris that the situation was dire; something needed to be done. French leaders were increasingly favorable to military action – but not in the form that action would ultimately take.

5 LEADING AFRICA FROM BEHIND

The creation of a safe-haven for al Qa'ida–linked Salafi jihadists in northern Mali was a phase shift in the North African terrorist threat to the region and to the West. Uncontested sanctuary gave al Qa'ida's allies the chance to accelerate their recruitment, build training camps, enrich themselves more fully from regional smuggling, enlarge their field of operations along multiple vectors regionwide, and plot attacks on enemies, near and far.

If the kidnapping scourge had focused French national attention on the Sahel intermittently for at least three years, the birth of "Malistan" in 2012 combined with the Merah attacks made Mali a top foreign policy issue in a presidential election otherwise focused largely on domestic issues. There was a creeping acceptance on both sides of the political aisle that the French approach to the problem posed by the spread of jihadists in the Sahel was not working and more needed to be done. Sarkozy, however, had eschewed direct action, likely out of a fear about the impact a mishap would have on a presidential campaign he was already losing.

When Hollande defeated Sarkozy in the May 6, 2012 elections, his foreign policy advisors knew Mali would be their first major test. What was at stake in the region was "immensely important" to France, as one senior French diplomat later put it.[1] It wasn't just that the French had a "moral duty" to do something in their former colonial space. The crisis was taking place "right in their backyard," a fact that gave France a special interest in addressing the problem.[2] At the same time, proximity also meant that Paris was better positioned and better informed about the issue than many other capitals, including Washington – although Paris by no means enjoyed perfect information about what was going on in Bamako's fraught political scene, let alone the desolate northern reaches of the country.

Most of all, France was the only Western power for whom Mali was genuinely a priority. The United States remained focused on Afghanistan and increasingly oriented toward the Asia Pacific. The United Kingdom was entering a period of intense introspection. Germany was still inclined toward its traditional "checkbook" diplomacy – in Africa and elsewhere.

Despite the growing French concern about the challenge the crisis in Mali posed, however, the new government was at first no more prepared to intervene militarily than its predecessor had been. Hollande was in fact in the process of accelerating the withdrawal from Afghanistan. Libya was meanwhile showing its first signs of faltering, and would serve thereafter as an aide-mémoire of the hazards and limits of military force used absent coordination with other forms of power. In keeping with past socialist positions, Hollande had moreover backed change in France's traditional paternalistic role in Africa. "I will break with the 'Francafrique' by proposing a relationship founded on equality, confidence and solidarity" read proposal 58 of his campaign platform. This would seem to imply an end to French unilateral interventions in its old colonial sphere.

France in 2012 thus seemed no more likely to intervene in Mali than did any other major power. Rather than acting directly in Mali, the French tried to prevail upon African states to take the lead on the crisis, insisting all the while on the need for an "African solution" to this African problem.

HOLLANDE'S CRISIS

International security issues did not figure prominently in the 2012 French presidential elections, where debate focused primarily on French economic challenges and discontent with Sarkozy's sometimes abrasive presidential style, which had worn thin with the French public. But Mali was one of few national security issues that did seem to matter. In the presidential debate on May 2, just days before the elections, there was no mention of Syria or Iran, and the only discussion of China or the United States was in the context of broader economic questions. The presidential candidates, however, spent several minutes arguing over Mali. "The terrorist threat also hovers over the Islamic Maghreb with al Qa'ida's rising power in the countries of the Sahel, including Mali, Niger, Mauritania, as well as Yemen and Somalia," said then-president Sarkozy. "Eight French hostages are held in this zone. How do you propose to free them, M. Hollande?" Sarkozy demanded. When he lost the election a few days later, the question would no longer be rhetorical.

When Hollande entered office, Mali was thus already a "very, very high priority for the president," as one senior member of his staff explained.[3] Some officials reported that France's desire to withdraw early from Afghanistan and Kosovo was driven in part by intense concern about threats from the Sahel, where French interests were implicated in multiple ways.[4] French intelligence resources had been shifted from Afghanistan to Mali, and the French military had in fact planned strikes against al Qa'ida in Mali on at least two occasions. Both times, however, President Sarkozy refused to pull the trigger. The first opportunity came during the 2011 Libya intervention, but the President was hesitant to open a second front in Africa. A second chance came as the crisis in Bamako was intensifying and French intelligence services had credible reports that al Qa'ida in the Islamic Maghreb leaders were gathered in a house in Timbuktu – sitting ducks for a military strike. The military tabled a plan for air strikes, but again the French president refused, fearing this time for his standing in the polls on the eve of the elections.[5]

France had economic interests in Mali and the broader region. Some 30 percent of French gas and hydrocarbon resources are imported from Africa.[6] Neighboring Niger was an important source of uranium for France's nuclear power plants, hence the presence of the Areva and Satom employees kidnapped from Arlit in 2010. Most of Mali's below-ground resources, which included gas and oil, uranium, phosphates, and manganese, however, are not considered profitable for extraction, and economic interests do not appear to have been a significant factor when it came to the decision to intervene in Mali.

France's nearly two centuries of colonial history in the region was much more important because it shaped French attitudes and brought the French and Malian societies closer together. There were many Malians in France, a large number of which were concentrated in the Parisian suburb of Montreuil, itself often referred to as the largest Malian city other than Bamako. This was a corner of the world well known to the French in general and the French military in particular. Colonial history engendered a sense of responsibility for the impoverished country, especially when coupled with what one senior French official referred to as France's "own neoconservative impulse" – France's yearning to serve as a global force for the revolutionary values of *liberté, égalité,* and *fraternité*.[7]

At the same time, any of the same forces that drew France and Mali closer – the immigrant community, proximity that allowed for daily direct flights between Bamako and Paris, and France's colonial past – also made concern about the al Qa'ida threat in Mali particularly acute in Paris. The hostage takings had become frequent fare on the nightly news in recent years, implanting the problem directly in the living rooms of the French public.

The special relationship between France and Mali was manifest most immediately and concretely by the conveyance of Diancounda Traoré to a Paris hospital after his beating at the hands of Sanogo supporters in May, which occurred only a few weeks after the French elections. An optimist by nature, the seventy-year-old interim president used his narrow escape from death to plead his case for action to top-level French leaders. Foreign minister Fabius, the president's advisors, and President Hollande himself visited Traoré regularly at his Paris hospital bed. Traoré used these meetings to stress the point that the crisis in Mali was "truly special."[8] What was happening in his country was not a typical case of African civil war, he insisted. It was about al Qa'ida, and thus a threat to everyone. Al Qa'ida was determined to get control over the whole country, creating an international menace, he argued, Mali was just the latest battlefield.[9] Traoré also tried to impress upon the French how weak the Malian army was, the fact that it was decrepit, for decades only an army in name, good for "parades and coups, but not war."[10] There was no way Mali would be able to handle the al Qa'ida menace on its own. His country needed French help, and especially the help of the French military.

These consultations strengthened the relationship between the new French leadership and Mali's battered interim leader. French trust in Traoré grew; French officials came to believe he was a sincere leader they could work with. After Traoré returned to Mali, Hollande had an interlocutor he could rely on. He was "our hub, our base" in Mali during the operation, a senior French official put it a year after the intervention.[11]

LEADING AFRICA FROM BEHIND

If the new Hollande team was immediately seized with the crisis in Mali, they were hardly eager to take direct military action themselves. The top French military brass promised they could defeat the jihadists on the battlefield, but the new French civilian leadership was ill disposed to the idea of launching headlong into a military intervention in Africa.[12] Instead, they focused on getting African countries to intervene themselves. Concern about campaign promises and whether or not the public would support another intervention figured in the calculus of the *Elysée*, but so did the fact that it was initially less than clear that Malians or their neighbors would be happy if their old colonial master restarted large-scale, unilateral military operations in the region. As foreign minister Fabius put it, therefore, a few months after the elections, while a military operation of some kind in Mali became more likely, "France, for obvious reasons, cannot be in the lead."[13] President Hollande was also concerned that if it looked like France was preparing for military action on its own, this could dissipate momentum for a multinational, African approach.[14] What emerged was thus akin to the strategy the United States had used to press France and other European allies to carry their water a year earlier in the Libya intervention, a strategy dubbed "leading from behind" in Washington. Military intervention had to be up to the African nations themselves. Africa would take responsibility for African problems.

Soon after entering office, Hollande's staff proposed holding a series of consultations with French allies and partners to raise awareness of the threat and assess the feasibility of military options. These consultations continued over the summer. Hollande met with Boni Yayi, the president of Benin, who held the chair of the African Union,

Mohammadou Issoufou, president of Mali's neighbor Niger, president Alassane Ouattara of the Côte d'Ivoire, and president Macky Sall of Senegal. In July, Foreign Minister Fabius toured the Sahel, with stops in Niger, Burkina Faso, Senegal, and Chad. Hollande also used his first call with President Obama to raise the issue, and, along with other French leaders, worked to draw attention to the problem with their European partners.[15]

Most African leaders were open to some kind of military intervention – indeed they had mooted the possibility in their initial negotiations with Sanogo in April – but the French ran into much more resistance when it came to Algeria.[16] A key regional power, Algeria had once been at the root of the regional terrorist problem (see Chapter 2). Abu Zeid and Belmokthar had retreated to Mali after being chased out of Algeria. Moreover, the Algerians had been central in negotiating the accords that ended Mali's 2006 Tuareg revolt and maintained ties with some of the jihadist groups in the region, especially Ghali's Ansar al Din. Throughout the first half of 2012, the Algerians pushed for a political solution to the crisis. As al Qa'ida strengthened its grip on the north, this increasingly irritated the French. In an effort to remain neutral, and because of the coup, Algeria froze military cooperation with Mali and withdrew its military advisors from the north. They then made a diplomatic push with their own Tuareg groups to get the rebels to return to the negotiating table, while at the same time refusing to treat wounded rebel fighters in Algeria.[17]

In mid-July, Hollande's top Africa advisor, Helène le Gall, and the Quai d'Orsay's special representative for the Sahel, Jean Félix-Paganon, visited Algiers for consultations with regional leaders on the crisis. Nevertheless, the French were becoming increasingly irked with Algeria's apparent willingness to work with Ansar al Din, which itself was now clearly allied with al Qa'ida, yet whose representatives had still visited Algiers earlier that month.[18] It seemed like the main objective of the Algerians was not to get rid of the terrorists so much as to push them south into the Sahara where they could be safely contained. "There is a troubling side to the attitude in Algiers," said one French diplomat.[19] Another put it more bluntly, "Algeria, who has suffered so much from terrorism, is adopting a policy that is being interpreted regionally as kind to terrorism!"[20]

Meanwhile the African negotiating efforts were continuing through the Economic Community of West African States. Burkina Faso's president Blaise Compoaré was also hoping for a diplomatic breakthrough – many believed largely to burnish his own regional prestige. Compaoré had played a high-profile role as a mediator in the Côte d'Ivoire, Niger, Togo, and other regional conflicts and had established bona fides with Tuareg groups in the region. He was eager to continue the diplomatic push before exercising the military option. He sent his foreign minister, Djibril Bassolé, directly to Gao and Kidal to negotiate with the jihadists in August.[21] These were the first direct talks with the jihadists at that level in the north itself, but they led nowhere in bringing the northern parties back into the fold. Needless to say, these efforts did nothing to stop the extremists from imposing *shari'a* across Mali's northern cities.

Algeria's reservations about military force aside, the coup in Bamako was getting real attention from Mali's other neighbors, who feared al Qa'ida might soon spread beyond Mali's own borders.[22] After all, a regional caliphate was their stated objective – like the Islamic State of Iraq and the Levant a few years later. African leaders continued to consider military action, even while pursing the diplomatic track. Sanogo, for obvious reasons, was set against the deployment of outside military forces on the ground in Mali. He continued to insist there was no such need; Mali's own army could handle the situation on its own. Other parts of the Malian government were also reluctant to accept foreign military on their soil.[23] On September 24, however, following a formal power-sharing agreement that in theory demoted Sanogo, Bamako yielded. Traoré officially requested a UN Security Council resolution that would authorize an international stabilization force to deploy onto Malian soil and begin the reconquest of the north.

French leaders recognized that given the grip the jihadists had on the North, an intervention was, by that point, highly desirable, even inevitable. Nevertheless, it still seemed like France would have a limited role. In the president's traditional summer address to the French diplomatic corps, Hollande again claimed France intended to break from its neocolonial past when it came to the crisis in Mali. He said the terrorist threat in the north was a "challenge to our interests, our

values, and our population," and that France was "directly implicated … we will have to act, not by the interventions of yesterday –
this is a bygone time – our role consists in supporting our African
partners; it is they who need to take the initiative, the decision, the
responsibility."[24] Yet at the same time, French diplomats continued
to insist that France would "only want to play a facilitating role," and
that "there is no question of sending troops on the ground."[25]

According to his advisors, however, Hollande did seek to nudge his
African counterparts along toward military action by offering them
reassurances of French military support. African leaders were aware of
the weakness of their own militaries – and often fearful of the menace
al Qa'ida loyalists would pose to their soldiers. No one wanted a repeat
of the humiliation that had spawned the chaos in Bamako earlier in
the year. Throughout the discussion about the African force, Hollande
thus quietly promised that the French military would be behind any
African intervention, ready to provide intelligence, transport aircraft,
and even close air support to ensure Mali's neighbors success on the
battlefield.[26] Again, this was leading from Behind, à la française.

On September 26, President Hollande thus delivered a speech
at the United Nations that aimed to press French allies to get fully
behind the African force with training, financing, and other support.[27]
Placing Mali alongside the crisis in Syria, the Iran nuclear issue, and
the Israel-Palestine conflict, Hollande said that Mali was a

> matter of urgency – and perhaps the first one we should deal with
> this week…. The situation created by the occupation of a territory
> in northern Mali by terrorist groups is intolerable, inadmissible and
> unacceptable, not only for Mali, who is directly affected by this ter-
> rorist evil, but for all the countries of the region and, beyond, for all
> those who may one day be the victims of terrorism.[28]

CLASH AT THE UNITED NATIONS

With French pressure, continued reports about the gruesome deeds of
the jihadists in the north, and concomitant fear the region was becoming a magnet for foreign fighters, who might soon turn their sites elsewhere, the international debate over what to do about the deteriorating

situation was heating up. France remained seized with the crisis and eager to push the international community forward toward its resolution. France wanted to see an international military force in place as soon as possible. The United States, however, was uneasy about the risk of moving too fast and raised several concerns, slowing the French down, piquing them, and generating rising levels of Franco-American tension.

According to French sources, Hollande and Obama spoke on several occasions about the crisis, either through meetings or videoconferences, and the French continued to raise the issue in top-level discussion with both the State and Defense Departments.[29] Then–White House advisor for homeland security, John Brennan, was meanwhile working with President Hollande's military advisor, General Benoit Puga, on a regional counterterrorism strategy.[30] Nevertheless, the French complained about the difficulty in getting the U.S. administration to focus on the issue. American interest in North African terrorism increased after the murderous attacks on the U.S. diplomatic facility in Benghazi, Libya on 9/11, 2012, but there were still strong reservations about any military action in Mali whatsoever.[31]

The truth is, the United States was divided internally between those who looked at the problem through a strict counterterrorism lens and those who saw it more broadly as a democracy promotion issue. Senior officials at the State Department in particular thought the French were charging much too hard at a military solution to what was an exceedingly complex issue. The State Department tended to view the problem largely through the lens of democratization and continued to withhold U.S. assistance to Mali until democracy could be restored. Any lenience on this front, they feared, would send the wrong signal to antidemocratic forces across Africa. Plans to support the Malian military or government in its effort to retake the north thus had to be put in abeyance until the situation improved. They tended to claim that foreign intervention needed to await the restoration of democratic governance in Bamako.[32]

As U.S. Assistant Secretary of State for African Affairs Johnnie Carson rightly testified before Congress in December, al Qa'ida was only one part of a very complex problem. Working with the illegitimate government in Bamako could send exactly the wrong signal to other regional militaries, he said. Military action was thus premature. The key thing was to restore democracy, and this meant negotiations with the secular Tuareg groups needed to take priority. There were real dangers, Carson stressed, in conflating the al Qa'ida threat with these other problems.[33]

Other parts of the U.S. government, however, ultimately including the White House, were increasingly focused on the counterterrorism challenge as Belmokthar, Ghali, Abu Zeid, and their associates entrenched themselves. While cognizant of the negative signal cooperation with the very imperfect interim government in Bamako could send to the rest of Africa, proponents of doing something about al Qa'ida in the north eventually won out in internal U.S. deliberations.

There was nevertheless a very real concern in all corners of the U.S. government about how any operation in northern Mali could actually work. U.S. officials seriously doubted regional militaries were in any position to take on a military operation in Mali, let alone counterterrorism operations in such a harsh climate. "It was troubling to hear heads of state talk about a West African Force that didn't exist," one senior U.S. official later lamented.[34] African forces had established that they could sometimes perform well within the rubric of a UN peacekeeping operation – and had done a particularly fine job at helping bring some semblance of stability to Somalia – but in this case very few had training for offensive action of the kind that was plainly going to be needed to retake northern Mali from the jihadists – let alone training in the extreme conditions of the Sahara.

The militaries of the countries that the French hoped would provide their forces were woefully ill-equipped. The Nigerian military had once been the backbone of the regional contributions to stabilization operations, including in Liberia and Sierra Leone. But Nigeria's expeditionary capability had been severely eroded in recent years as its army got bogged down with no less than three insurgencies on its own territory – in the Niger Delta, the north, and the middle belt. Senegal had a military many judged better suited for parades than military operations. Questions were also raised about Niger's military's human rights record.[35] Only Mauritania had units with any experience against al Qa'ida in the Islamic Maghreb, and they alone would never be enough to mount the operation.[36] Chad was one country that actually did have forces with experience in extreme desert conditions. Chadian troops had battled Qaddafi and also had more recent training in their own desert conditions. Chad's authoritarian president Idriss Déby, however, was hardly a model leader, and was suspected of having used his military to eliminate his political opposition. Equally, if not more important, Chadian troops had a rather regretful record when it came to human rights and the treatment of civilians.

Tension thus brewed between the United States and France on two fronts. First, whether or not the restoration of democracy ought to take precedence over military action. Second, whether or not the African forces that the French were pushing would be able to handle the task. To complicate matters, the head of the Economic Community of West African States's peacekeeping school in Bamako, Moussa Sinko Coulibaly, had associated himself with Sanogo, who was himself a graduate of the school.[37]

The French, for whom the terrorist threat was by far the most palpable, were undeterred by friction with the United States and persisted in seeking a Security Council resolution that would authorize foreign military intervention in Mali as soon as possible. Because French leaders were more comfortable with Diancounda Traoré than their U.S. counterparts, they were less concerned about the need for fresh elections prior to military operations to retake the north. Because they were prepared to offer significant support to the African mission, they were less concerned about the several issues that the U.S. raised concerning command and control and capabilities of African forces, especially for the more difficult counterterrorism tasks.

In December, the French tabled a draft Security Council resolution that would authorize the African force to deploy into the north. Both the United States and UN secretary general Ban Ki-Moon were skeptical. Ban refused to put UN funding behind the force, noting that required operations against the jihadists could be highly kinetic and thus did not fit easily into the rubric of UN peacekeeping.[38] U.S. ambassador to the United Nations Susan Rice called the French plan "crap."[39] Meanwhile the United States, though itself still internally divided on the issue, pushed for a two-stage process that kept the focus on getting a democratically elected government back in Bamako before anything was done to retake the north militarily.

According to the U.S. proposal, a regional peacekeeping force could be authorized to deploy into southern Mali to bolster and train the Malian army, but a second resolution would be needed to authorize any use of force against the jihadist-held areas.[40] There was genuine consternation in part of the Washington bureaucracy that the French were pushing too fast on the military front and consequent reticence about writing a blank check for the African force that still looked woefully unprepared for the mission.[41] From Paris, however, this U.S. caution looked like plain-old foot-dragging.[42] Franco-American friction peaked accordingly, as officials on both sides of the Atlantic later acknowledged.

As the contest over the Security Council resolution was playing out at Turtle Bay in New York, a new crisis broke in Bamako. On December 11, Prime Minister Cheick Modibo Diarra was arrested by Sanogo's backers, dragged to their camp at Kati and ordered to step down. Diarra's persistent support for an international force to retake the north had evidently pushed Sanogo, who continued to insist the Malian army was up to the task itself, too far. Diarra's ouster further increased the ambient tension and made prospects for getting a democratically elected government in place look even more remote than a week before. The French argued that Diarra's ouster was yet more evidence of the urgency of the situation and need for a UN resolution authorizing an international force.

Negotiations thus continued. Eventually, the French added language on elections that proved sufficient to win U.S. support for the resolution. On December 21, the Security Council approved Resolution 2085 under Chapter VII of the UN Charter. The resolution authorized the African-led International Support Mission for Mali for one year, but emphasized the need for further refinement to the military plans before the force began any combat operations. The need for a restoration of democracy and further efforts to find a negotiated settlement with the rebel groups that had severed ties with al Qa'ida came before the paragraphs authorizing the international force. Member states were called upon to offer funding, and the Secretary General was asked to hold a donor's conference and set up a trust fund to help finance operations, but specifics of who would actually pay were left to a later date.

As 2012 came to a close, therefore, the pieces were in place for a slow and steady effort to restore democracy in Bamako and begin full peace negotiations with the Tuareg rebel groups that would agree to renounce al Qa'ida. The European Union, in theory at least, would deploy a military training mission to strengthen the Malian military so that it could eventually play a role in the military effort to retake the north. Exactly how the European Union would train a military that was holding the democratic government hostage was far from clear – some delay until more propitious circumstances emerged seemed unavoidable. Also unclear was the extent to which the African-led force would deploy to Bamako as it built up capacity to take on the jihadists, a question that itself raised the issue of whether or not the Kati group would cooperate peaceably with such a deployment. In any event, the whole process was expected to take months at least to get underway. Most estimates pointed to September as the deployment date for the African force.

The implicit assumption behind all of this, and especially the U.S. position, was that the jihadists would stay where they were, north of the Niger Bend, while the international community got organized to take the country back. Less than a month after the UN resolution, that assumption was proven wrong.

VIEWS OF THE FRENCH MILITARY

Throughout these political and diplomatic machinations, the French military was quietly preparing to intervene.[43] French military officers are quick to stress that they view military intervention "as a last resort."[44] They followed orders and worked to support efforts to build up an African force, but they doubted the force would be able to do much on its own. Some form of French intervention in Mali was widely thought inevitable among their ranks. The only question was what exactly it would look like. Many officers shared U.S. skepticism about the likelihood that their African counterparts could shoulder a problem of this magnitude, not, at least, without a large dose of support from France. Much of the planning that took place on the French joint staff focused on a scenario in which France supported an African force, but even that planning tended to assume a very large French role.

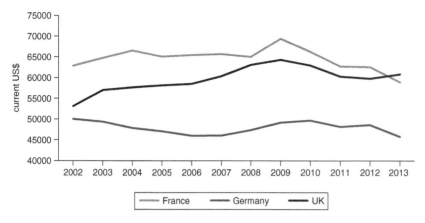

Figure 10. Total French Military Expenditure Relative to Germany and Britain (Millions of Constant 2011 Dollars).
Source: SIPRI Yearbook 2013. Note: SIPRI figures include some forms of domestic security and are therefore higher as a percentage of GDP than the figures normally cited in the NATO context.

The crisis in Mali came at a critical juncture for the French military, and especially the key service that it affected, the army. Amid mounting public skepticism about the utility of NATO operations in Afghanistan, President Sarkozy had decided to withdraw France's small but effective contingent from eastern Afghanistan ahead of schedule. The 2011 intervention in Libya had been largely the purview of the French air force and navy. Although French army helicopters participated and French commandos were on the ground, especially in the later stages of the war, the army in general played only a minor role. As elsewhere in NATO, the trend in war seemed to be away from the long-term large scale army deployments that had characterized the previous decade, and toward an era of precision wars fought with airpower and small numbers of special forces.

As pressure on the French budget intensified as a result of Europe's sovereign debt crisis, calls for defense cuts mounted. (Figures 10 and 11 show French spending trends relative to other European countries in recent years.) The Hollande administration had planned a new white paper on national security to explain how France would meet its defense commitments in a period of mounting austerity. Especially

Figure 11. Comparative Annual European Military Expenditures as Percent of GDP, 1988–2012.
Source: SIPRI Yearbook 2013. Note: SIPRI figures include some forms of domestic security and are therefore higher as a percentage of GDP than the figures normally cited in the NATO context.

given other priorities Hollande had laid out, many in French military circles feared the Socialists were planning deep cuts to the military, and it was rumored that the French military chief, Admiral Edouard Guillaud was scheming to ensure that any such cuts fell on the Army rather than the Navy.[45] As the crisis in Mali brewed, therefore, there was an obvious incentive for the Army to demonstrate that it remained essential to protecting French interests at home and overseas.

Since the end of the Cold War, the French military had been transformed from a large conscript force into a streamlined, fully professionalized modern military, while upgrading and modernizing its equipment to meet the challenges of the new international security environment. These efforts began in the wake of the Gulf War, which had brought several gaps in existing French capabilities to light. The major shift came in 1996, however, with President Chirac's decision to transition to a fully professional military force and shift investment to emphasize overseas expeditionary capabilities.

The growing emphasis on expeditionary capabilities favored the vestiges of France's old colonial army. Since the second empire, the French military had always housed two oft-competing forces, one focused on France's overseas empire, the other dedicated to defending France against Continental threats. The capabilities, doctrine, and culture of these two parts of the French military evolved in different ways. The colonially focused units were lighter and accustomed to long-term deployments overseas in which they worked closely with their foreign counterparts. The "Continental forces of the line" were heavier units, based permanently within metropolitan France. From the nineteenth century, these forces were focused almost exclusively on defending France's Eastern borders against a German attack, a mission that transitioned into defense against the USSR in the later half of the twentieth century. The colonial forces and the forces of the line were once formalized in the distinction between the French Foreign Legion and colonial regiments on the one hand and regular metropolitan French military units on the other. Such distinctions have been eroded some in the later twentieth century, but the humiliating defeat of French continental forces in 1940 and the overseas nature of French operations in Algeria, Indochina, and Africa during the Cold War helped sustain the distinction between those forces that were trained for overseas warfare and those that were relegated to defending French borders against an increasingly unlikely attack.[46]

Needless to say, France's postcolonial forces were among the best prepared within France and NATO for the out-of-area operations that became the norm in the post–Cold War global international security environment. After Rwandan genocide, however, France increasingly sought a multinational format for its operations and for a time shifted its operational focus back to Europe. French forces participated in NATO deployments in Bosnia and, after the United States, played a leading role in air operations in NATO's Operation Allied Force over Kosovo in 1999. French forces had never left their old colonial realm, of course, but the operational tempo in Africa in the decade after the Rwandan genocide significantly declined.

In the next decade, the focus of French military overseas operations again shifted back to Africa in a visible way, with French troops deployed in Côte d'Ivoire, the Democratic Republic of Congo, and Chad. Unlike French operations in Mali, however, nearly all these missions were conducted in closer and earlier coordination with the United Nations and European Union and conceived primarily as peacekeeping operations rather than offensive operations against an adversary such as al Qa'ida.

In 2003 in the Democratic Republic of Congo, for example, France provided the vast majority of the forces for the European Union's operation *Artemis*, which backstopped the much larger UN peacekeeping force when that force ran into difficulty. The French were able to leave the Congo behind in a matter of months but found themselves in Côte d'Ivoire much longer. There, operation *Licorne*, which was conducted solely under French auspices, aimed to stop a potentially very destabilizing civil war in 2002. French troops spent the next decade holding the line between rebel forces in the north and entrenched government in Abidjan. France finally tilted toward the rebel leader Ouattara in an effort to break the stalemate and garner some relief for itself from policing the standoff. French forces in operation *Licorne* would play an important role when it came time to respond rapidly to the crisis in Mali. So would French forces in Chad, Niger, Burkina Faso, and elsewhere across the region.

One of the central lessons French leaders took away from the experience of the 1990s, and the Kosovo air campaign in particular, was that their ability to contribute visibly to out-of-area operations would be crucial to their political and diplomatic clout.[47] This helped to justify continued investment in the Rafale multi-role fighter jet, which, while very expensive, offered a high-profile capability that might be useful for future airpower-heavy interventions. It also encouraged France to move toward greater deployability and interoperability with other allies. French leaders envisioned playing a supporting role in some operations, but a lead role in others, especially operations outside the NATO framework. As a "framework nation" France would provide the impetus and avant garde for interventions, especially on Europe's periphery.

While some European allies opted to save money by specializing, French military leaders have long insisted on the importance of maintaining a full spectrum of capabilities that would allow them to act autonomously. In keeping with the aim of flexibility and deployability, the French structured their land forces into eight combat brigades, of which two were light, two heavy, and four medium weight. Investments in technology designed to facilitate rapid deployability and expeditionary operations were a big focus of the French modernization program. Key investments included the Véhicule Blindé de Combat Infanterie (VBCI), a new combat infantry vehicle that would feature prominently in *Serval*, and the broader *Scorpion* modernization program, of which it is part, that is intended to provide a fully networked and digitized land warfare family of systems.

The post–Cold War French emphasis on expeditionary operations did decline somewhat in President Sarkozy's 2008 White Paper on Defense and National Security, which put military intervention as the last of five top spending priorities – the others being knowledge and anticipation, prevention, deterrence, and protection. All of these of course are important to intervention on some level, but the paper conceived of them, not without reason, as needs in themselves. French prepositioned forces in Africa were also to be reduced, in part to boost France's footprint in the Middle East. France had defense agreements with certain African countries such as Côte d'Ivoire, Gabon, and Togo that facilitated French intervention when those governments were threatened, for example, by civil war. Especially after the Rwanda experience, these agreements had come to be viewed as archaic. One objective of the 2008 white paper was to replace them with renovated partnership arrangements. Alongside this, the white paper called for a significant reduction in the number of French troops in Africa overall. As of 2007, some 10,000 French soldiers were deployed in Djibouti, Senegal, Gabon, Côte d'Ivoire, the Central African Republic, and at two locations in Chad. France would maintain some forward positioned forces, but these were to be reduced in number and concentrated in two bases, one in the west and one in the east – a reduction that was never implemented (as noted in Chapter 3).

At the same time that France was trying to reconfigure and reduce its role in Africa, French forces had been deployed in Afghanistan both as part of NATO-ISAF and as part of U.S. coalition operations under Operation Enduring Freedom (OEF). A small number of French special forces were engaged alongside the United States in counterterrorism operations in Spin Boldak and Jalalabad from 2003 to 2006, but most of France's 2,000 soldiers were confined to Kabul, where they did not see combat operations until the French took over responsibility for Kapisa province in the dangerous eastern sector in 2008.

Because their operations in Afghanistan had been more limited than the British and because they had expended no resources at all fighting in Iraq, the French were moreover better positioned for operations in Mali than any other European country. This was true despite the strain on the French defense budget. The United States, for its part, was still heavily occupied elsewhere. Although the U.S. presence in Africa had increased to nearly 5,000 troops, a force greater there than at any time since the Somalia intervention, the continent was still a lower level concern for U.S. leaders, who were in a strongly anti-interventionist mood to boot.[48] If there was to be an intervention in Mali, the French military would thus play a critical part. No other forces, African, European, or American, were up for the task.

From the French military's perspective, this was not entirely a bad thing. As the debate over the future of the French military brewed around the White Paper, a war against al Qa'ida in Africa offered a unique chance to demonstrate the military's enduring value against a serious threat that deeply worried the French public. Obviously, the outbreak of war always represents a human failure on some level, and the French military recognized this. But Mali was already under siege; in this case, that failure seemed to have occurred long ago.

6 CRISIS AND OPPORTUNITY

France's six-month attempt to lead the Africans from behind into a military action against al Qa'ida collapsed in a few short days in early January 2013 when several hundred jihadists breached the Niger Bend in an armed convoy and sped toward Bamako. For three days, French officials had watched anxiously from Paris as hundreds of jihadists assembled in their pickup trucks along the Niger. The French hoped the jihadists would stay in the north, and wondered what Ag Ghali and his allies might possibly expect to accomplish with an attack on Mali's capital in such small numbers. When the jihadists suddenly crossed the river and headed south, the attack came as a surprise for many onlookers, and a frightening one. Even if it would be almost impossible for a few hundred modestly armed jihadists to hold the city, the Malian military was torn and enfeebled, and the African force was far from ready to deploy. This left Bamako's population of more than one million defenseless against some of the most ruthless terrorists in Africa.

But if the jihadist thrust across the Niger River was dangerous it was also a classic example of an opportunity enfolded in a crisis. By crossing the river, the jihadists had made what many French officials would later come to see as their first big strategic error: The audacious threat to the capital not only gave France cause to intervene directly, it also openly exposed the jihadists to direct and violent strikes by the French military.[1] The French seized the opportunity and struck the enemy with the force of France's modern military machine, plunging themselves headlong into their largest military operation in Africa in half a century.

THE JIHADIST ADVANCE ON BAMAKO

In early January, controversy was brewing among the leaders of the various jihadist groups that now occupied northern Mali. With the UN Security Council resolution passed, the possibility of a foreign intervention was now real. Ag Ghali, eventually backed by his al Qa'ida allies, started pushing for rapid action to seize Bamako, in order to thwart any international action. But in Gao, Mujao leader Abu Kheirou resisted.[2] French intelligence services were watching these deliberations. Beginning on January 4, it was clear something was up, even if many observers still thought the jihadists would never be bold enough to cross the river.[3]

Sitting in Bamako, however, interim president Traoré felt certain the jihadists would attack. The African forces were nowhere near ready to deploy. More drastic measures would be needed to halt their advance. But the French were still wavering. President Hollande telephoned Traoré to ask whether he thought an attack was imminent. Traoré insisted it was. His own intelligence sources were telling him that the jihadists had every intent of crossing into the south and invading the capital. He was especially worried about what he feared were dormant jihadist cells dispersed throughout Bamako. Although these fears later proved exaggerated, they were not unusual – Bamako did have something of a reputation as an "R&R" spot for Algerian and other North African jihadists, according to one senior U.S. official.[4] Criminals and extremist elements already in the city could easily contribute to the violence and general chaos that was sure to ensue once the jihadists entered.

Then, on the night of January 9, the jihadists crossed the Niger and headed toward Konna. Dressed as civilians, an advance group rode the bus from Gao to Konna and toward Mopti. When the bus was stopped for an identification check, they opened fire with Kalashnikovs. Ansar al Din followed close behind them, supported by al Qa'ida and Mujao, which after initial hesitation had decided to join the attack.[5] When the jihadists took Konna, Traoré received another call from the French president. This time, Hollande wanted Traoré's invitation to intervene.[6] In a hastily drafted letter, the Malian president requested that France come to his country's aid immediately. A similar letter was sent to UN Secretary General Ban Ki Moon, asking the full support of the international community.

On Friday morning, January 11, President Hollande convened an emergency meeting of his national security team to consider France's options. Unlike parliamentary systems in many other European countries, and even in comparison with the American system, the French crisis decision-making process can move rapidly. This is in large part because the primacy of the president in French foreign and security policy is well established and a cornerstone of the Gaullist Fifth Republic. In contrast with Germany, for example, the French parliament has no say in the decision to send French soldiers into battle. Although, as in the United States, the French president must eventually seek parliament's approval, the initial decision to go to war is this President's alone. Moreover, the U.S. process can involve a lengthy and often bureaucratic set of preparatory meetings intended to coordinate bureaucratic interests and shape decisions for the president and his top national security advisors, whereas in France, the process is much less iterative.

The rough French equivalent of such a top-level U.S. meeting is the *conseil de défense*, or defense council, which brings the president together with a select group of ministers – normally the defense and foreign ministers along with the French chairman of the joint chiefs of staff – the *chef d'état-major des armées*. The French council, however, has no subordinate councils or committees, and this accelerates the decision-making process, at least relative to the U.S. model.

Foreign Minister Fabius was perhaps the most seasoned political figure in the new French government – a former prime minister with even more experience than the president himself. But Fabius had taken only modest interest in African issues and throughout Hollande's administration had focused on big issues in the Middle East – especially Iran and Syria. Moreover, as a key representative of a more left-leaning branch of the Socialist Party that had often clashed with Hollande's favorites, he was not a political ally of Hollande. Another key player was the president's personal military advisor, General Puga. A combative former paratrooper, Puga had been brought into the *Elysée* to serve as Sarkozy's advisor, and it surprised many when Hollande decided to keep him on. Puga played an important role in the decision to intervene, although, according to those close to him, speculation about that role was too often exaggerated in the press. Close observers described Puga less as an advocate for a specific strategy than as an expert who tirelessly explained the military risks and implications of the various strategies at hand to his chief.[7]

JEAN-YVES LE DRIAN

The key individual shaping the debate over intervention was in fact the French defense minister, Jean-Yves Le Drian. Normally, the French defense minister is one of the weaker figures in the French government, especially when it comes to wartime operations, because the Fifth Republic's constitution clearly makes defense issues the president's purview, and there is a direct link between the military and the president via the *chef d'état-major particulier* (in this case General Puga). Most French presidents had taken full advantage of this prerogative. "For Sarkozy, the Defense Minister just didn't count," said one French officer.[8] But in this case, things were different. Le Drian was no figurehead and had a sound grasp of defense issues from substantial personal experience. A leading political figure from the Atlantic port city of L'Orient in Brittany, which was home to some of France's most important naval industry, as well as a key base for France's naval special forces commandos, the defense minister had served on the defense committees in parliament for many years and had a reputation for being intensely detail oriented.[9]

Le Drian had also earned the respect of a military corps that otherwise tended toward suspicion about the Socialists. Throughout the summer and fall of 2012, as the crisis unfolded in Mali, the French government was under enormous pressure to bring its burgeoning fiscal deficit under control, lest it succumb to the sovereign debt crisis that had wracked several of its southern European neighbors. As noted in Chapter 5, given the pressing need to rectify France's financial problems, many in French military circles feared the new president would eviscerate the military. The Socialist Party's relationship with France's military, historically dominated by Catholic conservatives, has not always been smooth. As discussions about the white paper and

French national budget played out, however, Le Drian would play a crucial role in defending the defense ministry from the draconian cuts that some other members of the government sought, ensuring at least that any cuts to the defense budget would be no deeper than those any other ministry suffered.[10]

Moreover, Le Drian had been on top of the Mali dossier from the moment he arrived in office. He was personally seized with the challenge posed by the Sahel – which he thought rivalled only the crisis in Syria in importance.[11] Le Drian recognized that the social, political and economic trends in the Sahel, as a whole, augered poorly for the future and admitted that the strategy in place simply wasn't working. French citizens were still being abducted, the terrorists groups were expanding their reach, and, based on the intelligence he was getting, the possibility these groups might succeed in setting up a safe haven within striking distance of France was frighteningly real.[12]

Perhaps most of all, Le Drian and President Hollande had been close political allies for decades. The president trusted his judgment on both the political and the military risks of the problem – a rare combination. Because foreign minister Laurent Fabius was – at the outset at least – not especially interested in African issues, this left all the more space for Le Drian to play a key role in shaping French policy on Mali.[13]

Le Drian and his staff assessed the situation to have three important negative consequences that mattered for France: the direct impact on Mali, the risk the crisis posed to the broader region, and the danger of attacks on France if the jihadists were allowed to hold onto their safe haven. Le Drian was convinced that this was not a problem that could be ignored without risking dire consequences.[14]

He would thus come to play a major role in shaping the policy, taking daily updates – sometimes several a day – as events unfolded on the ground.

HOLLANDE TAKES THE PLUNGE

As the emergency *conseil de défense* convened on the morning of January 11, the jihadists were well across the Niger and descending on Bamako, but their intentions were still opaque. To some of those watching, the

advance looked a lot like an old-school Tuareg *razzia* aimed at deter-
ring or otherwise fouling up the African troop deployment.[15] Other
observers, however, were convinced the objective was truly to sow
terror in the capital. With the Malian army still in serious disarray,
Bamako's population was badly exposed.[16] If the jihadists moved into
the city, the civilians would risk life and limb.

That al Qa'ida's allies could ever have expected to hold a city
of a million even with a force of a thousand was dubious. Yet, the
very fact that they were attacking at all was already audacious and
unexpected. Given this behavior, it was hardly unthinkable that they
might actually have intended to hold Bamako through terror. In these
circumstances, as a French military officer put it, not acting could
have entailed "great risks for the population of Bamako."[17] If they
did enter the city, the military problem would become much thorn-
ier, and the fragile consensus at the United Nations was apt to be
completely derailed. From any perspective, crossing the Niger River
and heading into southern Mali violated the awkward status quo that
had been established since the initial revolt a year earlier. Even if
the jihadists only wanted to disrupt and delay the deployment of the
African forces, they could easily have undermined the whole international strategy.[18] Taking Sevaré alone would strengthen their grip on
the north significantly, because the town had an airport and served
as a key crossroads for controlling the routes from the north toward
Bamako.[19] The risk was thus real any way one looked at it. The Niger
River had become Mali's Rubicon.

On one level, the military task, if not insignificant, was certainly not
beyond the known capabilities of a country like France. French troops
would not face a committed adversary with anything like the weaponry
of a modern state. Mali offered a largely permissive environment for
French airpower, with no air defense systems to worry about. Although
the enemy was widely suspected of having some Libyan man-portable
air defense systems, the chances they knew how to operate these were
slim (though of course greater than nil). French forces were familiar
with the terrain, and their adversary had just concentrated its forces
in the open, making it much easier to strike with airpower and other
standoff fires.

Other risks loomed, however. To begin with, it was uncertain how
France's millions of north African residents would react to images of

French soldiers and warplanes attacking targets in Africa on the nightly news.[20] A greater risk was that African terrorist groups might take advantage of the intervention as an excuse to attack French embassies, consulates, businesses abroad, or even more precious targets in France itself. Then there were the domestic political risks. Despite French public worries about jihadists in Africa, it was still uncertain exactly how another African military intervention would play in the press, especially given that eight French hostages remained in al Qa'ida's hands. Overt French intervention put their lives in jeopardy – gruesome murders could easily create a political uproar in Paris. Perhaps most troubling of all, there was the potential for a serious quagmire. With domestic approval ratings already sagging after only nine months in office, all Hollande needed was to be accused of military adventurism in a part of the world where he had promised to tread more lightly. With the lessons of the Iraq and Afghanistan wars fresh in the minds of French leaders, nothing was less attractive than the prospect of a multi-year counterinsurgency in a former West African colony.[21]

The risks aside, as the defense council met, there was quick and firm consensus within the highest levels of the French government that the al Qa'ida advance was a potential disaster in the making. Fabius and Le Drian were on the same page, and the president was quickly convinced that immediate action was imperative.[22] As soon as he saw that this was an organized attack, conducted by multiple groups, his mind was made up. There was no discussion at all of going to NATO or the EU to organize a broader coalition. Some French leaders saw the EU as pusillanimous, and both organizations were viewed as slow, cumbersome, and prone to costly delays. The situation called for an immediate military response, and France needed to be in the lead. "There was not much debate," said one senior official who participated in the meeting, "everyone understood that we had to move fast."[23] France would take the plunge.

COMMANDO OPERATIONS IN SEVARÉ

French special forces were in action within hours. The Fourth Special Forces Helicopter Regiment, stationed in Burkina Faso as part of regional counterterrorism operation *Sabre*, struck a column of jihadists from the air as they moved from Konna toward Sevaré. A handful of French commandos had deployed into Mali to bolster the collapsing Malian army at Sevaré a few days before. Now, flying low and taking small arms fire from the ground, two French Gazelles, guided by forward air controllers, destroyed several jihadist pick-ups en route toward the town.

Only a handful – likely a few dozen at most of the 250 soldiers assigned to *Sabre* – participated in this initial strike. Amid the firefight, ground fire pierced the bottom of one of the helicopters, fatally wounding a pilot, Major Damien Boiteux. A short time later in Ougadougou, Boiteaux died of his injuries, the first French casualty of the war.[24] The other helicopter was forced to crash-land not far from this first point of contact with the enemy, creating an urgent and dangerous demolition mission for *Sabre*. But the special forces dispatched the job quickly.

The initial enemy advance was stopped by this attack, but the situation was precarious. When French special forces arrived at Sevaré they discovered that the Malian troops, who they had ostensibly come to support, had all fled.[25] A jihadist riposte, including against the small band of French special operators in Sevaré, seemed likely. Even though these were elite forces they were seriously exposed, hundreds of kilometers from Bamako.

Back in Paris, Hollande held a press conference, announcing that France had intervened. Referring to the "brutality and the fanaticism" of the terrorists, he cited the threat to Mali's population, the fact that France had 6,000 expats in the country, and the threat to the very existence of the Malian state itself. The operation, he said, would last as long as necessary, concluding that "the terrorists should know that France will always be there when their fundamental interests are concerned, or when there is a risk to the rights of a population, in this case, Mali, which wants to live free and with democracy."[26]

Soon, larger-scale operations began. Within twenty-four hours, air operations began to target jihadist positions in the north. The first and second night of operations, four Mirage 2000D strike fighters flying from N'Djamena, where they had been stationed as part of France's Operation *Epervier*, struck targets in jihadist strongholds in northern Mali, hitting training camps, weapons depots, and other jihadist infrastructure. They were supported by two KC-135 refueling aircraft.

A total of six Mirage 2000D, two Mirage F1 CR, three KC-135, one C-130, and one *Transall* C-160 were available in Chad.[27]

Meanwhile, the French scrambled to build up a larger force on the ground. A unit of some 200 soldiers from the Twenty-First Marine Infantry Regiment and the First Foreign Legion Regiment serving with operation *Epervier* in Chad deployed in a C-130 to Bamako. Back in France, a company of 200 soldiers from the Second Marine Infantry Regiment was deployed through the French rapid response system, *Guépard*, to Bamako, arriving on January 12 in A310 and A340.

The airstrikes continued the night of Sunday, January 13, with the longest distance air raid ever conducted by the French military. Four Rafales flying from Saint-Dizier in France, supported by two KC-135 tankers, flew nine and a half hours to strike targets in Mali.[28]

On Monday, additional forces arrived in Bamako, this time from operation *Licorne* in Abidjan, composed of troops from the First Paratroop Regiment, the Third Marine Infantry Paratroop Regiment, and the Seventeenth Marine Engineers Regiment. Two hundred troops and sixty armored personnel carriers had departed Saturday to drive the 1,400-kilometer route to Mali's capital. On the night of January 14 and 15, two RAF C-17s delivered tanks and logistics for the Second Marine Infantry Regiment, a light armored unit in Bamako.[29] Cobbled together, the companies deployed from Chad, Côte d'Ivoire, and metropolitan France formed the first joint tactical task group – *groupe tactique interarmes* (GTIA) – of the operation.

The formation of the first tactical task group brought the total number of French forces in Mali to 800 by January 15, with 1,700 participating in the operation overall. Meanwhile, intelligence had indicated that Mujao was assembling as many as 200 4x4s in the town of Diabaly.[30] An armored unit of the first task group departed on January 15 with the objective of taking Markala, which lay 150 kilometers south across the river and where one of only two bridges across the Niger was situated – the other being farther north at Gao. Arriving on January 17, French forces took the bridge and set up surveillance aimed at stopping Mujao from making a successful push south.[31] The large skiffs that were frequently used to transport goods across the river, which could each hold more than ten vehicles, were meanwhile forbidden from moving, under threat of destruction by

French fighter jets that had begun to patrol the river.[32] Air operations in the north continued simultaneously with French jets striking eight targets on January 15, ten targets on January 16, and five on January 17, and continuing surveillance operations in the north. In addition to the RAF contribution to transporting French forces in the theater, Denmark and Belgium had now joined the airlift effort.

As this small armored unit held the second line south of the jihad-ists in Markala, Paris decided to further increase the force size to 2,500 by adding three more joint tactical task groups, an air mobility group and part of a mechanized brigade.[33] As the buildup in Bamako con-tinued, French Air Transport command leased Antonov 124s from Russia to accelerate the throughput. French tactical transport helicop-ters soon arrived in Bamako from France in a Canadian C-17, and by January 18, one week into the operation, the French government reported 1,800 troops involved in the operation in theater, with 2,700 total participating.[34]

On the night of January 19, another unit arrived at Mopti to strengthen Bamako's forward defenses and relieve the small special forces team that still occupied Sevaré. Meanwhile, French forces at Markala ranged further to the small town of Nionno. On January 21, French and Malian forces reoccupied Diably, across the river to the north from Markala and also Douentza, which lies across the Dogon plateau east of Konna. Another company of the Third Marine Regiment arrived in Bamako on January 21 to secure the rear operating base the French had by now largely set up there. Buildup from France contin-ued, with the support of French allies, which by January 22 included the United States. The French *Mistral* class amphibious assault ship *Dixmude* was also underway toward the Senegalese coast with several hundred additional forces and a logistics unit aboard.[35]

On January 22 the First Mechanized Brigade officially took com-mand of tactical operations on the ground.[36] By January 23, less than two weeks after the initial attack, thousands of French soldiers were on the ground and the buildup was continuing. France was clearly in control of the regions south of the Niger Bend.

Despite long-standing orders to plan for only a supporting role to the African force, operations went smoothly when the orders came to go in themselves – after all, not a few French planners had anticipated a heavy French role. Most of the necessary plans were in fact already in place. There was also little need to collect intelligence about a situation the French had been following closely for months if not years. Because they were acting unilaterally, there was no need for coordination with other countries – let alone a NATO decision-making process. "We were able to act very quickly because we had a long period in which we recognized that it was absolutely necessary to do something in Mali," said General Grégoire de Saint-Quentin, who would soon become the commander of French operations on the ground.[37]

Still, if the French military had long been contemplating intervention in Mali, they could not have known exactly what form it would take – let alone that it would come at the moment that it did. The advance on Bamako was audacious and could not have been foreseen. Even for those who were convinced there would eventually be an intervention, which was most of the military, it was a surprise – although from a certain perspective, also opportune. "There was always going to be a French intervention on the ground, but it was far off," said one senior French official.[38] The military may have expected to intervene at some point, but in the event, the decision was sudden.

The initial French attacks had surprised and seriously disorganized the enemy. French forces continued to flow into the theater. Figure 12 depicts the movements of the initial commando raid (1), the composition of the first task group (2), and subsequent force flow by sea (3). With the south secure, the chief question was where to go from here.

WHAT TO DO NEXT?

Before French troops intervened, Hollande's popularity had been low. Although 65 percent of the French public had a favorable view of their new president immediately after his May 2012 victory over Sarkozy, the vitriol the public had once directed at Sarkozy's excesses rapidly turned to complaints about Hollande's indecisiveness and lack of leadership skills. His polling figures fell steadily as a result. If Sarkozy's antics were speared as unpresidential, Hollande's quiet and "doughy" style seemed even more so. Rising unemployment and a controversy

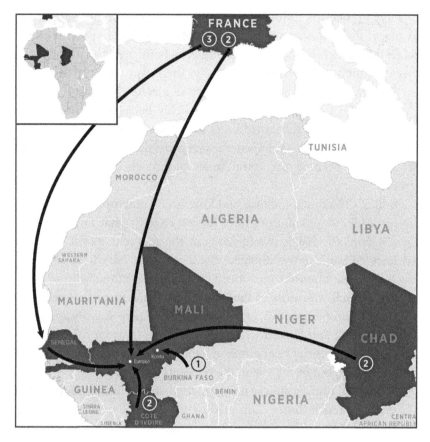

Figure 12. French Force Movements into Theater.

over gay marriage further compounded the *Elysée's* problems. At the end of 2012, Hollande had lost nearly half of his support. His popularity ratings dropped to 37 percent.[39]

Amid this political gloom, French public reaction to Hollande's decision to mount an intervention in Mali was a rare ray of sunshine. In polls conducted over the weekend of February 12–13, the decision to intervene proved very popular, with 63 percent of those polled favorable and only 37 percent opposed.[40] These figures did not necessarily mean that the popularity of the president himself would rise in tandem, though, given the continued weight of the domestic economic troubles on public opinion. Historically, French presidents (like other democratically elected leaders) have both gained and lost from military interventions. Mitterrand had gained substantially from his decision to join in the first Gulf War, but the more recent Libya intervention had given Sarkozy only small bumps in popularity, with no lasting effect – no doubt because of the very disappointing long-term results. Jacques Chirac's decision not to join the 2003 U.S. intervention in Iraq, meanwhile, had been wildly popular with 80 percent of the French public backing it.

As it turned out, Hollande did gain a point in the polls, and given that his popularity had been in a seemingly terminal slide since his election, even this petite bump meant something. Leading opposition figures, including former prime ministers François Fillon and Jean-Pierre Raffarin, as well as Sarkozy advisor Henri Guaino, insisted on the need for unity in the face of "islamist terrorism."[41] Several important French foreign policy experts came out immediately in favor of Hollande's decision, along with major French dailies including *Le Monde, Le Figaro,* and *Libération*.[42]

France's closest allies also moved quickly to proclaim their support for the French decision. British prime minister David Cameron said he was "deeply concerned about the recent rebel advances in Mali, which extend the reach of terrorist groups and threaten the stability of the country and the wider region," and offered British support.[43] Both the German foreign and defense ministers – no doubt eager to avoid a repeat of the Franco-German split over Libya less than two years before – made similar statements supporting France and offering material support.[44] Russian officials also made similar statements. (Meanwhile, far right Russian nationalist politician Vladimir Zhirinovskiy said in a January 14 debate on *Ekho Moskvy Radio* that Russia ought to follow France's lead and send troops to Syria to help President Assad fight jihadists there, an idea that at the time was viewed as a direct affront to U.S. efforts to get Assad to step down.)

In Mali itself, the response was hugely supportive, as was the wider regional reaction. At a meeting of the UN Security Council on January 22, for example, representatives from Benin, Burkina Faso, Chad, Côte d'Ivoire, Mali, Niger, Nigeria, and Senegal all praised French action. The head of the African Union, Boni Yayi announced himself jubilant, saying, "I'm in heaven."[45] Regional public opinion polls also showed high levels of support for intervention in Mali, even before it happened.[46] Later polls showed support, for example, from publics in Nigeria and Senegal.[47]

If the enthusiasm with which the initial French moves into Mali were met was welcome, Hollande's advisors were wary opinion could turn sharply and suddenly against them. The fickle French public might be especially prone to flip-flop if things started to look like they were going badly.[48] Progress was easy to show at the start, but what would follow?

Soon enough, sharp critics started emerging. Only a week into operations, the opposition started taking shots at the *Elysée*. One theme was an alleged lack of strategy. Interviewed in *Le Monde*, Laurent Wauquiez, the vice-president of the leading party of the center right, the *Union pour un Mouvement Populaire*, charged that Hollande had no strategy and was acting recklessly without any support from France's European partners.[49] On *France 24*, former foreign minister Alain Juppé called for the government to define its strategy and warned that France was isolated. The initial intervention was needed, he said, but sending in more French ground forces was a potentially big mistake: "The presence of French soldiers in a region where our country was a colonizer ... was perhaps not the best thing to be considering."[50]

Villepin, meanwhile, penned a sharp opinion piece in the *Journal du Dimanche* pillorying Hollande's decision to go to war. "Let us not give way to the reflex of war for war's sake," he wrote, "this is not the French way." All such wars of the last decade have failed, he warned, leaving behind failed states, armed militias, legitimizing terrorism, and undermining regional peace. In Mali, none of the conditions for success are in place, he said, complaining that France was isolated and alone. "How has the neoconservative virus been able to win everyone over?" he asked pointedly.[51] Villepin's piece was rather fatalistic, but given his personal stature, the critique bit.

Predictably, jihadist Web sites depicted the intervention as a crusade against Muslims and immediately began inciting their followers to attack France. A posting on a leading jihadist website, Ansar al Mujahedin Network, urged followers to "send lone wolves to France to strike inside of France," and carry out attacks modeled on Merah's the year before. Their instructions were often specific; one post urged the attacks should be "carried out by gunfire rather than explosives because it takes a long time to prepare explosives."[52]

Meanwhile, from Gao, Mujao leader Abou Dardar made similar threats of attacks on French soil: "France has attacked Islam and we will strike France in its heart," he promised, while another jihadist spokesman warned France to "stop your assault against us or you will be digging your children's tombs."[53] "Our jihadists are not a bunch of sheep waiting to be slaughtered inside a closed pen," Mujao spokesman Omar Ould Hamaha proclaimed, adding, "Listen closely to me. Our elements are constantly on the move. What they hit is a bunch of cement. France is going to reap the worst consequences possible from this. Now no French person can feel safe anywhere in the world. Every French national is a target."[54]

Amid these initial operations and their reactions, French civilian and military leaders had meanwhile been hit with a serious failure thousands of miles east, on the shores of Somalia. Shortly after French forces had successfully stopped the jihadist advance on Sevaré, another, more complex, special forces operation had been launched to free the French secret agent, Denis Allex, whom al Shabab had captured on Bastille Day in Mogadishu more than three years earlier. At midnight on January 11, only a few hours after the firefight in Sevaré, fifty French commandos flying in six Eurocopter EC-725s had descended on an al Shabab camp in Bulo Marer, southwest of Mogadishu. A forty-five-minute firefight ensued, in which seventeen jihadists and one French soldier were killed. But the French were forced to retreat, and Allex was summarily executed by Shabab shortly thereafter.[55] By early morning of January 12, it was clear in Paris that the rescue operation was a complete failure.

The Bulo Marer operation had been risky. There was likely no connection in the timing, but as discussions about French strategy played out over the next few days, the failure would serve as a reminder of the acute risks at play.

As the dust settled over the first few days of operations, the concern that France was alone, plunging headlong again into Africa without the support of allies, hung over the decision makers, all of whom feared the real potential for quagmire.[56] A British editorialist put it aptly at the time, "Having suddenly jumped in with both feet, France faces the daunting prospect of fighting a protracted, increasingly nasty counter-insurgency campaign without adequate or whole-hearted backing from its NATO and regional allies."[57]

A week into the operation, therefore, as Hollande's defense advisors gathered for their daily meetings at the *Elysée*, the big question was what to do next. The initial success had been everything that they could have hoped for – in military and political terms – but a number of unknowns loomed ahead. How would the jihadists react to these initial French strikes? After moving into the north, French forces would have to fight within populations where many people were known to be loyal to the Tuareg revolutionaries and some of the jihadists. The prospect of a protracted urban insurgency in the north also pervaded discussion. Intelligence sources indicated that at least one Algerian explosives expert had traveled to the theater, and strategists in Paris fully expected to face a perilous threat from improvised explosive devises of the kind that had proven so lethal against U.S. and allied forces in Iraq and Afghanistan.

Jihadist capabilities were yet another big uncertainty – especially whether or not they had man-portable air defense systems that could shoot down French helicopters, as defense experts expected they did after so many had slipped from the West's grasp in the aftermath of the Qaddafi regime's collapse in Libya eighteen months earlier. Most immediately, commanders simply wondered, where did they all go?[58] In addition, the sheer size of the country posed risks of its own. Compared to Afghanistan, where the French had controlled a province that was only a sliver the size of Mali, moving farther into the north would demand an ability to operate across extreme distances, creating even greater logistical challenges and increasing the risk that a single logistical failure might turn deadly and transform a winning operation into a national tragedy. If for example, French logistics lines were cut off by an ambush, it could leave French forces stranded and soon dying of exposure in the extreme heat of the Saharan desert. So far, the objective had been to keep the enemy from Bamako. "In the desert, it's going to open up like a sinkhole," said one trepidacious French colonel.[59]

As if to hammer the dangers of intervention home for the domestic French audience, another regional crisis unfolded just as the gears of the French war machine started to grind. On January 16, Belmokthar and a band of some thirty fighters seized a gas facility at In Amenas in southern Algeria. The world watched with alarm and then horror as the crisis played out. The jihadists took hundreds of Algerian, European, and other residents hostage; hundreds more remained hidden in the facility. Despite the pleas for negotiation from the families of those held, Algerian forces mounted a full, frontal attack the following day. Several of Belmokthar's footsoldiers were killed, along with thirty-seven hostages. Belmokthar himself escaped.

The In Amenas attack was widely viewed as a riposte to France's decision to intervene in Mali. Although planning almost certainly would have needed to begin before the French troops deployed, the crisis was a sobering reminder of the risk the jihadists posed – also to Algeria, which would cooperate more willingly with the French operation thereafter. Belmokthar had succeeded in terrorizing many, but if intended to deter intervention, his gambit would ultimately fail.

In a second press conference on Tuesday, January 15, held during a visit to the United Arab Emirates, President Hollande had emphasized that French goals in Mali were limited. "France does not intend," he said, "to stay in Mali." France had only three goals: to secure Bamako, to stop the terrorist aggression, and to allow Mali to regain its territorial integrity. He stressed (somewhat curiously given his own military's assessment) that the African force that would take over was on the verge of deploying to relieve French troops. France was the "decisive" actor that had launched the attack, but it was not planning to stay forever.[60] Indeed, France was not planning to stay long at all. On January 13, Fabius told a group of reporters that "regarding the aspects that more directly involve France, it is truly a question of weeks," insisting that even if France were likely to continue in a supporting role thereafter, they had no intention of being on the ground indefinitely.[61] This would not be Afghanistan, French leaders repeated again and again in their public statements. Hollande was hardly the first national leader to pledge a rapid exit from an intervention. Nor would he be the first to find himself backpedalling from this position.

Having pushed the jihadists back to the Niger, the French had three basic military options. The first was simply to dig in, consolidate their positions around Bamako and in other towns south of the Niger Bend, and turn things over to the Malian or African force as soon as it had reached a minimum level of readiness. French forces had already successfully chased the jihadists out of the south, and dealt thereby with the immediate threat to Bamako that precipitated the crisis. By holding ground, France could still claim to have averted the imminent threat to Bamako and restored the status quo, but without taking on the risks of a protracted operations in the north.

A second option was to retake a few of the major towns in the north – Gao and Timbuktu in particular. This would relieve the civilian population of these towns from subjection to *shari'a*. Strategically, taking these towns would also provide better protection for Bamako, especially given that Gao was the main chokepoint for access to the far northern areas around Kidal and beyond where the rebels and jihadists had started their uprising a year before. Operations could then be turned over to the international force.

In retrospect, the first option, which offered the chance to lock in the gains to date at relatively low political and military risk, must have been tempting. In comparison, the second option was the riskier. But President Hollande actually chose a third option, more aggressive than either of these two – no doubt in part because he wanted to avoid repeating the Côte d'Ivoire experience, where France had patrolled the north-south border for a decade, in part because the memory of the unfinished business in Libya was still fresh. French forces would thus not only retake the north, they would hunt down al Qa'ida and its allies there, destroy their infrastructure and kill as many as possible. As they advanced into the desert they would meanwhile keep the pressure up to get the international force to deploy. This way their troops could focus on the jihadists, not just in Mali, but wherever else they might flee. And this they would begin immediately. "We have decided to conquer the towns while our deployment is still underway," said General Jean-Pierre Palasset, adding that this would have been "a heresy with our allies, but something that could cause considerable surprise with the enemy."[62]

The announcement to the French public was made by Le Drian on Sunday, January 20, on the French talk show, "C Politique." "The objective is the total reconquest of Mali," the defense minister said.

"We will leave no pockets" of resistance. French forces now had four main missions, he explained. First, stop the terrorist advance with airpower. Second, bomb the jihadists' rear bases to smithereens. Third, keep Bamako safe and secure. Fourth, help the Malian forces reconstitute themselves so that they might defend their own country against the jihadist scourge.

7   *SERVAL*

The first two weeks of French operations saved Mali from falling into the hands of al Qa'ida's allies. With the Niger Bend now secure, Hollande was determined to chase the jihadists out altogether, and then withdraw as fast as possible. The sudden French attack seemed to have caught the jihadists by surprise, and the French leadership now sought to exploit this advantage to the maximum. In the *Elysée*, Hollande pressed the military to speed ahead, despite the risks – to an extent that surprised even some of his military advisors. France had paid the price of intervention from the moment it took action, the president reasoned, and now it was time to get as much out of the effort as they could.[1] Clearly the last thing the French president wanted was to be bogged down in an African quagmire. "The orders to the troops were to keep the initiative. Don't give them time to regroup," explained the commander of the operation, General Grégoire de Saint-Quentin, in his underground Paris bunker a year later.

No one knew what lay in store for French forces across the Niger, however. Political success meant not only delivering large numbers of jihadists, it also meant prevailing on the local and regional forces to take over as much as they could handle, as soon as possible, so the French troops could exit swiftly.

This would thus become a war of speed, long distances, and rapid engagements, not to mention punishing heat. From an operational perspective, the emphasis on speed meant there would be no significant fortifications for the troops, who would move rapidly in small units in a sometimes-haphazard charge into the northern desert. The orders recalled General Patton's words to his troops on the eve of their departure for the North African campaign in World War II: "If you have any doubts as to what you're to do, I can put it very simply. The idea is to move ahead, and you usually know where the front is by the sound of gunfire."[2] The French troops, though, would not have the benefit, such as it were, of the sound of gunfire for orientation. Instead, the vast expanses of the Sahara opened up silently before them. Moreover, the French would have to make this charge with a disparate force cobbled together from different parts of their military and sometimes operating alongside a shaky and variegated African force, with Mali's own forces towing behind. To complicate the situation even more, the Malian forces were largely unwelcome in the key Tuareg areas the French intended to retake. To facilitate operations – and no doubt partially out of necessity – decision making was thus devolved as far down to the unit level as possible, with low-level officers enjoying an unusual breadth of autonomy in their movements to retake the Niger Bend. Similarly, the operational commander in Mali, General Barrera, had broad "tactical autonomy to free the country and destroy the enemy," as he later put it.[3] Autonomy was easier, French officers later pointed out, given that there were few foreign forces to coordinate with on the ground.[4]

French forces enjoyed a major advantage as long as the jihadist groups stayed in formation and tried to stand and fight rather than adopt hit-and-run guerrilla tactics. "This is not the Russian campaign," said a French official, referring to Napoleon's disastrous 1812 foray to Moscow. "They are rather small in number. A thousand men occupying part of a state that no longer exists."[5] The fact that the French forces overmatched the jihadists, however, hardly meant the operation was a risk-free lark. French forces had limited intelligence on al Qa'ida and its allies intensions, whether they would attempt a stand, and if so where and how. If the jihadists went to ground and started an urban insurgency in Gao, Timbuktu, or elsewhere, French fortunes could soon turn for the worse. In the meantime, there was enough to deal with in keeping the troops supplied along logistics lines that stretched out over a thousand kilometers across the desert while simultaneously accelerating the timeline for the deployment of the African force. At the outset, Malian forces offered the only hope of relieving the French from their sudden military commitment, but that was a dubious prospect at best.

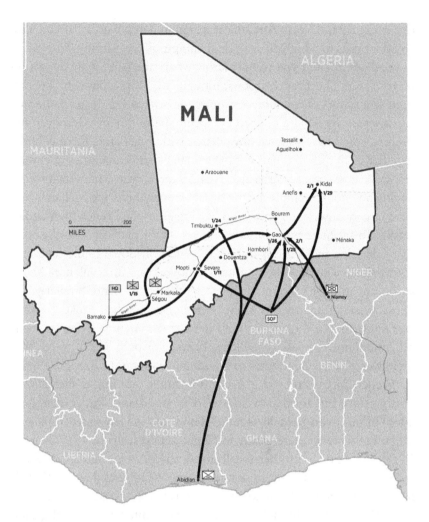

Figure 13. French Troop Advances as of February 2, 2013.

OPERATIONS

Figure 13 depicts the French advance to the Niger Bend as of February 2. Because of the hostage crisis and the growing possibility of intervention in some form or another, the French had developed a good picture of what the operating environment and enemy were like.[6] French human and technical intelligence were rich. The French intelligence agencies had moved resources from Afghanistan to Mali several years before to develop sources that could help cope with the region's growing kidnapping problem.[7] In later 2012, in anticipation of the intervention, the French military conducted multiple reconnaissance flights with Rafale, Mirage F1, Atlantique-2, and special forces C-130s and Harfang drones.[8] The French would also benefit from their two recently launched Pléiades surveillance satellites and the two slightly older Hélios II, as well as imagery from German and Italian satellites under a European pooling arrangement.[9] Nevertheless, intelligence would be at a premium throughout the operation as French commanders endeavored to divine the whereabouts and intentions of their enemy. Moreover, the battlefield was enormous, so the main challenge for French forces, especially early on in the operation, was logistical. Mali is 1.2 million square kilometers in size, or roughly twice the size of France itself; Bamako lies 4,000 kilometers from Paris and shares 7,420 kilometers of border with seven countries. The distance from Bamako to Timbuktu is almost 1,000 kilometers, to Gao, slightly more than 1,000, to Kidal, 1,600, and to Tessalit, 1,714.[10] The land the French forces traversed was moreover some of the most inhospitable on the planet. Infrastructure was broken down or nonexistent. Roadways between these cities were very few, and often in poor condition. Existing runways for aircraft were too short for many aircraft and almost always in bad condition. The runways in Kidal, for example, were so poor, bumpy and short, that taking off would still be an adventure for UN pilots flying there more than a year later, even after improvements had been made.[11]

The French movement into northern Mali would stretch French logistical capacities to their maximum. Because French units were under orders to go as far and as fast as they could into the north, they were often out of communications with higher headquarters for up to ten hours a day.[12] They carried only one day's supply of fuel, water, and food. They bathed once a week.[13] Stretched this thin, any break in the logistics chain could have been fatal – and also embarrassing for the military. If French soldiers started dying of dehydration, this would have been very bad optics in Paris, to say the least.

Overall control of the intervention rested with France's chairman of the joint chiefs, Admiral Guillaud. Strategic command was exercised from Paris by lieutenant general Didier Castres, the deputy director of operations for the French joint staff. The fifty-four-year-old Castres had previously run the French joint staff's command center and served on the staff of the chief military advisor to President Sarkozy. Operational command went to brigadier general Gregoire de Saint-Quentin, a fifty-two-year-old veteran of the French First Special Forces Army Group. A soldier who at close to two meters tall literally towers nearly a head above everyone else around him, Saint-Quentin was the son of a French naval pilot who had fought in Indochina and the grandson of a World War I pilot. Commander of the French detachment in Senegal for the preceding two years when *Serval* was launched, his assignment to lead the operation on the ground initially caused a stir in the upper echelon of the French officer corps. "Certain three stars did grind their teeth hard," said a French Army colonel, "but Saint-Quentin had established solid links with several African military chiefs. The special forces… were already deployed: he was clearly the right man for the job."[14] Saint-Quentin's performance in the operation would earn him a promotion to the head of the French special operations command. Within Mali itself, tactical operations would fall to brigadier general Bernard Barrera. Fifty-one years old and a classmate of Saint-Quentin at Saint-Cyr military academy, Barrera was also the son of a military officer once wounded badly in the Algerian war. He commanded the French Third Mechanized Brigade – "the Africans" – the unit on alert for rapid deployment from France in the event of a crisis as of early 2013.[15] Tactical air command fell to French Air Force colonel Laurent Rataud, in Chad.

IN SEARCH OF ALLIES

If the French were ready to take unilateral military action in the face of what they saw as an imminent crisis, they had no illusions about needing support from their allies as soon as the intervention got underway. Paris considered getting other countries involved quickly to be essential not just for political optics, but also for operational ones. French capabilities were already stretched – and bound to be stretched further – as the French army continued its charge north into the Sahara. Deploying and supporting forces for an operation this big and so far away from France was beyond what the French were accustomed to or really equipped for. However eager they may have been to get on the ground and fight, the French military was keenly aware of these gaps. The fact was, fighting a war was costly and would cost even more without allies.

Most of all, the domestic political cost of going it alone was mounting. Hollande enjoyed broad public support after his initial decision to intervene, but it didn't take long for naysayers to start quipping "where are the others?" and criticize what had essentially been a unilateral decision to go to war. France was at risk of looking isolated, even rogue – it was immediately clear to French leaders that they needed a coalition to succeed.[16] No sooner had they intervened, therefore, than the French started a full court press to bring as many allies on board as they could. France's willingness to put its own troops on the ground in harm's way upped the pressure on all of France's allies to back them up with concrete contributions.

The French thus immediately put out a request to their allies for tactical and strategic lift, refueling, medical evacuation, field hospitals, drones, and access to data from reconnaissance satellites.[17] Like the United States, many French EU partners had been reluctant to join the French in pushing for military action in Mali over the course of the previous fall. The EU's proposed training mission seemed to keep getting pushed back and some thought France's European partners were less concerned about the situation than France, or in any case less willing to help out.[18] With French forces on the ground, however, several European countries lined up quickly with contributions. The fact that the target was an al Qa'ida franchise strengthened European support and made it less likely French allies would see the war as simply another instance of French neocolonialism.

The British quickly promised two C-17 transporters to help ferry French forces and equipment into theater. One took off from RAF Brize Norton in the United Kingdom on Sunday, January 13, only two days after the French launched their operations. The same day, Diancounda Traoré inadvertently revealed a Canadian pledge of a C-17 in a tweet, forcing Prime Minister Stephen Harper to acknowledge that Canada was indeed deploying one of its four C-17s for a "non-combat" role for a period of one week.[19] (It would later extend this commitment for most of the operation.)

On Monday, Denmark announced that it would contribute a C-130, which would deploy the following day. The Belgians also moved fast. A few days before the French intervened, Belgian defense minister Pieter de Crem had already promised support for European training efforts. After some initial questions about whether Belgium would be ready to deploy forces outside an EU framework, Belgium promised significant additional support. It had eleven C-130s in the Congo as well as field hospitals and much needed A109 helicopters for medevac. It deployed two C-130s to Mali on January 17 and would send the helicopters soon thereafter.[20] Other countries followed suit eventually, as shown in Figure 14.

Like Canada and the United Kingdom, the United States also promised to send forces immediately after the French intervened. Indeed, on January 11, when Le Drian telephoned Secretary Panetta to notify him that France had intervened, Panetta promised that the United States would be 100 percent behind the French.[21] Despite this pledge, however, the U.S. effort to help the French in these fragile early stages of the intervention was soon entrammeled. A Franco-American spat brewed as French forces pushed forward on the ground and the French request wended its way, unmet, through the U.S. national security bureaucracy.

The challenges to the French request for support were several. First of all, there was the question of authorities for war and whether or not assisting the French required a notification to Congress under the War Powers Resolution. This depended in part on how one interpreted the question of whether or not by helping the French, the United States was engaged in "hostilities." In the 2011 Libya intervention, the Obama administration's initial decision not to formally notify Congress had created a great deal of bad air that still permeated some White House discussions with Capitol Hill.[22] After some deliberation, officials decided that offering the French intelligence, surveillance, reconnaissance (ISR) support surely did not require notification since these operations were ongoing from long before the French intervention. Intelligence sharing began more or less immediately, and a Global Hawk unmanned aircraft arrived within a week.[23]

ISR was easy to turn on (some 30 percent of French intelligence ultimately came from the United States), but meeting France's other requests turned out to be more difficult.[24] It was less clear that fulfilling the additional French requests for U.S. C-17s and refueling support wouldn't require congressional notification. The administration also cited concerns about the optics of more robust U.S. participation in the operation and risk of retaliation in the form of attacks against U.S. interests across Africa. Nevertheless, the decision to go ahead with providing the C-17s, which were not directly supporting combat, was made fairly quickly. Even here, however, further challenges arose. On a technical level, the United States needed to know the specifications of the loads they would be transporting into theater – for example the dimensions of the armored vehicles, where their balance points and tie downs were, and so forth – that the French needed loaded onto the C-17s.[25] A team from the U.S. air base in Ramstein, Germany had to fly in and work for seventy-two hours straight to get all the critical data into the U.S. flight system.[26] The first U.S. C-17 finally took off from Istres, France on January 21, loaded with dozens of French troops and some forty tons of equipment.[27]

It still remained unclear who would foot the bill for the planes. The United States proposed that France cough up $20 million for their use.[28] When the French refused, there was an outcry against perceived U.S. cheeseparing in the press. That the United States might refuse to contribute financially to a key ally's fight against al Qa'ida struck many observers as untoward, although why the U.S. should subsidize what was essentially a French operation was an equally sound question. "The Obama administration's foot-dragging in providing support to an ongoing French intervention in Mali is baffling – and disturbing" said the *Washington Post* in a stinging editorial on January 18 titled, "Stiffing an Ally." Financial concerns no doubt weighed on the United States, but U.S. officials later argued that the real problem was internal to the U.S. military. Because the U.S. combatant command that would be providing the force, U.S. Transportation Command (TRANSCOM), lacked its own funding for the operation, it was unclear where the funds to cover the costs within the U.S. government itself would come from.

Eventually, the U.S. rescinded its demand for payment for the C-17s. But two weeks into French operations it remained to be seen whether or not the French request for refueling support would be met. France owned fourteen air-to-air refuelers (3 KC-135s and 11 C-135FRs), but half of these were undergoing maintenance and unable to fly. Two more were fenced off for national defense missions and thus unavailable for operations in Africa. The remaining five were deployed to N'Djamena, and flying in the operation, but these two were only sufficient to keep French jets in the air over Mali for some six to twelve hours a day.[29] This meant French ground forces, already exposed from their long logistical lines, had only intermittent close air support, a factor that increased the risk that they might be successfully ambushed by the enemy. Finally, on January 26, two weeks after the initial request, the U.S. agreed to add tankers to its existing contributions. According to a senior French military official, this made the U.S. refueling aircraft the most important of the U.S. contributions – at least in the initial phases of operations.[30]

At least one senior U.S. military official was exasperated by the delays. "It was embarrassing, very frustrating," he said, that the United States was unable to immediately send the French the aircraft they were asking for. "The French were doing something we want done," he said; after all, this was al Qa'ida the French were fighting – a threat everyone agreed was a priority.[31] The French had an invitation from Mali's government and a UN Security Council backing. It wasn't as if the U.S. aircraft were engaged in some other, more important operation. They were just sitting on runways, waiting for the go-ahead from Washington. As a former French air force general quipped, President Obama had the authority to order an MQ-9 Reaper to take out an al Qa'ida leader with a Hellfire missile, but he apparently couldn't arrange for U.S. refueling aircraft to back the French in their effort to hunt exactly the same leader down.[32]

French officials later claimed that they fully understood that the delays were procedural and not political in nature. They had bureaucratic regulations and procedures of their own, of course.[33] They would also note, though, that the U.S. military machine is set up for either inter-vening itself or for building up the security forces of weak states.[34] Plugging into a French-led operation seemed to be something alto-gether new. In Libya, the United States had taken a back seat, but the whole operation was under NATO auspices. In this case, the rela-tionship was very different. The alliance was not involved, and U.S. Transportation Command was effectively providing services to the French in the same way that it would normally provide them to another U.S. combatant command. This was uncharted territory.[35]

U.S. Special Operations Command, which already had a robust relationship with its French counterpart, was also closely involved with the operation. The commander of U.S. forces in Africa would likewise remain in close contact with French military officials throughout. As the French pushed further north and set up operational headquarters at Gao, the United States deployed a small cell along with them to facilitate U.S. intelligence support to French operations.[36] The United States also supported the regional African force by deploying a plan-ning cell to help their deployment and operations. Because of the coup, the United States was restricted in what it could provide directly within Mali, but was able to support the regional efforts with training and other measures in Burkina Faso, Nigeria, and Liberia.[37]

U.S. contributions continued throughout the operation. U.S. senior military officers from U.S. Africa Command, including its commander General David Rodriguez, would visit French headquarters in Gao. The United States maintained liaison cells in Bamako, Paris, and in Mont-Verdun at French air-operations command outside Lyon. U.S. military and civilian leaders meanwhile kept in regular contact about the operation in Washington, Paris, and Stuttgart, Germany, where U.S. Africa Command is located.

At an operational level, most of the allied contributions came off fairly well. The Danish case is a good example. The Danes have a total of four C-130s in their fleet, one of which was in Afghanistan in a joint UK-Danish air wing. The Danes nevertheless started gearing up for a contribution from the moment they heard the French had intervened. Denmark has a close relationship with the French, as well as the United States and the United Kingdom, and the opportunity to show support for a European operation after years of fighting with the United States in Afghanistan and Iraq had a certain political benefit. Vaccinations for Danish crews were ordered up almost immediately. Teams meanwhile started investigating the possibilities for assistance, and after finding that ramp space and other limitations in Bamako, Chad, and Central African Republic were too limited, settled on Senegal as a base of operations.[38]

The small Danish team set up first in France to help transport French equipment into theater, flying twenty-hour round-trip flights via Corsica. The Danish crew offloaded the equipment with as little time on the ground as possible since their vaccinations were not yet fully in effect and there was little space anyway. After a week, the crew deployed to Senegal, whence it flew logistics into Bamako and eventually the north. They even jerry-rigged a way of offloading fuel from the C-130s for use by French ground forces.[39]

Ultimately, then, despite the public charges that France had isolated itself, French officials' claims that support was actually much stronger than it seemed from the outside were hardly groundless. The French had been pushing their European partners for months about the situation in Mali, and when the crisis broke, fifteen other members of the European Union eventually responded positively to French requests.[40] In February, the German Bundestag approved sending German refueling aircraft to Mali. Like the analogous U.S. tanker contribution, the German input was an important one – for political and military reasons.

French allies ultimately provided 75 percent of the airlift and 30 percent of the refueling for the operation.[41]

OPERATION ORYX: TAKING TIMBUKTU AND GAO

As the buildup in Bamako progressed and deliberations over objectives in Paris continued, the *Sabre* special forces team that had been relieved at Sevaré on January 21 had begun hop-scotching across the north. Their movements were extraordinarily fast and prepared the ground for the conventional forces that would follow. But as at Sevaré, these units were far too small to hold a town for long. For this, larger scale conventional forces were needed. French planners recognized quickly

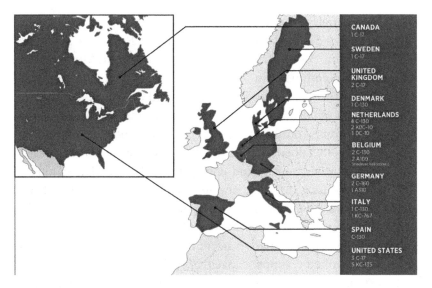

Figure 14. Allied Airlift and Tanker Contributions to *Serval*.

that the vast expanses north of the Niger Bend necessitated control of the airstrips in the main northern towns so logistical lines could be set up to support operations there. Of the two major towns along the Niger itself, Gao and Timbuktu, Gao was the more important from a strictly military standpoint, since it was the only route toward Kidal and the Ifoghas. It was important to chase the enemy from Timbuktu, but there were no roads leading from there northward, even if from a political and symbolic perspective, Timbuktu was more significant, given the town's history and the outcry that had arisen when it initially fell to the jihadists. Plans for an initial assault on Gao, a longstanding hub for regional smuggling operations, were thus overturned when President Hollande intervened and directed the military to concentrate on taking Timbuktu first.[42] Operations against both objectives began with some thirty bombs dropped by French aircraft flying from Bamako and N'Djamena. They struck logistics and other key targets in these towns on the nights of January 25 and 26.

French commanders now had fourteen multi-role fighters at their disposal, six Mirages based in Bamako and eight Rafale flying from N'Djamena. Intelligence collection was eventually bolstered by multiple intelligence collection platforms, including five Atlantique 2s, a C-160 Gabriel, and two of France's Harfang drones, along with a Royal Air Force Sentinel R1, two U.S. Air Force Predators, and a U.S. Navy P-3 Orion. Air operations were commanded from Mont-Verdun, with a forward command in N'Djamena.[43]

The tip of the spear of the French entry into Gao and Timbuktu was planned as an airborne assault. Airdropping forces offered the chance to get many troops on the ground fast and concentrate them quickly. Operationally, this jibed with the political pressure to move as fast as possible. Yet an airdrop behind enemy lines also entailed significant risks given the long distances and logistical challenges involved. The overriding concern of planners during preparations for and execution of the seizure of the north was to avoid leaving French troops vulnerable in the vast desert expanses north of the Niger, exposed to enemy attack, with limited resupply capacity. The French were still operating with very limited intelligence about the enemy or their intentions. It was clear the enemy was avoiding contact, but the French assessed (correctly) that they likely were regrouping and intended to fight back at some point. Exactly when was unknown. This made every move into the areas they controlled in the north risky.[44]

In light of these risks, Barrera decided to delay until a ground convoy could be deployed north to protect the paratroopers. On January 25, therefore, the first joint task group moved on Timbuktu. It encountered serious encumbrance along the way. Driving on the unimproved road from Léré, the heavier-laden trucks sunk into the sand and the whole column was forced to stop repeatedly to dig them out. Finally, the column was split in two to accelerate their movement. The faster vehicles charged ahead.[45] Meanwhile, the helicopter air mobility group split into two sub-groups and deployed to Sévaré and Diabali to support the ground movement.[46]

These forces reached Timbuktu on the early evening of January 27, seventy-two hours after their departure, moving with support from the air mobility group, as well as Atlantique 2 surveillance aircraft and drones. There had been no resistance. At roughly the same time 250 French Foreign Legion paratroopers of the fourth task group flew from Abidjan, dropped from five C-130s flying at 1,000 feet, and landed on the airstrip north of the town. On January 28, the legionnaires secured the routes that ran northward out of the town and set up joint patrols with the Malian forces.[47]

The decision to wait until the ground forces arrived before the drop on Timbuktu obviously reduced its potential impact.[48] It certainly made the air drop look like overkill. After the fact, there was speculation that the operation had been pushed unnecessarily by General Puga, who, as a young officer, had participated in the legendary 1978 Kolwezi air assault that freed some 2,000 European hostages from a rebel group in Zaire.[49] It does indeed seem redundant and it is difficult not to conclude that eagerness to give the paratroopers the chance to show their stuff figured into the plans. But the airdrop certainly did no harm. The French were not clairvoyant, and the drop could have been vital if the resistance on the ground had ended up being stiffer.

By the time Timbuktu had been secured, the assault on Gao had already begun – and likely would have concluded before Timbuktu was taken, were it not for the political imperative of seizing the better-known city first. Indeed, in reality, Gao was mostly captured before Timbuktu. On January 26, a small special forces team launched an initial assault on the town, taking the airport and seizing the bridge across the Niger. They met with moderate resistance, and killed fifteen of the enemy. Simultaneously, an armored squadron of ERC 90 armored cars from the first task group moved from Sévaré to relieve the special forces. This operation obviated the need for a repeat of the Timbuktu airdrop, so the French paratroopers instead landed their aircraft on the airstrip and secured the airport.[50] The town was itself officially secure on January 28. On February 5, the French moved tactical command to the city, where it would remain for the rest of the operation.

When they entered the near-deserted town, the French discovered the jihadists had wrecked the Catholic church and burnt all the bibles and other books in a room behind the choir stall. French airstrikes had meanwhile leveled administrative buildings that had served as the quarters for Mujao leaders, as well as the camps where their fighters had trained. Pictures of the jihadists' bodies, torn apart by French bombs, circulated morbidly on telephones around the city. The French did not disclose any estimates of civilian casualties from the strikes.[51]

On the morning of Saturday, February 2, President Hollande descended on Sevaré, where he was met by interim president Traoré and his defense, foreign, and development ministers (Figure 15). They then hopped north to Timbuktu, where a crowd of thousands waved

Figure 15. President Hollande Arrives in Mali, February 2, 2013.
Source: Courtesy of *Elysée* Palace.

banners thanking France and dancing to show their gratitude for the deliverance from *shari'a*. The French president visited the 700-year-old Djingareyber mud mosque and the Ahmed Baba library for ancient manuscripts, both critical parts of the region's cultural heritage that had been vandalized by the occupiers.[52] In brief remarks to a crowd in front of the city's independence monument, the French president declared that "terrorism has been pushed back, it has been chased away, but it has not been defeated yet."[53] Back in Paris, *Le Monde*, recalling George W. Bush's premature 2003 "mission accomplished" speech aboard the USS Abraham Lincoln, editorialized that the task had only just begun.[54]

The warning was well placed. The speed with which the enemy abandoned the main cities of the north came as a real, but welcome surprise, especially given what many anticipated would be a bloody urban fight.[55] All in all, it had taken less than two weeks to secure the south, and only a week more to retake the key towns across the Niger. But the relief was only temporary. High-level officials in Paris continued to press the military to move with the utmost speed. "There will be no stagnation," promised Foreign Minister Fabius, implying that the government was fully appreciative of the lessons of the war in Afghanistan.[56] Within a few days, the infantry units that had disembarked from the *Dixmude* at Dakar on February 28 completed the near 3,000-kilometer trek to Bamako then on to Gao. The relief of the troops assembled from Chad and Côte d'Ivoire at the outset of operations was underway. The units that had arrived from France with Barrera would stay on, but the others were soon rotated out. In addition to the new troops that had come by sea, which constituted the second joint task force, French forces in the North soon also included a battalion sized paratroop unit and an armored unit of similar size arrived from Niamey. These latter two (known as the third and fourth joint task forces – GTIA 3 and 4) would take responsibility for operations in the north, while the task of holding Gao and fighting in its environs would fall to GTIA 2.

Despite the success of the initial operations, serious risks remained. There was precious little intelligence about where exactly the enemy was and what their intentions would be.[57] A few weeks earlier the jihadists were entrenched, ruling these towns. Where had they gone? Were they hiding in the cities and their environs to lay ambush for French forces when they were at their most exposed, stretched northward in a few thin ribbons into the Sahara? The further their soldiers moved north, the more exposed they became. The greater the chances that the jihadists could kill – or worse yet capture – French soldiers in significant numbers. "In this kind of terrain," said one French general, "the further you go, the weaker you get."[58]

An initial indication came on February 5, when Mujao fighters launched 122 mm rockets into Gao, and on February 8, when a suicide bomber attacked a Malian army checkpoint there. The suicide bomber's head was found intact, allowing his identification as a local Arab youth who had been living in a Mujao camp.[59] Two days later, a street fight between French forces and the jihadists broke out in Gao's tangled inner city streets. It ended when a Tigre attack helicopter fired five 30 millimeter rounds into a house where the fighters were hiding. The mayor of Gao, who had fled to Bamako during the occupation, sounded the alarm, claiming that Mujao had in fact never left, but simply shaved their beards and disguised themselves as regular citizens. Left unchecked, these fighters were ready to wage a long urban insurgency – or at least go on a kidnapping spree against the growing number of Westerners in the city – he warned.[60]

The initial occupation of Gao had been followed by a fierce sandstorm under the cover of which many of the Mujao fighters were able to escape.[61] Fearing that the nightmare scenario of an urban insurgency was developing, supported from neighboring towns, the French quickly drew up a plan to retake the town of Menaka, which lay 300 kilometers to the east and was a suspected rear base for Mujao attacks on Gao. A French sub-task group, accompanied by Malian forces set out on February 7 late at night, arriving twenty-four hours later. They took Menaka's airport on February 10 and entered the town on February 12. By that time, however, Mujao had fled, dispersing yet again around the villages in the Gao region.

By the second week of February, General Saint-Quentin was ensconced in his theatre headquarters in Bamako; Barrera was in place at his tactical headquarters in Gao. In these conditions, and given mounting questions about why France seemed to be the only country committed to the operation, the French political leadership was already growing eager to get out as fast as they responsibly could. But there was yet another problem emerging. The Malian government and its military still made little if any distinction between the Tuareg rebels and the jihadists. One purpose of Hollande's February 2 visit was in fact to relaunch dialogue between the Tuaregs and the Malian government. As French forces pushed north into Tuareg lands, it was imperative to reassure the Tuareg populations that the French had no designs on them. Keeping the local population on their side would be critical to their success. This meant checking the ambitions of the Malian troops, who were chomping at the bit to get back into the northern towns and exact their pound of flesh for their humiliation the year before.[62]

Meanwhile, French forces were facing up to the challenge of sustaining themselves in the desert. Water of any kind was the greatest scarcity. Eight to ten liters a day were available for troops in Tessalit and Gao, but even this was a light ration given the heat. The fresh water was supplemented by three liters of brackish water for bathing every other day. In the Ifoghas the only available food other than Meals,

Ready-to-Eat (MREs) were onions, which were eaten raw by troops on patrol there. Coupled with the lack of bathing water, this regime can only have made for a rather pungent French force. Eventually things improved, and troops got one beer a week, served at the ambient temperature; said one general, "It didn't taste good, but at least it was a beer."[63] The enemy had cut the telephone lines and destroyed the cell towers in Tessalit and Timbuktu, so soldiers got five minutes of time per week on a satellite phone to call their families. There were no beds in most of the forward bases; troops slept on makeshift mattresses on the ground. Eventually showers were installed in Gao, but elsewhere it was still the "whore's bath" with a few bottles of dirty water a day.[64]

In these unsanitary conditions, microbes were nearly as big a problem as the heat. The troops avoided malaria – rife in southern Mali – but nearly everyone came down with multiple bouts of dysentery, which only added to the sanitation problem and risk of death from dehydration. Most of the troops got sick at some point. Parched soldiers frequently collapsed from heat exhaustion or desiccation and had to be medevaced to the field hospitals where they would recuperate for two or three days and then head back out into the field.[65]

BATTLE IN THE IFOGHAS

The rocky Ifoghas Mountains rise from northern Mali's desert landscape several hundred kilometers northeast of Gao (Figure 16). Largely composed from huge black boulders, the desert sand runs through them in oversized rivulets. The mountains are home to occasional oases that have been crucial to the survival of passing trans-Saharan traders for centuries. Belmokhtar and Abu Zeid spent years developing rudimentary depots and fortifications throughout them. This was the area where many of the French hostages were thought to be held – "needles in a haystack," according to Barrera – an ever-present concern for soldiers and commanders alike in the region.[66] The battle for the Ifoghas massif would be the critical and most violent of France's war.

On a superficial level, French and Chadian operations against al Qa'ida in the Ifoghas resembled U.S. and NATO operations against al Qa'ida

Figure 16. French Forces in the Ifoghas.
Source: Courtesy of French Ministry of Defense.

and the Taliban in the eastern provinces of Afghanistan. Both areas were remote – the Ifoghas even more so. Both areas required troops to oper-ate in extreme conditions – rugged mountainous terrain in Afghanistan, and the extreme heat of the boulder-littered Ifoghas. In both cases, the enemy was some form of al Qa'ida, which had allied itself with a disaf-fected local group. But the parallels stop here. To begin with, the spaces in eastern Afghanistan were smaller. Troops there regularly returned to established forward operating bases, rarely spending more than a night sleeping under the stars. In the Ifoghas, French forces and their allies moved constantly for up to a week, harkening back to a type of expeditionary operational mobility rarely practiced by Western armies since the first half of the twentieth century. But if the conditions in the Ifoghas were in some ways even more difficult than in Afghanistan's east, at least the enemy lacked support from the population. The loy-alty of many locals in the region was never in question the way that it so frequently was for soldiers operating in more hostile Pushtun areas of Afghanistan. This was of course chiefly because there was really no population – or very little – in the Ifoghas to begin with. This fact itself gave the French much greater latitude in their use of firepower, because it meant civilian casualties were unlikely – especially compared with urban settings. Furthermore, the French operations were classic, conventional maneuver warfare against an enemy that used guerilla tactics when possible but sometimes fought as a conventional force.

The Ifoghas are bordered on the western side by the two remote towns of Tessalit and Kidal, where the revolt had begun. With Gao and Timbuktu now under French control, these towns became the next objectives. Initially their seizure was planned on a model similar to operations to take Gao and Timbuktu, with paratroopers in the lead, followed closely by armored units. On January 29, however, the same French special forces group that had taken Gao also seized the airstrip at Kidal, and the paratroopers from the fourth task group were able to land in their C-130s directly on the tarmac. They relieved the special forces and secured the city, joined by Chadian troops soon after.

Plans to capture Tessalit were meanwhile delayed by the sandstorm that blew across the desert in the first few days of February. An armored company initially based in Niamey, Niger was then transferred to Gao, which they departed on February 6 in their aging AMX-10RCs – a light armored vehicle mounted with a 105-mm gun – along with two *camion équipées d'un système d'artillerie* – a 155-mm howitzer cannon mounted on the back of a sizable truck – to make the 500-kilometer push to Tessalit. On February 8, a now-familiar scenario played out on the Tessalit airfield, which special operations forces had seized that morning and handed over to French paras from the fourth task group. The armored company arrived midday, as did Chadian reinforcements from Kidal. The French thus had the fourth task group paratroopers, the third task group of AMX-10RCs, with the two 155-millimeter howitzers, a logistical subgroup, a medical unit, and a command post ready to deploy into the Ifoghas. In total there were some 400 French soldiers in Tessalit, and 200 in Gao.[67]

As French forces pushed deep into Tuareg lands, new political concerns arose. If the jihadists had fled Kidal, secular Tuareg rebel forces were still present in force. The rebels had pledged allegiance to France within hours of the intervention, many hoping perhaps that French might further their political objectives vis-à-vis Bamako. But it was uncertain how they would react to French troops occupying their home base. The secular rebels were not France's enemy, but to avoid complicating matters with Bamako, the military had orders from Paris to eschew direct negotiations with the rebels. French forces would remain neutral when it came to the internal split that had rent the country apart a year before.

The objective was thus still the jihadists. There was still no intelligence reporting on current al Qa'ida presence in the Ifoghas, although there was a good deal of intelligence that had been collected in recent years about the bunkers, casernes, and other defensive structures the jihadists had built in the mountains. The working assumption was that there were a few hundred enemy fighters. The French just needed to find them.[68]

On February 16, initial reconnaissance began with the first of several operations in the Ifoghas, code named *Panthère*. On February 19, the paratroopers of the fourth task group headed back into the Ifoghas. After recon of a small town south of Tessalit on the trans-Saharan road, they turned toward the mouth of the Ametetai valley, which runs east-west through the northern portion of the mountains. Their objective: destroy a set of known enemy logistics depots previously identified by intel. The paratroopers arrived at seven in the morning, with air support from two Mirage 2000Ds. After surveilling the area for two hours without sign of active enemy forces, they decided to move on the spots where the logistics depots were located. Arriving on site, however, the unit suddenly came under heavy fire – to the surprise of the unit's leader given that intelligence reports had indicated limited recent enemy activity in the area. "They clearly wanted to stop us and deny entry into Ametetai Valley," said one officer involved in the ordeal.[69] A paratrooper from the foreign legion, thirty-three-year-old chief sergeant Harold Vormezeele, was killed.

It was too risky to pull back, so the fight lasted several hours, with fixed-wing air support, but no helicopters, which were still in Gao, at least two hours away – too far to be of much use. After four hours of fighting, the French troops had identified all the enemy combat positions and killed at least twenty-four of their fighters. But they were still unable to enter the valley and so withdrew one to two kilometers to set up a permanent surveillance outpost before returning to Tessalit.[70]

Thus the battle of the Ifoghas began in earnest. From the ferocity of the initial encounter it was evident Abu Zeid's forces did not mean to withdraw.[71] The February 19 attack forced French commanders to shift their operational focus from the effort to subdue Mujao around Gao to fighting al Qa'ida in the Ifoghas. The French called for support from Chadian forces. Barrera decided to shift two of his three task forces northward from Gao.[72] In Tessalit they set up a makeshift camp that would serve as a forward operating base.

Before attacking, however, they would pause to regroup. Logistics flowed in gradually until there was enough fuel, water, food, ammunition, and medical supplies for the impending operation. Initially, most supplies came via air-bridge, but as costs mounted and the aircraft began to falter in the harsh environment, the load was gradually shifted to the ground. Trucks from Bamako could reach Gao, but there they had to be offloaded to desert-ready vehicles for the convoy's three-day trek via the trans-Saharian to Tessalit. Logistical movements of this size were entirely new for French forces and required no small amount of improvisation.[73] Meanwhile, they kept close watch on the valley to make sure that Abu Zeid's forces couldn't escape.

The operation to clear the valley began on February 22, with the bloodiest day of the whole intervention for the French allies. At the request of the French, more than 1,000 Chadian forces, trained by the United States and France, several riding in U.S. provided vehicles, and led by none other than the son of Chadian president Idriss Déby, mounted the initial attack into the valley from the nearly inaccessible eastern end. The Chadians, who had departed Menaka on February 29 were by far the most capable of the non-French foreign troops in country. The brunt of Abu Zeid's defensive lay-down was concentrated in front of them. They charged the enemy positions fearlessly, and to their peril. In the intense firefight that ensued, twenty-six Chadian soldiers were killed and sixty-two wounded. Many of Abu Zeid's fighters were killed, but many also escaped. In over six weeks of operations, this was the first deadly combat on any significant scale.

Several French and American officers interviewed for this study heartily applauded the Chadians for their extraordinary bravery, while at the same time noting that it was that very same bravery that led to such bloodshed. The "Chadians are very courageous but they attack a position like the French in 1914," said one French officer who fought in the Ifoghas.[74]

On February 24, Barrera flew via helicopter from Gao to Tessalit. From there he took off for the eastern flank of the Ifoghas for consultations with Déby and the other Chadian leaders, returning to Tessalit late that night to establish the forward command post. By February 26, Chadian forces had recovered and were deployed to block Abu Zeid's escape via the eastern end of the Valley. French armored units from the third task force were deployed for similar purposes at the western end, while the French paratroopers moved in trucks and then on foot into the center of the valley from the north, through a small inlet. These groups would work in tandem to flush the jihadists into the center of the valley, where the paratroopers cut them in half and sent the enemy into disarray.[75]

Operating conditions in the valley were extreme. The threat of exposure for the French forces rivaled the threat from Abu Zeid's troops. At one point, the temperature soared to 60 degrees Celsius – 140 degrees Fahrenheit. "Fire fell from the sky."[76] With body armor, their weapon, ammunition, grenades, and a rucksack with two days of water and other supplies, some soldiers were carrying close to 100 pounds on their backs.[77] At night, when the temperature would fall precipitously to as low as 14 degrees Celsius – below 60 degrees Fahrenheit – they slept on the desert ground, between the boulders of the massif.

In such conditions, even well-trained troops could scarcely be expected to keep up for long. But the nature of the task they faced was slow and arduous. The terrain of the Ifoghas, pockmarked with hidden caves and piled high with huge boulders, offered excellent cover for ambushes by small enemy units. If French forces failed to detect one of those units, they were at risk of merciless attack from behind. The troops thus plodded along, going from rock to rock, and hill to hill. The operation was like looking for pins in a haystack, or, in the words of the defense minister Le Drian, working *à la fourchette à escargot* to root out and destroy the arms caches they knew were hidden beneath the rocks.

It would take five days to reach the heart of the valley, where Chadian and French forces converged. The operation continued for another six days to search additional caves for jihadist logistics and weapons, and track down any remaining fighters in the area. All told it took ten days to clear the valley.

The Ametetai Valley was the first and most significant of the operations in the Ifoghas, but other similar operations would follow. French forces returned to the forward operating base in Tessalit between each foray, where they regrouped and reequipped. Conditions in Tessalit were somewhat better than in the Ifoghas itself. Supplies were airdropped by C-130s from Bamako. But there was still no electricity and the only water for bathing – which soldiers sorely needed after several days eating onions and sleeping in the desert – came from a well. There were no bunks; troops still slept on the ground.[78]

For a month, French and Chadian forces would continue combing the valleys of the Ifoghas mountains. After the Ametetai came the In Tegant and then Terz and Assemalmal valleys. Armored units also raided along the Algerian and Nigerian border on the outskirts of the mountains. Pockets of enemy resistance remained. When possible, French forces would try to draw them out of their hiding places so that attack helicopters could strike their positions. But air support was not always an option. Often, the enemy was too close. The determination and ferocity of their commitment astonished some French officers who had become more accustomed to the hit-and-run tactics preferred by the Taliban in Kapisa province, Afghanistan.[79] This was clearly not a "typical African" group with limited discipline and commitment, officers noted. It was a determined bunch of extremists who were more than willing to give their lives to defend their Ifoghas base. French troops suspected widespread enemy use of Ketamine, an anesthetic that reduces fear.[80] Fear of precisely this fanaticism appeared to be adding to the hesitations some African militaries had about joining the fight.[81]

French and Chadian forces eventually killed close to 400 jihadists and seized 130 tons of munitions and equipment, according to French sources.[82] Objects found included passports from Egypt, Tunisia, and Canada, computers, GPS, rifles, AK-47s, RPGs, rocket launchers, and large amounts of ammunition and other weapons.[83] This was a significant stash that meant real damage to al Qa'ida's regional strength. It came at the cost of three French soldiers lives: Vormezeele, on February 19; Corporal Cédric Charenton in an assault on March 2; and Corporal Alexandre Van Dooren, on March 16, when his tank was destroyed by an improvised explosive device in Terz.

Among those dead was al Qa'ida in the Islamic Maghreb ringleader Abu Zeid, although the exact circumstances of his death are still unclear. After an initial report in early March that French forces had killed the al Qa'ida deputy in operations on February 27 in a heavy combined arms strike on the hamlet of Garage in the western In Tegant valley, Chadian President Déby claimed his own forces had in fact already eliminated Zeid a few days earlier.[84] In either case, one of al Qa'ida's regional ring leaders was dead, as France officially confirmed on March 23 after DNA testing. French forces also captured the first French national, Djamel Ben Hamdi, who evidently had grown weary of jihad and turned himself over to a French patrol in the Ifoghas. Belmokhtar was also reported dead in strikes. But these reports, unlike those of Zeid's death, soon proved false.

PROBLEMS IN GAO

Even as the main focus of French operations was in the Ifoghas, Mujao was proving tenacious in its hold on the Gao region. Barrera was forced to split his units and own attention between the two areas. After ten days in Tessalit, he had returned to Gao. The general remained concerned Muajo attacks there might force him to pull forces back from their efforts in the mountains: "We feared complex attacks, in several places, staggered in time."[85]

The second task group had continued to track the fighters through a series of operations code named *Doro* that concentrated especially on the smaller towns to the east. French intelligence estimated that there were still some hundred Mujao fighters left in the region. If disorganized by the initial French attack, these fighters continued to put up a fight. In addition to the attacks on February 5, 8, and 10, some twenty fighters mounted a larger attack on February 21.

French troops used classical counterinsurgency tactics, focusing their efforts on growing public support, cutting off the insurgents' financing, and hitting them hard and fast whenever they could be located. As in the Ifoghas, the French viewed intelligence operations as critical to success. French documents later listed among their key sources "Malian gendarmes, a liaison officer from the French intelligence service, local sources, information taken from the enemy, and tactical collection devices."[86]

On February 28, French forces launched a small-scale amphibious operation to clear suspected terrorists from Kadji, a small cluster of islands in the center of the Niger River. On March 1, they fought a Mujao pocket in a *wadi* northeast of Gao for seven hours, killing fifty-four of them. On March 6, Mujao sought to ambush Malian units on patrol with French counterparts. Here the French took another loss, sergeant first class, Wilfried Pingaud, but the outcome was much worse for Mujao: fifteen of their fighters were killed, many from close air support, but some in close combat fought with pistols alone.

Subsequent confrontations in Gao resulted in the deaths of another twenty-two Mujao fighters. All was not calm in Timbuktu either, where attacks against a smaller French force were also not uncommon throughout March. By mid-April, some 200 jihadists had been killed in the wider Gao region, and 75 tons of equipment had been seized.[87] As would later become apparent, this was not the end of the local jihadist movement, but it did amount to a serious degradation of their force.

BRINGING THE AFRICAN FORCES IN

French positions in February and March are shown in Figure 17. At the start of April, there were 5,300 French forces in the region involved in the operation, with 4,000 in Mali itself. France was now clearly signaling that it planned to begin drawing down. The first task group had already been relieved at the end of February. By late March, the pressure to draw down had grown as intense as the pressure to build

Figure 17. French Troop Advances through March.

up eight weeks earlier. "We engaged in a race against the clock in the opposite direction of what we'd done two months before, going from one task group up to four and now four to one" Barrera would later note.[88] France shifted the bulk of its forces from the Ifoghas back to Gao or out of the theater altogether. The fourth task group departed the Ifoghas area at the end of March. The third task force disengaged at the end of April, and the second task force in May. Both of these left behind elements that would form a new tactical desert group to continue operations against the jihadists. Conventional and special forces operations continued in April and May, but their tempo was reduced, especially in the Ifoghas. By July, the French contingent had been reduced to 3,200, roughly three quarters of its strength at the height of operations. A new operation, *Serval 2* was begun.

Even in the initial stages of the operation, the question of how France would transition responsibility for operations over to an African lead, as was originally intended, were in the forefront of discussions in Paris. The president was ready to go in fast and move fast, but he also wanted to get out as fast as he could without provoking a broader collapse. This was not just because of domestic pressures – it was also due to concerns that the longer French forces stayed, the greater the chances they would overstay their welcome, lose the support of the population, and end up in exactly the kind of quagmire they were so adamantly insisting would not befall them. *Serval* was built as an intervention force, not a stabilization force, explained one of its commanders later.[89] And there was, above all, also the cost to worry about. The longer the French stayed in theater, the more the operational costs would mount, and the harder it would be to make ends meet down the road. The French leadership thus felt enormous pressure to demonstrate concretely that their presence was going down and the transition was taking place.[90]

Beginning in February, a three-tiered transition strategy consisting of French forces, UN blue helmets, and Mali's own military started to take shape. The French would draw down and be replaced – or at least augmented – by a UN force. Meanwhile, the European Union would embark on an intensive effort to train Mali's own military so that it could eventually relieve the United Nations.

The strategy was far from uncontroversial. The French pushed the United Nations to take over as much responsibility for Mali's security as possible. The United Nations pushed back, and concerns about the effectiveness of the African forces, of which any UN force would be composed, resurfaced. Despite the fact that the West African troops had successfully deployed into Mali, complaints about their lack of basic equipment like C-130 transport aircraft or helicopters, their amateurism, and their indiscipline were widespread. The U.S. assistant secretary of defense for special operations and low intensity conflict, Mike Sheehan, accurately called them "not capable at all … a completely incapable force" in testimony before the Senate Armed Services Committee.[91] The commander of the African force, Pierre Buyoya, defended his troops noting that it was unfair to compare them to French forces, but Sheehan's assessment was on the mark.[92] There was little to no chance the African troops could take on a role akin to that of the French.

As these discussions were percolating, secretary general Ban Ki Moon set out on a fact-finding mission and reported back to the Security Council that indeed, there was no way that the United Nations could be expected to take over operations from France. "The challenges that confront Mali run deep and are not susceptible to any easy solution," the secretary general reported, noting that "Operation *Serval* has achieved impressive gains." As to the requests he had heard that a UN force "undertake combat operations against terrorist groups with the aim of restoring Mali's territorial integrity," his answer was a straightforward no. "The United Nations is not configured to oversee such operations at a strategic level," he said, "nor are its peacekeepers typically trained, equipped or experienced in the kind of operations that would be required to implement such a mandate. Moreover, an effort of this nature falls well outside the scope of the United Nations peacekeeping doctrine. It is also doubtful that the Organization would have the ability to absorb the numbers of casualties that could be incurred through such combat operations."[93]

Instead, Ban offered two alternatives for UN involvement. At the low end, it could strengthen its political presence in order to support mediation, humanitarian assistance, human rights, and other areas alongside the existing African force. Alternatively, it could undertake a more ambitious integrated peacekeeping mission under a Chapter VII mandate that would incorporate both the existing African force and the small UN operation on the ground.[94] On April 25, the Security Council passed Resolution 2100, voting for the second option and creating the UN Multidimensional Integrated Stabilization Mission in Mali. The Security Council authorized thereby the use of force and laid out a broad mandate for the operation: The mission would stabilize key population centers, support state-administration countrywide, support security sector reconstruction, develop disarmament programs, support national dialogue efforts, support presidential elections, protect civilians under imminent threat of violence, support humanitarian work, help preserve Mali's national culture, and support national and international justice. To accomplish this ambitious set of tasks, a force of 12,640, of which 11,200 would be soldiers and 1,440 police, was authorized, with an initial deployment date of July 1. The budget of $800 million per year was significant, but much less than the budgets the UN had agreed to dedicate to operations in Chad and the Democratic Republic of Congo.[95]

In theory, the UN forces should be somewhat of an improvement on the African forces in place. The reality, however, was little change, since, at least at the start, the bulk of the UN troops were drawn from the 6,000 West African and Chadian forces already on the ground under auspices of the Economic Community of West African States. What took place on July 1 was thus not a deployment of a UN force so much as a re-hatting of the African forces already there. Some adjustments were needed to meet UN standards. For example, Burkina Faso's contingent was too small to constitute a UN battalion and had to be supplemented, while the Chadian contingent did not initially meet UN human rights standards for the involvement of child soldiers. Mostly, however, the African forces on the ground simply switched their national berets for the familiar blue of UN peacekeepers.[96]

Where the other 6,000 troops would come from was unknown. As one international official put it diplomatically, "we don't have all the details" about what the force will actually look like.[97] The challenge was not just to come up with bodies, moreover. To carry out the ambitious tasks it was charged with, the UN mission would need aircraft for mobility and attack, engineering, intelligence analysis, French speakers, and troops with experience operating in the desert. Beyond these requirements, which were in short supply in all UN missions, troops that participated in the operation had to be willing to take on risks of a kind that non-African troops did not normally accept. The infernal temperature of desert bases, meanwhile, acted as a further deterrent to finding suitable volunteers for the task.[98]

A final deterrent both to volunteers and to UN operations itself was sincere fear of facing off against al Qa'ida and its allies. UN forces had never before been deployed anywhere they might have to fight such fierce and committed jihadists. Cognizant of these limitations, officials went to lengths to stress that even though UN forces were operating under Chapter VII authority, and thus, authorized to use force, it was not, strictly speaking, a peace-enforcement mission. "This is not an enforcement mission, this is not an anti-terrorist operation" explained Hervé Ladsous, the UN undersecretary general for peace-keeping operations, immediately after Resolution 2100 passed.[99] The United Nations did not, in other words, intend to use force proactively to squelch an insurgency or hunt down terrorists as the French had done – even if they might have to kill people to protect themselves or civilians. The distinction could not be altogether strict, however. If the jihadists attacked UN forces, they clearly needed to fight back to defend themselves. How would the UN fare in these conditions? At a minimum, then, the distinction served as an expression of the inherent limitations of capabilities of the UN force.

Unable to find relief from the critical counterterrorism mission, the French were thus forced to slow their drawdown of *Serval*, an eventuality clearly laid out in Resolution 2100, which expressly authorized "French troops ... to use all necessary means ... to intervene in support of elements of MINUSMA"[100] (Figure 18). They would remain in Mali in force for years to come.

"ABSOLUTELY EXCELLENT"

Throughout the mission troop morale was high among French troops. As French forces pushed forward in a conventional maneuver operation, advancing on specific axes and into enemy territory that could be clearly marked on a map, the satisfaction among the troops was palpable. The population welcomed the French forces as they advanced. Despite the extraordinarily unpleasant living conditions, troops reported a sense of satisfaction often lacking from other recent combat, especially in Afghanistan, where victory had been so elusive. When Assistant Secretary Sheehan testified before the Senate Armed Services Committee in April that "the French operation was absolutely excellent," Gallic pride surged. Even the Americans respected what they had done.[101]

All in all, French operations involved 4,500 troops at their height. Moving forces into the theater required 17,550 tons of freight on 300 flights and six ships. The army fired 34,000 small arms rounds, 58

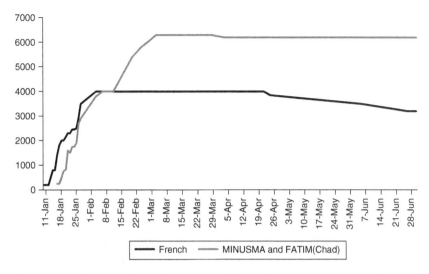

Figure 18. French Force Buildup and Drawdown, January–June 2013.
Source: French Ministry of Defense, *Mali Operations*.

missiles, 753 artillery shells, 80 105-mm tank shells, and 3,502 30-mm rounds from their Tigre attack helicopters.[102]

From this expenditure, the French haul was some 200 tons of arms and munitions taken from the jihadists, including artillery, rockets, hundreds of Kalashnikovs and other rifles, dozens of vehicles, twenty suicide vests, sixty improvised explosive devises, several GPS units, computers, telephones, and even a cache of old aerial bombs. Specific numbers regarding how many enemy forces were killed are difficult because many perished in air strikes, and some of those wounded who escaped may have died later. The official French estimate was that they killed 300–400 in the Ifoghas and 200–300 around Gao.[103] This represents somewhere between a third to half of al Qa'ida in the Islamic Maghreb and its allies' fighters when they crossed the Niger in January. The fight was thus not over. But the French had struck a resounding blow.

8 THE ELUSIVE "POLITICAL" DIMENSION

It was under these tenuous circumstances, with the bulk of the original jihadist forces chased from Mali's territory, French forces bent on withdrawing as fast they could, and an uncertain transition to a UN peacekeeping force under way, that the focus began to shift back toward Mali's fraught political scene and the daunting state-building task ahead. American officials – especially the State Department – had emphasized the importance of the political dimension of reconstruction all along, stressing the need for reconciliation between the Tuaregs and political elites in Bamako as well as the restoration of democracy through national elections. French political and military leaders likewise recalled the desultory outcome of the NATO intervention in Libya two years earlier, where initial military success had been followed by a rudderless and almost nonexistent international postwar effort – and consequent strategic failure.[1]

As they withdrew, the French were thus sensitive to the possibility that their military gains could soon slip away absent rapid progress on political fronts. Al Qa'ida was at bay, but Mali's problems ran deep. As Traoré put it, "the fact that Mali collapsed in so few days was not a good sign."[2] There were no illusions that the military itself could offer a permanent solution for the challenge. "It's not the French army that will ensure Mali's future," a senior official said a year after *Serval* was launched.[3] Addressing the political piece of the problem would be critical.

Three major challenges called for immediate and near-simultaneous attention. First, political, military, administrative, and other institutions had to be rebuilt on multiple fronts. Major efforts to reduce corruption and strengthen the postwar state were clearly required. To truly regain its sovereignty and independence, the Malian state also needed reliable security forces that could hold the north without direct support from France or the United Nations. These were a long way off.

Second, Traoré's interim government had functioned as well as one might have hoped, but it was widely agreed that Mali needed to get an elected government back in place as soon as possible. Without an elected government, the United States would be limited in what it could contribute to reconstruction. More importantly, most officials thought it would be fruitless for the interim government to try to move ahead toward a settlement with the north.

Third, there was the ongoing, fundamental problem of Tuareg separatism. Even if many Tuaregs had ended up cooperating with the French in their effort to chase al Qa'ida and its allies out, this did not at all mean they had reconciled themselves with Bamako or given up the dream of autonomy and independence. Elites in Bamako meanwhile continued to harbor deep skepticism and even downright hostility toward the Tuaregs, many still conflating the jihadist and secular groups. The separatist conflict could thus easily flare up again. With troops in the north, the international community was now in a stronger position to impress on Bamako's political elites the need for negotiation and compromise. Tuareg communities had to be made to feel the positive economic effects of their liberation from al Qa'ida's rule.

REBUILDING THE MALIAN ARMY

France's European partners had proven lukewarm about the French push for intervention in Mali throughout the fall of 2012. Although they recognized the problem was serious, the possibilities for direct military support from the European Union were limited. For most of the last decade, the French had preferred intervention under the European Union flag to NATO or unilateralism. *Serval* was thus a clear break from a pattern that had begun to change with the NATO intervention in Libya. Facing tepid support for intervention and lack of capabilities from key allies, the French had decided to go it alone.

But this didn't mean that the French were prepared to let the rest of Europe off the hook. Throughout the fall of 2012 the French government had wrangled with their European counterparts to get at least a European Union training mission in place to take on the critical challenge of reforming the Malian military. Despite political declarations in favor of helping Mali, however, many European countries dragged their feet when it came to actually making concrete commitments.[4] The French decision to intervene changed the dynamic, forcing the issue in Brussels. The European Council agreed to the deployment of a European Union training mission on February 18, just as French forces were setting up to begin their labor in the Ifoghas.

Reconstituting the Malian army had to be a key part of the international postconflict reconstruction effort. The European Union objective was to restore the army to a point where it had not only the tactical proficiency to hold the north, but also the organizational backbone to do so.[5] This was a huge task before 2012, but given the coup and collapse of the military in the face of the revolt, what was needed now was no less than a root and branch reconstruction. Mali's military was in a decrepit state, with only some 1,500 men still in arms. Factionalized before the revolt, it had become even more so in the aftermath of the Sanogo coup. Unsurprisingly, capabilities and equipment were extremely limited. Many soldiers had to share rifles. Mali once had a small air force of twenty MIG-21s, but only two of these remained, and the country's sole pilots refused to fly them because they were in such poor shape. Three old Ukrainian helicopters were of little more use and largely sat rusting on the tarmac.[6]

The European Union mission drew on 541 staff from 22 different countries – the major contributors being France, Germany, and Spain. The French again made up the bulk of the force, contributing 207 soldiers, with Germany in second place at 73. This was a substantial size for a mission of this kind, although it was not the largest such EU mission. Many of the soldiers were of course there to protect the mission itself – in total there were 180 instructors.[7]

The failures of earlier efforts to train the Malian army weighed heavily in the European approach. Determined not to repeat the mistakes of the past, the European training mission set out a two-track strategy to strengthen the rank and file while simultaneously building a better defense ministry from the top down. A small number of staff worked in the ministry in Bamako to help it improve its basic administrative and other skills. The bulk of the work, however, took place at the lower level at Koulikoro, a training camp on the outskirts of Bamako that had been built by the French in the late 1990s. The objective was to create eight, unified, self-supported battalions. The first of these was pulled together from what remained of the army, supplemented with some new recruits, between April and July. This battalion was roughly ten percent Tuareg.[8] Subsequent battalions were trained also on a three-month basis, but with larger portions of new recruits. Many soldiers had had no training before entering Koulikoro. The training focused on building a basic counterterrorism and stabilization capability. Units focused on four areas – reconnaissance, area control, defense, and offensive operations for eliminating isolated pockets of resistance.

The initial fifteen-month authorization for the European effort would clearly not be enough to overcome the many deficiencies of the Malian army. The mission was thus extended by two years on April 15, 2014, with the aim of training an additional four battalions.

THE OUAGADOUGOU INTERIM ACCORDS

In June, representatives of Mali's government and the Tuaregs met in Burkina Faso to discuss peace terms between the secular rebels and the government. The government was represented by Moussa Sinko Coulibaly, the secular Tuaregs by Bilal Ag Acherif, and the High Council for the Unity of the Azawad (HCUA) by Algabass Ag Intalla – all three important Tuareg leaders. By this time, many of the secular rebel groups – the MNLA and the HCUA in particular – had been fighting alongside the French forces against the jihadists. MNLA had announced its support for the French intervention early on and was still in Kidal after the jihadists were chased out, cooperating tacitly with French troops. The precise details of that cooperation are murky – French troops not being permitted to negotiate with the rebels. Needless to say, Bamako objected strongly to the Tuareg presence, insisting the rebels disarm and allow government forces to occupy turf in and around the city. The rebels resisted, insisting, for their part, that Bamako stop legal proceedings against some of their imprisoned fighters and release them. After several days of difficult negotiations, President Hollande had to intervene personally, backed by President Ouattara, to convince Traoré and the rebels to ink even a preliminary agreement.[9]

Signed on June 18, the Ouagadougou Accords called for a cease-fire, cantonment of rebel forces, the return of Malian state authority to the north, national elections, and continued peace negotiations. The rebels agreed to disarm in principle, but only after a final peace agreement had been signed. In the meantime, however, they would begin cantonment and the Malian army would deploy to Kidal. More in-depth peace negotiations were to begin sixty days after the election of a new government in Bamako.

The ceasefire became effective immediately. A monitoring and evaluation committee with representatives of all concerned parties, including the government, the rebel groups, the Economic Community of West African States, the African Union, the United Nations, the European Union, Algeria, France, Mauritania, Niger, Chad, and Switzerland, was set up to oversee the implementation of the Accords. Finally, a commission to investigate war crimes was established. In addition to the government and rebels, Nigerian president Goodluck Jonathan and Burkinabe President Compaoré also signed the agreement, with witnesses from the United Nations, European Union, Organization of Islamic Cooperation, and the African Union.[10]

The accords were met with applause from European and other capitals. The reality, however, was that the Ouagadougou Accords were only a first step. Contrary to what some claimed, they could hardly be considered "historic" given the fact that two similar agreements between Bamako and the Tuareg rebels had fallen apart in the last twenty years, levels of distrust were high, northern rebel groups were far from united, and the military situation between the two sides remained tense.

IBK'S ELECTION

How soon to hold elections after a war is one of the perennial issues of postconflict stabilization. Some experts hold that elections are inherently contentious and thus risk a disruption of the postconflict stabilization process, while others argue that elections are necessary to move ahead on any front – unelected governments lack legitimacy and can thus be timid or controversial in their own right. In this case, the latter camp won out. Nearly all the actors on the ground agreed that Mali needed elections and needed them soon. Traoré himself was particularly focused on holding the elections sooner rather than later. If elections were delayed, any momentum that had been generated by the government's near-death experience in January would be lost. Moreover, if a workable solution to the Tuareg issue seemed impossible with an interim government in place in Bamako.[11] At the same time, however, with the continuation of the conflict in the north and the French occupation, there was also good reason to doubt that effective presidential elections could be held so soon. The end of July was only six weeks off when the Ouagadougou accords were signed. Organizing free and fair elections in the vast country where security was predominantly in the hands of foreigners and where tensions in some areas still ran high looked like a tall order. Nevertheless, the United States and other powers pushed for the rapid timetable in hope of getting a legitimate government in Bamako that could negotiate more effectively with the rebels, doing away with the military junta once and for all, and opening the door to the resumption of foreign assistance.

As it turned out, July and August polling took place with relatively little violence. Of the twenty-eight registered candidates, Ibrahim Boubacar Keita won a commanding majority of 40 percent of the vote in the July 28 poll, twice the amount of the second-place finisher, Soumaila Cissé. In the August 11 runoff, Keita won 78 percent, giving him a substantial mandate to lead the country out of its crisis.[12] Forty-eight percent of registered voters (3,345,253) participated in the process, significantly more than had in any election since 2002. No major security incidents were reported, and incidence of voter intimidation was very limited.[13]

Keita, or "IBK" as he was more widely known, was a member of the old guard, a close ally of former president Konaré, a former foreign and prime minister, several times a presidential candidate against ATT, and president of the national assembly from 2002 to 2007. IBK had spent twenty-six years in France, where he attended lycée and taught at the University of Paris-I, Tolbiac. A member of the socialist international, he had run a 2013 campaign that emphasized his conservative Muslim values and determination to restore Mali's territorial integrity. He maintained close ties with a religious organization known as Sabati, which was linked to Mali's High Islamic Council and also enjoyed widespread support among the Malian military – including from Sanogo (although his party strongly denied any link).

The new president was inaugurated on September 4. He quickly formed a government that included many figures from the old guard, but also some new faces. Oumar Tatm Ly, for example, a Parisian-born specialist in economic and financial affairs who had worked for two decades at the Central Bank of West African States became prime minister. IBK proclaimed his determination to eschew the bloated, consensus politics of the ATT period and the ineffective governance that it produced. Some feared that this emphasis on a strong hand was a possible precursor to an authoritarian slide, while others worried that his rhetoric about national unity would leave him in a tough position in subsequent negotiations with the Tuareg separatists.[14]

RECONCILIATION STALLS

At first, the new Malian government engaged energetically in a reconciliation process, starting soon after its election. A ministry for national reconciliation and development of the north was created, and a national dialogue was launched with a series of conferences that aimed to promote broad discussion of reconciliation, development, decentralization, and other issues in the north. The government saw the broad process as a way of avoiding a straightforward face-off against the rebel groups.[15] Two conferences were held in the fall of 2013, both in Bamako. It was a positive sign that hundreds of representatives of northern groups attended. Unfortunately, however, representatives of the armed groups themselves did not.

The conferences were a step in the right direction and signaled a recognition that something needed to be done about the nation's division. But this recognition did not amount to a will to take the difficult steps necessary to make a clear break with the past. Many observers were skeptical that the conference would amount to anything, given the fact that such conferences had regularly attended the end of previous Tuareg conflicts, yet produced little in terms of concrete results for the north.[16]

Meanwhile, meetings between the government and rebels did take place, but they did so informally, outside the established framework. The secular Tuareg rebels had been greatly weakened over the course of 2012 as the jihadists pushed them aside. Although the MNLA was still the strongest of the remaining rebel groups, it remained divided over whether or not to negotiate with Bamako.[17] At the same time, a second Tuareg rebel group, the High Council for the Unity of the Azawad (HCUA), had emerged. This group appears to have been the initiative of the Amenokal of the Ifoghas tribe, Intallah ag Attaher, who had led the tribe, ruling the Kidal region, since 1963 and now sought a means of reconciling the Tuaregs as a whole before the upcoming peace negotiations. In May, 2013, Ag Attaher split with the other Tuaregs to become president of the new group.[18] His son, Mohamed Ag Intalla, was made the group's secretary general. Another son, Alghabas ag Intallah, meanwhile disbanded the Islamic Movement of the Azawad, which he had led since breaking away from Ansar al Din earlier that year, and joined the group as vice-president.[19] The High Council was thus closely linked to the MNLA, drew heavily on the Ifoghas tribe, and brought in many former moderates of the now-defunct Ansar al Din – men who otherwise likely continued to be regarded with suspicion by MNLA leaders such as Najim. (Ansar al Din had been designated a foreign terrorist organization by the U.S. State Department in March 2013. Ag Ghali's whereabouts were unknown, but he was reported to be hiding out with a few remaining holdouts.)[20] The HCUA was strong in several towns of the Kidal, Gao, and Timbuktu regions.

As noted above, both Tuareg groups were signatories to the Ougadougou accords. Alongside them, a third group, the Arab Movement of the Azawad (MAA) also took on a role in the process. Traditionally uncertain both about its relationship with the Tuaregs, against whom it had fought in early 2013, the Arab northerners were the furthest from the traditional rebel fold.[21]

Sadly, two years after the French intervention, little progress had been made on reconciliation. The North-South divide endured. The situation only got worse in May 2014 when an attempt by a faction within the Malian army to wrest control of Kidal from the rebels ended in humiliation. Tuareg military leader El Haj Ag Gamou, in an apparent effort to settle old scores, marched on the town with over 1,000 government troops armed with tanks and rocket launchers, but was outgunned, and at least forty troops were killed in the fighting. He had to fall back to the safety of UN and French protection. Infuriated French officials blamed the incident on Ag Gamou, cursing him for "pouring oil on the fire".[22] The intra-Tuareg conflict, with heightened tensions between Ag Gamou's Imghad tribe and the Ifoghas and other pro-rebel tribes, added a whole other dimension of complexity to an already fragmented and shifting security situation. In the wake of Ag Gamou's failed assault on Kidal, anti-government armed groups seized government vehicles, fuel and other supplies and used them to retake the neighboring town of Anefis. Some of Ag Gamou's forces meanwhile defected to the rebel side in fear of reprisals against them.

The May 2014 outbreak did not, luckily, spark a broader conflagration, but years after the initial revolt, lasting reconciliation between Bamako and the Tuaregs was still a long way off. A year later, the Malian military continued to contest de facto Tuareg control of Kidal and its environs, and the Bamako government was increasingly backing an anti-Tuareg militia known as the Gaita, which was in open conflict in Menaka and elsewhere against the new Tuareg umbrella group, the Coordination for Mouvements of the Azawad. Algeria brokered a preliminary peace accord among key groups in May 2015, but the chances the accord would lead anywhere were low.

These developments were unquestionably a cause for major concern given the role this ancient conflict had played in opening the door to jihadist advances back in 2012. International concern that the country was heading in the wrong direction, despite *Serval*'s gains, was growing.[23]

JIHADIST VIOLENCE CONTINUES

Moreover, even if *Serval* had struck a blow to the jihadists, their attacks against forces in the North would continue. Within weeks of the investiture of the new government, jihadists managed new attacks against government and UN forces. In August, Belmokthar's Mulathamin and Mujao had joined forces and formed a new group, known as al Murabitun. Although Belmokthar was now widely suspected of having decamped to southern Libya, Kheirou, Hamaha and others were suspected to still be in the environs of Gao. Other former members of Mujao were reported to be returning to the town, sparking fear and protests from many locals.[24] Despite the death of Abu Zeid, other groups remained active in Timbuktu and Kidal under the leadership of Ghali's cousin al Targui.

On September 28, 2013 al Qa'ida in the Islamic Maghreb car bombed a military camp in Timbuktu, killed two assailants along with two civilians pulling a cart nearby.[25] On October 7 and 30, Murabitun shelled military installations at Gao and on October 8 sabotaged two bridges on the outskirts of town, destroying one. On October 23, Al Targui's forces attacked French and Chadian troops in Tessalit repeatedly with a car bomb, two suicide bombers, followed up with a small-arms guerilla-type attack.

On November 2, Ghislaine Dupont and Claude Verlon, two French journalists working for *Radio France Internationale* were kidnapped and then executed, likely by a jihadi outcast seeking a way into Al Targui's good graces. The kidnappers were claimed by some locals to have been living among the secular Tuareg rebels.[26] Subsequent attacks included a November 30 suicide attack on a barracks at Menaka, attacks on peacekeepers at Kidal on December 13, and more shelling of Gao on December 25.

Further attacks by Mulathamin, Ansar al Din, and al Qa'ida in the Islamic Maghreb, continued in 2014 and 2015. To complicate matters, in 2015, a new jihadist group appeared to have emerged, the Macina Liberation Front. Attacks from these groups, though mostly smaller scale, caused significant losses among United Nations forces in Kidal, Tessalit, and elsewhere in the North. By May 2015, thirty-five UN peacekeepers had been killed – a heavy toll for a UN peacekeeping mission, even one operating under a Chapter VII mandate. With twenty-eight deaths and seventy-five injuries in 2014, the UN mission in Mali became the most deadly UN mission that year.[27]

FROM *SERVAL* TO *BARKHANE*

Although these attacks were signs of the very difficult road ahead, even in 2015, Mali was still far better off than it had been before the French intervened. The tough road ahead, however, clearly called for continued French presence. France had once hoped to draw its forces down to 1,000 by the end of September 2013 but was forced to delay repeatedly. Some 200 French soldiers remained in Kidal with similar size forces in other towns in the Kidal region, with larger numbers in Gao and Bamako.[28]

France began to plan for the long haul. In January 2014, a new force posture for North Africa was previewed. It would focus on dealing with the rump threat from Belmokhtar, al Targui and their comrades, who had now begun to use the southern Libyan province of Fezzan as a rear operating base for their attacks in Mali and Niger. In December 2013, French forces had killed another eighteen jihadists as they moved from Libya back toward Mali. The new plan was designed to broaden the scope of French operations beyond Mali, to include also Burkina Faso, Mauritania, Niger, and Chad. Responsibility for Mali's internal problems would fall, in theory at least, to Malians themselves, supported by the UN.

The new French posture drew on the French strike fighters deployed in Abidjan, the new Reapers the French had just acquired from the United States and based in Niamey, the helicopter units stationed at Gao and the special forces unit still in Ouagadougou. Forward operating bases were also set up in Tessalit, Faya-Largeau in northern Chad, and at Madama, not far from the Libyan border in northern Niger. This posture was intended to allow for the most rapid response possible against the remaining jihadists and any new threats that could arise. The whole system would be backed by French forces in Abidjan, Dakar, and Libreville. This meant some 3,000 French forces would remain in the region, with the primary purpose of continuing to track and kill the jihadist groups – as opposed to stabilizing Mali.[29] This was half the French troops deployed in Africa, a sum that made France the largest non-African military force on the continent.

In July, France officially dubbed this new operation *Barkhane*, and turned the page on *Serval*. The 1,000 troops remaining in *Serval*, most of which were in Mali, would be folded into the new force. Hollande made a tour of the key African capitals involved, announcing the new cooperation. *Serval* may have been a success, but it would only be one of the many chapters in France's long history of military operations in Africa.

MALI'S SHAKY PROSPECTS

A year after the French launched *Serval,* one observer noted that "after having made the observation that the 'Malian model' had been nothing but a house of cards, Mali's partners now have a tendency to fall back into the illusion of the 'return of the sovereign state.'"[30] The situation has improved little since. IBK's emphasis on sovereignty in the wake of the crisis may be understandable, but the government is and will remain utterly aid-dependent for a long time. Months after his election, IBK's honeymoon with the international community had worn thin and charges of corruption had resurfaced. Even if many jihadists had been chased out, as noted above, the security situation remained fragile. The threat of ISIS expansion into Mali was, by mid-2015, no longer far-fetched. The poisonous north south division had not improved, despite the Algerian brokered talks.

On the institutional level, it remains uncertain whether or not the demand for reform among the population – a key ingredient when it comes to strengthening a weak state – will be large enough to bring about the change needed to move Mali on the path toward self-sustaining stability.[31] Some elites in Bamako are near despair when it comes to their countrymen's civic spirit, desire for democracy, and willingness to tolerate rampant corruption.[32] "In such a poor country, it is hard for democracy to develop," said one. Even if Malians have grown accustomed to democracy and a democratic culture has taken root, leaders will still face an uphill battle to avoid another relapse into war. This does not mean they are doomed, but the challenges are real. Mali at least has the support of other states in the region, whose leaders have recognized the criticality of keeping the country on track and not allowing the jihadists to move back in. Its capacity for dealing with the problem in any significant way, absent outside help, however, will be extremely limited for many years to come.

9 THE ROAD AHEAD

The French intervention in Mali was unexpected but, if unexpected, it was in many ways unexpectedly successful. This is true despite the challenges that persisted in Mali after France's drawdown. Without the French intervention, the situation in Mali was and would have remained even worse. *Serval* was thus only the first step in a long-term effort, but it bears close study given the challenge the world faces in coping with the unnerving proliferation of Salafi jihadist groups across the Middle East and North Africa. The threat from Bin Laden's al Qa'ida has been greatly reduced, but the world now faces a new problem with al Qa'ida's offspring – al Qa'ida in the Islamic Maghreb, Boko Haram, al Shabab and others – as well as now established competitors such as ISIS. Needless to say, military force is not alone the solution to these threats. It is part of the solution, however, and to expect progress without the use of force would be naïve. Developing appropriate military strategies is pressing. To design a strategy for combatting Salafi jihadists in North Africa and understand accurately the options for military strategy there – and in other regions – requires assessing what the French accomplished in 2013 and why.

DID THE FRENCH MODEL SUCCEED?

The French model in Mali involved a small to medium sized conventional force, many times larger than a typical special operations unit, but a fraction of the size of the forces deployed by the United States and its allies in Iraq and Afghanistan. The primary objective of the force was counterinsurgency, especially the prevention and destruction of a terrorist safe haven. The operation, though longer than French leaders hoped, was still limited in duration, with French forces starting to redeploy or draw down only a few months after it began. To destroy the safe haven in Mali, the French military took ground, but it left much of the responsibility for holding the ground up to UN and Malian forces. Parallel initiatives were undertaken on state-building and resolving the underlying conflict that opened the door to al Qa'ida in the Islamic Maghreb in the first place.

Most French officials and experts are decidedly positive about what this model accomplished. "A major success" said one, "even better than we expected."[1] "No country wants another country to intervene in its own affairs, but without the French intervention, there would be no Mali today," explained Traoré. Hollande's reception in Mali was also not disingenuous. Most Malians, as well as most regional leaders, were grateful once France took action against the terrorist threat.

The French intervention has also had many detractors. Some seem to have a bone to pick with Hollande or the French military. In *Papa Hollande au Mali*, for example, the French journalist Nicolas Beau charges that the intervention was a "fiasco;" "amateurish and arrogant" – lacking in international support and political vision.[2] A more balanced but still critical writer predicted that jihadism was "a force in retreat" at the time of the French intervention, but will be revived as a result.[3] It is clear now, however, that jihadism in Africa was not in retreat in 2013. Others doubted the risk posed by al Qa'ida in the first place.[4] Presumably these critics would have preferred to permit the jihadists into the unprotected capital to test their good intentions. Still others question whether "tens of amputations or executions justifies the deployment of thousands of soldiers."[5] But this critique ignores the many other rationales for intervention, especially the national security rationales. Still others questioned whether the French might have accomplished more with a limited campaign of drone strikes.[6] Manned and unmanned aircraft were used to positive effect but alone could not have restored Mali's integrity. In the absence of reliable Malian troops, French ground forces were needed for this task.

Judging the success of modern military interventions is tricky. Scholars have identified many pitfalls and inadequacies in the way interventions are usually judged. For example, assessments of operational success too often focus on inputs alone – the number of troops deployed, humanitarian movements made, tons of equipment moved, number of flights accomplished, and so forth. These data can be useful in assessing the tactical success or comparative magnitude of an intervention, but they offer little insight if any into whether or not an intervention succeeded in broader strategic terms. Another possibility, judging success by the numbers of lives saved, is sometimes held up as a standard for so-called "humanitarian interventions" but it is inherently subject to serious data collection challenges, and ultimately tells only part of the picture anyway, even if an important part.[7] Other judgments of military interventions unrealistically hold up a maximalist, ideal outcome such as the degree of democracy after five years as a benchmark across all cases.

All such measures, moreover, fail to assess costs alongside benefits. The success of an intervention needs to be judged not just based upon what an intervention achieves, but also what these achievements cost. Counterinsurgency operations, for example, sometimes fall into the category of threat prevention or humanitarian relief. When they do, the operation should only be undertaken if it can be successful at a cost commensurate with the importance of these national interests. Costs and benefits themselves moreover need to be assessed not only from a financial and military perspective, but also in a broader political and moral framework. When judging an intervention, it is, above all, critical to keep in mind what would have happened absent intervention. Far too often, judgments about the success of an intervention are based on assessments of the explicit or implicit comparisons to the prewar status quo. This is a common but misleading error. Crises evolve, with or without foreign interference. The key question is thus what direction they would likely have taken had the military operation never happened. In other words, in assessing the costs and benefits of a particular case, analysts must think in terms of counterfactuals – what would have happened if nothing had been done.[8] For example, a robust assessment of the costs and benefits of the U.S. war in Iraq requires some defensible picture of what Iraq and the Middle East would have looked like today if the war had not occurred. Similarly, an assessment of the wisdom and appropriateness of the 1999 NATO intervention in Kosovo requires a serious effort to understand what the political and strategic situation in the Western Balkans and Europe more broadly would have become had NATO not intervened.

Finally, judgments about success or failure need to take into account a sufficiently long view. It is often very difficult to ascertain whether or not an intervention has accomplished its strategic objectives at the time military operations wind down. Postintervention, postwar challenges very often derail hard-won military gains – as was the case in both Afghanistan and Libya. It is possible, however, to assess fairly early on whether or not a country has a fighting chance of emerging stronger in the medium term. While the processes that cause states to collapse are varied, there are certain things that the international community can do to improve the chances of postwar political – hence strategic – success. Key among these are ensuring security, addressing underlying political problems, and offering financial, administrative, and other assistance to strengthen weak institutions and improve governance. Without such measures – or in cases where the needs are much greater than the international community is prepared to fill – the strategic impact of military intervention is bound to be limited if existent. In such cases, it may still be necessary to intervene militarily to stave off a major humanitarian tragedy or national security threat, but policymakers should be wary that in doing so they are at best applying a salve when deeper surgery is likely needed.

Judging *Serval* thus requires looking at the operation from multiple angles. A good place to begin is simply whether or not the French achieved their own stated objectives. This they clearly did. French goals in the operation as outlined by President Hollande on January 15 were threefold: to secure Bamako, to stop the jihadist insurgency, and to allow Mali to regain its territorial integrity. All of these had been achieved satisfactorily by the spring of 2013, only a few months after they intervened: al Qa'ida in the Islamic Maghreb was hardly destroyed, but it had taken a serious hit. Bamako was secure, or at least as secure as it had ever been. Mali's territorial integrity had been restored, at least in the sense that the country was under the control of Malian state or its French and African protectors.

The damage to the jihadist groups was real and should not be under-estimated. In January 2013, they were joined in a common, if fractious, front against Bamako. They had free reign in the north, where they had stockpiled weapons, set up paramilitary training camps, ran smuggling operations, and could move easily across the broader region. They controlled a territory the size of France, albeit one far less populous. They had built close links with the Tuareg tribes, especially in the Ifoghas, and set up administrative, judicial, and governmental structures in Gao, Timbuktu, Tessalit, and Kidal. Alongside certain areas in Syria, Pakistan, Yemen, and Somalia, this made northern Mali one of the world's better-established terrorist safe havens. It was a decade in the making, and the French destroyed it in a few weeks.

It is nearly impossible to know the exact number of jihadist casualties, but several hundred jihadists were clearly killed by French forces in air strikes or close combat in the Ifoghas and Gao.[9] This represents at least a third, and possibly as much as half of the overall jihadist fighting force of over a thousand in January 2013. The jihadists were deprived of their training camps, and more than 2,000 tons of weapons were destroyed, seriously attriting their stockpiles. Their ability to finance operations with profits from smuggling was diminished. In addition, their organizational structures were damaged, both within some of the groups and especially between them. Although Mujao and Belmokthar's groups later joined forces, the broader collection no longer forms a common front. The elimination of Abu Zeid, who played an important personal role as a link between the Ifoghas tribes and the jihadists, makes it more difficult for them to reestablish links to the local communities in the future.[10]

It is important to emphasize that, from a national security perspective, the biggest problem in Mali was that the north had become a true safe haven for the jihadist insurgents, their allies from elsewhere in Africa, and even the world – one that was particularly menacing to the French. Here was an area where the jihadists had near-complete control of the governing institutions and no local adversaries to contend with. This compared favorably with contested areas where al Qa'ida affiliates were powerful but forced to fight for their territory – as was the case for jihadists in Syria at that time. A safe haven in Mali was a boon that allowed the jihadists to strengthen their planning,

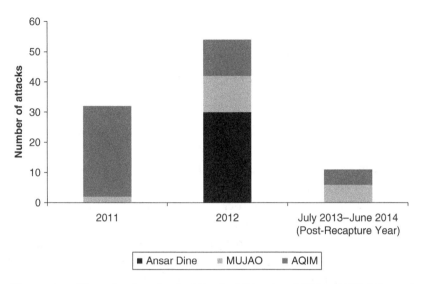

Figure 19. Terrorist Attacks in North Africa by AQIM, MUJAO, and Ansar al-Din Before and After French Recapture of Northern Mali. *Source*: Jane's Terrorism and Insurgency Intelligence Center (JTIC) Events Database.

organization, financing, recruiting and training – including of foreign fighters. The French operation took all this away, a fact reflected in the overall decline in attacks attributed to al Qa'ida affiliates after the initial phases of *Serval* were complete (Figure 19).

Indeed, looking back at what *Serval* accomplished, it is hard to imagine a better outcome given the situation in January 2013. On the eve of the intervention, the country was divided, *shari'a* had been imposed in several parts of the north, the government had collapsed, and a military junta still exercised significant influence in Bamako. Only a year later, the country was reunited, the jihadists chased out, and a democratically elected government in place. Had it not been stopped by the French, the jihadist advance on Bamako would have been disastrous. Even if it was intended only to delay the deployment of the UN force the advance could easily have undermined existing international strategy by causing ECOWAS to falter. If the jihadist charge toward Bamako had succeeded and they had occupied even parts of the city, the international community would have faced enormous difficulties in getting them out. Certainly a much, much larger operation would then have been necessary.

Mali has a very difficult path ahead, to be sure, but there is little question that its prospects were far better after the French intervened than before.

The larger issue, however, is whether or not the French will be able to achieve strategic success, the longer-term success that has proven so elusive in so many other major military engagements of the twenty-first century. This is much harder to judge.

If the jihadists were struck a serious blow, they were clearly not eliminated. As noted in chapter eight, Al Qa'ida in the Islamic Maghreb survived; key figures decamped for Libya and continued to plot attacks from there. Fighters once in Mali were also reported in Burkina Faso, Chad, Mauritania, and Morocco.[11] Belmokthar's *Mulathimeen* unified with Mujao to create *Murabitun*, which continued a low-level insurgency in Gao and conducted attacks elsewhere. It had a rear operating base in southern Libya and possibly also western Algeria, along the border with Morocco, where the Polisario had been strong for decades and Mujao leader Abu Kheirou had links. *Murabitun* threatened attacks against France and pledged to unite Muslims "from the Nile to the Atlantic."[12] Further attacks on regional targets were likely.

The threat of Salafi jihadists is moreover regional, and now includes ISIS in Libya in addition to al Qa'ida in the Islamic Maghreb and other groups. Nevertheless, as French officials rightly point out, Belmokthar and Abu Zeid had invested years intermarrying and building networks and trust in the north. These networks will be more difficult to replace than the foot soldiers the French killed. Rebuilding similar networks elsewhere will take time. Rebuilding them in Mali will be even harder, now that the population has been treated to al Qa'ida's brutal interpretation of *shari'a*. The Malians may have a conservative, Muslim culture, but it is not a brutal one.

Reports of ransoms paid for the release of hostages continued, however, to give the appearance that the French government was working against its own objectives in the region, financing the very enemies its troops on the ground were trying to hunt and kill. Ransoms are obviously not the only source of financing the jihadists have – they continue to exploit regional smuggling networks – but ransom payments that can reach into the tens of millions of dollars buy a lot of weapons and foot soldiers in such an impoverished part of the world. The lure of money is moreover an excellent added seduction to waging jihad. As long as the weapons keep circulating, and economic and social conditions still offer a favorable market for jihadist recruits, ransom payments will clearly work against long-term French and U.S. aims.

Intertwined with the question of whether or not the jihadists will be able to regroup is the question of whether or not Mali's enfeebled state has a fighting chance of avoiding collapse again. After successful initial military operations in Afghanistan, Iraq, and Libya, all three states fell victim to political conflicts that spilled over again into war – a sobering reminder of the difficulties of postconflict reconstruction. Depressingly little has been done to resolve the fundamental north-south conflict that allowed the jihadists to infiltrate Mali in the first place. Its government remains corrupt. Its democratic politics and institutions may be even weaker than they were on the eve of Sanogo's coup. The efforts by the European Union, France, the African Union, and others in the country may be insufficient and cannot alone guarantee a relapse will not occur. Exogenous shocks or policy missteps could easily shatter the progress that has been made. Other problems like China, Russia, ISIS, and Ebola will meanwhile continue to consume international resources and attention, increasing the challenge of achieving strategic success in Mali.

If *Serval* had a decidedly positive effect, therefore, it cannot yet be considered a strategic success. But it was a critical stepping stone on the road to strategic success. Without *Serval*, political progress in Mali (and perhaps its neighbors) would have been near impossible, and the jihadist challenge would be even greater than it is today. No single intervention could have resolved, once and for all, the complex problems of this fragile region. But overall *Serval* has done far more to help than to hurt.

The success the French did achieve with *Serval* came at a relatively low cost. The French lost eight soldiers, and the financial cost of operations for 2013 was estimated at 647 million euros. The operation may also have encouraged the attack on the French embassy in Libya in April 2013, and other retributive attacks could still follow. But French citizens and facilities were targeted before the intervention as well, so the cost in this sense is marginal at most. Politically, however, France seems to have gained in the region, where its willingness to go after the jihadists was welcomed by leaders who feared the safe haven's poisonous effects on regional stability. Charges of neocolonialism have been muted with most regional powers, including even Algeria.

The final costs of the operation cannot be known since follow-on operations are ongoing. But this is a positive thing. The fact that French forces remained in Mali for a long time after the initial intervention in somewhat smaller, but not inconsequential numbers, could be seen as evidence the operation was not entirely successful. Ideally, French forces would have been able to immediately withdraw and hand the situation over to the African forces or the Malians themselves. But to fault the French for staying on is unfair. Indeed, in Libya, the international community closed up shop far too soon, and the country suffered the consequences. Similarly, in Iraq, the unexpected contraction of the U.S. presence to nil at the end of 2011 has helped create the conditions for the return first of al Qa'ida in Iraq and, eventually, ISIS. In Afghanistan in 2001, the United States had striking success with a strategy similar to that used by the French in Mali, but then largely departed, leaving security up to the warlords and enfeebled Karzai government. When the Taliban then returned, the United States was forced to deploy 100,000 troops to save the country from collapse. France has been right to avoid the same mistakes in Mali. They have remained, in smaller numbers, but act as a force multiplier and enabler for the UN stabilization operation. They should be expected to stay for a long time in this role. It is easy to put too much emphasis on exit strategies, at the expense of strategic objectives. Anyone who favors U.S. deployments in Europe and Asia should be no less open to the potential benefits of European deployments in Africa, provided, of course, they serve broader strategic objectives and can be sustained politically and financially. As Heisbourg argues, "exit *per se* should not be of the essence."[13]

REPLICATING THE FRENCH MODEL

Serval worked both because the conditions under which France fought were favorable and because the French fought well. The operation was not especially difficult from a strictly military perspective. France faced a surprisingly bold, fairly well organized foe that had reinforced positions in the Ifoghas mountains, but was outnumbered more than threefold, had minimal training, and was relatively badly equipped even by insurgent standards. This was not Hezbollah, in other words. Jihadist foot soldiers were skilled in the use of Kalashnikovs – skilled enough to kill a French special operations pilot from the ground in the initial battle – and they had some old tanks and other heavy weapons, but evidently no training in how to use them. The ground-to-air rocket launchers that had been a major concern during the operation were never used, likely because the jihadists lacked the skills to fire them, or because the batteries were dead.[14] In short, the jihadists were greatly overmatched by the French, who controlled the air, had far greater intelligence, more forces, and far more advanced weaponry. When it came to conventional war, the jihadists simply did not stand a chance.

For this reason, the big fear in Paris at the time the operation launched was that the enemy would go to ground, melt into the population, and then strike back with a brutal terrorist campaign of improvised explosive device (IED) attacks, suicide and car bombings, and small-scale guerilla warfare, buffeting Mali into more intense ethnic conflict. This in turn would have soured the French public on the war, and potentially inspired third-party attacks against France itself. This had been al Qa'ida's strategy after its initial defeats in Afghanistan and Iraq, and on the surface there was no reason to think they wouldn't try again.

But for the most part, they didn't, or at least not on the scale the French feared. The most likely explanation is that they were simply caught off guard, overconfident about the strength of their grip on the north and too quick to judge the European powers timid and feckless. The jihadists' somewhat meager efforts to switch to nonconventional terrorist attacks in Gao and Timbuktu demonstrated how unprepared – mentally and otherwise – they were for any such strategy. Belmokhtar, Abu Zeid, and others had been operating in the north for a decade. When they then moved to occupy the north, they had faced almost no resistance from the Malian army. They were accustomed to being in control, taking hostages, and basically doing whatever they wanted. "AQIM was a group that was used to having complete control," explained General de Saint-Quentin, "They were organized into *katibas*, they had committees set up in each village to manage relations with the local populations. This was an occupation force, not an insurgent force prepared for offensive asymmetric warfare."[15]

The jihadists did use some IEDs – killing soldiers in the process – but even here their capabilities in retrospect seemed limited. The exposed desert conditions also made them more difficult to operate.[16] One possible reason that the IED threat never amounted to much is that it would have required more complicity from the local population than the jihadists actually enjoyed. France had fairly widespread support from Mali's population throughout the operation. Although some parts of the Tuareg population clearly supported the jihadists, overall support from the Tuaregs and other groups was more limited, and can only have declined when the jihadists began enforcing *shari'a* (as Droukdal feared). This was a major handicap for the jihadists compared with Taliban forces in Afghanistan or al Qa'ida in Anbar province, Iraq during the height of the violence there. For the southern political elites, who had just seen their government collapse and recognized that they were at risk of falling into the hands of a terrorist group, it was not hard to get beyond anticolonial objections to a French intervention.

Perhaps the single most important factor that worked in favor of French success, however, was strategic. The jihadist decision to stand and fight in an effort to hold territory in the initial stages of the conflict and later in the Ifoghas was a huge mistake. When they massed their technicals on the Niger Bend and headed for Bamako, they immediately created both a motive for French intervention and offered a conventional target for French airpower. France could make the case that the urgency of the situation called for rapid action and thereby trump those at the United Nations and elsewhere, including in certain parts of the U.S. government, who continued to insist the situation was not ripe for intervention. The move also allowed France's far superior weapons systems to inflict maximum damage on enemy forces. The reasons why Ag Ghali and his al Qa'ida cronies opted to push their advantage and attack cannot fully be known, and it would be unwise in future cases to count on enemies making such mistakes, but it is nevertheless a reminder that however important it is to assume that insurgent adversaries will be perfectly rational, we should not forget that they are also constrained by their own processes, structures, and dynamics and thus no less prone to error than any other human organization.

Although the desert environment was vast and especially inhospitable to ground forces, French warplanes had little difficulty locating, targeting, and striking the enemy in it. The air operating environment was thus highly permissive, with no significant air defense systems to contend with – in contrast, for example to Assad's Syria, or even Qaddafi's Libya. Had there been, it would have made the operations much riskier for French pilots and made U.S. military support all the more critical. France had very good tactical intelligence about enemy capabilities, where those capabilities were located, and comparatively good intelligence about the dynamics of the enemy groups themselves. In contrast to the Libya intervention, where allies started the campaign with very little knowledge either of Qaddafi's forces or the rebels they were supporting, in the case of Mali, French, American, and regional intelligence services collectively had excellent "situational awareness."

The real military challenge was not the enemy so much as the environment. The fact that the French managed to take such a large country with only 4,500 forces, backed by a somewhat larger but by no means overwhelming African force, is significant. Long and vulnerable logistical lines, serious in any conditions, were all the more serious given the oppressive heat, which rendered any break in supply potentially fatal for the troops. Vehicles ran out of gas and broke down in the sand, gumming up supply lines and exposing troops to potential ambush. The French managed these challenges well.

That said, it is also true that, while vast, northern Mali is very sparsely populated. As noted above, if wide-open desert was a challenge in some ways, it was also a boon to striking and targeting, especially when compared with triple-canopy jungle conditions elsewhere in Africa. Moreover, as they retreated, the jihadists' options for shelter were limited; the same desert environment that facilitated their initial inroads also limited their options for safe harbor when they came under attack.

French forces also deserve credit for the alacrity with which they repelled the initial attack, put the rebels back on their heels, and then chased them down. Speed, in turn, resulted from a number of factors, among which the most important were France's prepositioned forces in the region, the bravery of their special forces' initial attack, high alert forces in France, the fact that so much planning had already been done and so much intelligence collected, and the readiness at the highest levels for considerable risk by attacking with small, joint units that enjoyed a high degree of operational autonomy and sufficient latitude in their rules of engagement. This would not have been possible without a tolerance for greater political risk in Paris and at the *Elysée* itself. Speed would also not have been possible if France had not been willing to act unilaterally – a term French leaders are quick to avoid given that their intervention had political sanction from the United Nations and the Malian leadership, but which is nevertheless accurate in describing their initial military foray.

Sound political and diplomatic strategy also increased the chances of French success. The French took a multilateral approach to the problem as a whole. Although they went in alone, they had the backing of the UN Security Council and the government of Mali. They sought and obtained the support of regional actors, the Security Council, and key allies throughout the operation. Regional support was possible because West African leaders recognized the risk the extremist groups posed to their own countries, which, if not all as fragile as Mali, faced many of the same problems. French policy was also flexible enough that it could change course when the strategic context changed in the second week of January 2013.

One of the points French analysts and officials sometimes make when discussing *Serval* is the extent to which their forces operated for days on end, sleeping under the stars, with limited water, food, and infrequent trips to bases that were themselves extremely basic. They occasionally contrast this approach with what they perceive to be a slower, more ponderous U.S. approach, involving less roughing it.[17] Although this view may reflect accurately the somewhat limited French experience with U.S. forces in the Balkans and Afghanistan, it is hardly accurate as a blanket statement about the willingness of U.S. forces as a whole to rough it. It would be churlish, moreover, to compare the hardships U.S. soldiers faced in Afghanistan to those the French faced in Mali. But if these comparisons can be put aside, it can be acknowledged that the French forces benefitted from their willingness to endure the strenuous conditions that came with the desert environment and limited French resources. Similarly, the willingness of the French military and political leadership to push ahead with Napoleonic audacity and without waiting for the full logistical complement to arrive surely helped them succeed.

French commanders have argued that another reason they were able to accomplish so much with such a small force was the emphasis they placed on adaptability and resiliency in training their officers. The jargon is *système D*, a training that emphasizes the ability to find creative solutions for tactical problems that arise on the ground. This training surely also played a role in French success, but it was much less important than the fundamental strategic advantages that the French enjoyed over their adversary.

The French also leveraged local forces effectively as the United States would later try to do against ISIS. This was true both for the UN force that provided a stabilization role, and especially true for the Chadians, who fought in a combat role alongside the French. Coordinating with these disparate entities was no doubt a complex and often frustrating challenge for French officers, but it ultimately allowed them to leverage a relatively small force to its maximum advantage.

Perhaps most importantly, the French did not lose sight of the fundamental political and economic challenges that Mali faced during the operation itself, and continued to press – along with the United States and others – on the need for reform and north-south reconciliation. French military and civilian officials stress that they do not think the military can be the solution to the problem. Many of the same will also point out that this was a fairly straightforward offensive military operation – not a stabilization operation on the model of the Balkans, much less a counterinsurgency amid a partially hostile population as eventually occurred in Afghanistan and Iraq.

In such operations, of course, chance plays a large role, and there can be no surefire formulas for winning. Moreover, the operation was ultimately just a battle in a broader regional conflict. Success notwithstanding, said one senior French officer, "nothing is decided definitively." France needs to prepare itself for a long war against the extremists in the region.[18] This battle is continuing and will last several years. The French (and hence the West) could still fail in this, as discussed later in this chapter. Nevertheless, in situations where broadly similar circumstances obtain – that is, a mostly cooperative population, good intelligence, tolerance for some risk and losses, an enemy that presents at least some conventional profile, a second-tier force that is prepared to hold the territory, regional support, and willingness to stay the course over the long term, the chances of success in using such a model to destroy a terrorist safe haven should be good. Notably, even though the French force was relatively small, it was still four times the estimated size of the jihadist ranks and far outclassed them in all military aspects.

The French model clearly had certain advantages over both a larger-scale and a smaller-scale operation. Had the French relied, for example, solely on drone strikes or small special-operations teams, it would have been much more difficult to destroy the safe haven. A sustained air campaign alone might also have done damage to the groups, but absent ground forces it would not have been able to flush the jihadists out as thoroughly or as quickly. Neither of these strategies, moreover, would likely have been enough to deal with the initial jihadist charge on Bamako, which is of course why the French chose to use a larger force in the first place.

The use of conventional forces to destroy the safe haven was probably necessary as it is hard to see how special forces alone could have had the same effect over such a large area – unless they were deployed in unusually large numbers. Special forces played a critical role in chasing the jihadists out of several northern towns, but conventional ground forces were needed to retake occupied territory and claim it for the legitimate authorities. There is also little reason to use special forces for a task that conventional forces can do equally well. At the other end of the spectrum, a large-scale French occupation would clearly have been more costly, and more likely to provoke a backlash both within Mali and regionally. There was a risk of backlash even with the smaller force the French deployed, but the smaller footprint can only have helped to keep the country and its neighbors on their side.

A final lesson of the French experience in Mali, has to do with subtle differences in how the French view the role of military force in relation to political aims. Both France and the United States view their militaries as political tools, on a certain level, but debate in the United States too often opposes military and political approaches to national security problems, with the military strategy depicted as a separate option from diplomacy. In contrast, the French approach tends to prefer the discrete use of military force in support of larger political ends. This is in large part because the French military is petite in comparison with its U.S. counterparts – but there is virtue in necessity here.

With *Serval*, military power was deployed to get a political process that had run off the rails back on them; it was never seen as the solution to the broader problem of Mali's state weakness, or even the deeper issues that generated the terrorist threat, even if it was clearly viewed as the solution for dealing with that immediate threat in the concrete form it took in January 2011. Military power was used to promote political ends and create space for political processes to take hold.

Many U.S. military thinkers obviously recognize the limitations of the use of force and the importance of political, diplomatic, and economic measures for treating the diseases that threaten international security today. This is why Secretary Gates was so frustrated about the fact that Defense Department funding so outstripped that of the State Department. The frustration with the limits of the use of force, however, is one of the central reasons the United States hesitated, for three years until the advent of ISIS, to intervene in Syria. The massive investments in Iraq and Afghanistan – so much cost for so little evident benefit – have made many throw up their hands in despair and seek to return to the isolationism that characterized U.S. foreign and security policy before World War II. But *Serval* demonstrates that even a relatively small force can achieve military objectives decisively enough to have a positive impact on the broader strategic and political picture. The Powell Doctrine that calls for decisive wins, in other words, need not always require tens, let alone hundreds, of thousands of troops – even if in some cases it clearly will. The French managed as close to a decisive win in Mali as possible – at least militarily – without such a force.

THE IMPACT ON FRENCH SECURITY POLICY

Given multiple overlapping crises in the Middle East, a revanchist Russia and a rising China, U.S. resources and leadership for dealing with the problem of jihadism in Africa are apt to be relatively limited. The United States has increased its involvement in and attention to Africa since the 1990s, but the continent is still a lower priority for U.S. foreign and security policy. If anything is to be done about the security problems there, France will thus have to play a major role. What are the chances that it will?

On a certain level, France's centuries-long historical relationship with West Africa is the best explanation for its willingness to intervene in 2013. The longstanding relationship between France and its former colonies has shaped the attitudes of French elites, the capabilities and posture of its military, and the outlook of publics both in Africa and France itself.[19] France's intervention in Mali was shaped by France's neo-colonial past. It was not, however, neocolonial in the sense that it was driven by the same narrow interests that often drove France to intervene in Africa, for example, in the 1970s. Unlike the majority of France's earlier interventions in Africa, the French objective in Mali was not to defend traditional economic and political interests, but to stamp down on a burgeoning and aggressive al Qa'ida franchise.

Belief that France was the only country likely to risk intervention also factored into French thinking. Here, perceived shifts in the global political system reinforced this thinking.[20] Several interviews with French leaders indicate that the French perceived the United States to be unwilling to intervene, especially in Africa. The U.S. "pivot" to Asia, combined with U.S. policy of leading from behind on Libya contributed to this view. True, the United States had created Africa Command in 2008 in recognition of the continent's importance, but the command is small compared to other regional commands and staffed largely with experts in strengthening partner militaries, not combat operations.

U.S. strategy, in other words, has been to look long-term in Africa and hope that stronger African institutions, military and civilian, will over time alleviate the problem of African jihadism. Without objecting to this approach, the French thought that U.S. counterterrorism strategy in the region has left something of a gap when it comes to addressing more immediate threats such as that of al Qa'ida in the Islamic Maghreb. Although U.S. special operations forces operate in Africa, and the United States has increased its military role in the last twenty years, the U.S. conventional footprint is very limited, and the United States has not shown any signs of revising its traditional reticence about deep involvement on the continent. France, which remains, alongside the United Kingdom, the United States' most capable allied military, has sought to fill this space with continued military action against the terrorist threat in Africa.

To a certain degree, the factors that contributed to the French intervention in 2013 are not new. What is new, on the other hand, is the nature of the threat the jihadists posed and its proximity to the metropole. The French understood better than almost any other country in the world how much jihadist groups were threatening the region. This understanding created an acute sense of their own vulnerability to attack. France had been attacked by African terrorist groups in the past, and al Qa'ida in the Islamic Maghreb had trumpeted its designs on France for years. In December 2005, just before he created al Qa'ida in the Islamic Maghreb, Abdelmalek Droukdal had moreover singled France out as al Qa'ida's number one enemy in Africa.[21] He would do so on several occasions thereafter, and sometimes be joined by Bin Laden himself.

Moreover, in the years prior to the intervention, French citizens had frequently been kidnapped by al Qa'ida–linked groups. The kidnappings led the evening news and created intense anxiety – especially for French political leaders who failed to remedy the expanding scourge. The French government's initial attempts to fix the problem by doling out millions of euros in ransoms only made the problem worse – and eventually brought rebuke from the United States. Efforts to use French special forces to deal with the problem went awry or even backfired at least twice. On top of the kidnappings, the French got a chilling reminder of the threat of homegrown terrorism with the Merah murders, just as Mali was falling apart.

Finally, long-standing French political traditions and the interests of the French military also played a role. The constraints of French military capabilities have made Africa a logical place for France to seek to continue to project power in the twenty-first century, and thereby retain some semblance of its former great power status. Africa is a continent where the French have experience, tradition, and utility, and where no other major power is ready to dedicate so many of its precious resources. Moreover, the French have long seen themselves as defenders of universal human rights, and these were under assault in the jihadist-controlled areas of Mali.

By intervening, the French opened a key new chapter in its war on al Qa'ida – one in which they intended to play the leading role. It is safe to assume the French will intervene again if needed. The lessons they took away further support this conclusion. One of these lessons was that their prepositioned forces in Africa were essential and should not be reduced, as had originally been planned. Prepositioning either in small special forces contingents that deployed in the early hours of the operation from Burkina Faso or the garrison that sped the arrival of French troops via Dakar or the quasi-permanent standing relationships that France enjoys with countries such as Chad all allowed France to react quickly and sustain operations more easily than if they had needed to do the same solely from metropolitan France. This African force posture is thus slated to continue for the foreseeable future. France will remain a military force in Africa even as it pulls back from commitments elsewhere in the world.

Serval was also indicative of a broader French return to Africa, or at least a reversal of the trajectory of France's African role, which had long been toward withdrawal and minimization. "Africa is again a priority for France," said one French general.[22] The Arab Spring and the subsequent collapse of Libya "lifted the cover" off a host of problems in the region, above all failed states and a resurgent al Qa'ida. With the United States increasingly working to rebalance away from the region, France seeks to play a lead role in managing African problems. In addition to maintaining its forward deployed forces, it will also seek to sustain and possibly even develop closer defense relationships with its African partners. As discussed later in this chapter, however, these aspirations could be challenging if France is pulled northward into reassurance deployments in Eastern Europe, or if French defense resources are further diminished.

The experience also boosted French special forces, which, as in the United States, have increasingly become a tool of choice for policymakers who recognize their role as often invaluable surgical instruments of modern irregular warfare, especially against disaggregated foes like al Qa'ida and ISIS. The key role French special forces played in *Serval* – both in the initial phases and as an avant garde later in the operation – was no doubt instrumental in ensuring that France would continue to invest in them, and continue to seek support and cooperation from the United States. The 2014 French defense budget increased the number of French special operations forces by 1,000 – a thirty percent boost, in part due to their success with *Serval*. France meanwhile invested more in technologies that would allow the French intelligence services to share information more easily with their American counterparts – increasing the opportunities for future cooperation in this critical area.

Serval also strengthened the view that France should aim to play the role of a "framework nation" in crises like these. By this, most French officials mean that France should be prepared to intervene in a crisis, if necessary alone, in order to set the stage for takeover from a larger, preferably multinational force. Importantly, France is not going to plan for long-term stabilization or counterinsurgency operations on the Afghanistan and Iraq model. "We're not going into operations that last several years, like Afghanistan," one French general emphasized.[23] French analysts tend to regard such operations as too costly, and in many cases counterproductive for a Western power to undertake anyway in Africa. Instead, the French objective is a long-term effort to address root causes of jihadism, punctuated by interventions with military force. This, the French believe, is liable to be at least as effective as long-term deployments of French boots on the ground, will be less costly, and runs less of a risk of generating resentment among the population. French operations will rely, like U.S. operations, on small-footprint special forces whenever possible. Larger operations like *Serval* will occur, but when they do it will be a signal that other efforts are failing – just as it was in January 2013.

Mali also reinforced the conviction, closely related to France's role as a framework nation, that France must maintain its ability to act autonomously – in other words, without need for recourse to U.S. or other allied capabilities, however much these are appreciated when they augment France's own. The importance of autonomy is in part a question of national pride for the French, but some French generals will also argue rather convincingly that France's autonomy is intimately bound up with its national security elite's capacity for strategic thought. This, in turn, is an essential part of why the French remain so much better prepared for expeditionary operations than many other countries in Europe, notably Germany.

Primarily, however, maintaining autonomy is prerequisite for rapid reaction. As in Libya, when France resisted using NATO structures for *Operation Odyssey Dawn*, on the grounds that it would slow down decision-making and reduce the ability to seize the initiative and exploit the advantage of surprise, the French similarly saw their ability to act autonomously in Mali as a key aspect of their success. U.S. or other efforts to persuade the French to abandon multipurpose forces in favor of greater specialization in the name of cost savings will correspondingly continue to meet with resistance.

None of this is to argue, however, that France will not face difficulties combatting African jihad. Even if the French military achieved the objectives they set out for themselves in Mali, this was by no means an easy operation for them. Looking ahead, the biggest problem will be financial. Rising operational costs from recent deployments have forced the French to postpone much-needed investment and repairs to their military. The military's operational budget for 2013 was 647 million euros, but the actual expenses came to over 1.2 billion.[24] This means that other areas – especially maintenance and investment – have suffered. The high tempo of operations also means that French equipment is often wearing out more quickly than initially predicted, often with no replacement programs in the pipeline. Just as the British military was badly worn down by the huge effort they put into the Iraq and Afghanistan wars, so the French risk wearing their own equipment out much more quickly than they can replace it.

France may still aspire to conduct multiple operations at the same time, but given the toll operations are taking on the French military, doing so will become increasingly difficult for anything but the least taxing of cases. Moreover, without some increase in the French defense budget, it may become difficult for the French to conduct significant operations back to back, with little time in between for recovery and rebuilding the force.

The French will continue to seek financing for their military operations from any source they can. Their European allies – and especially Germany, with whom relations remained strained throughout *Serval* (though not on account of it) – will continue to be the main hope for additional financing. France will aim to get the European Union to take on as much of the postconflict reconstruction and stabilization as possible. Even if these European missions rely heavily on French forces, France will look to the European Union as a vehicle for burden sharing. As one expert put it, "France would like to see a bargain in which they fight but the Europeans pay."[25]

Similarly, in order for the framework nation concept to work, African and European militaries need to be ready to contribute. Regional states still have a long, long way to go on the capacity-building front, as the initial struggles of the United Nations force in Mali made clear. Without more work to strengthen these militaries, the strategy the French used in Mali will be tough to repeat – indeed, the regional peacekeeping forces are still a major weak link in operations in Mali today.

Finally, should the situation in Mali go south, publics in France and elsewhere in Europe may be less likely to support future operations – politically or financially. Success in Mali so far is imperfect, but the region is much better off than it might have been. Continued success there – as in most military operations – is the sine qua non of long-term public support.

COOPERATING WITH THE FRENCH

That it could pull off an operation like Serval with relatively limited help from other countries is a point of pride within the French military. The French capacity for meaningful autonomous action demonstrated by operations in Mali, even when it rested on shaky foundations, was praiseworthy. If the French are to continue their role as a security provider in Africa and elsewhere, however, they will need support not just from Europe, but also from the United States. Despite the initial fillips over who would foot the bill for the U.S. aircraft flying in support of the French operation, overall enthusiasm for what France and the United States achieved together was high. According to a senior French diplomat, this was "a very good illustration of what we have in common and what we can do together."[26] One former French general judged that relations between the French and the United States on military matters "have not been this good since World War II."[27] This was another sign that any wounds incurred from the 2003 U.S. invasion of Iraq or the more recent French exit from Afghanistan had largely healed.

French officials are quick to express their gratitude for the whole panoply of U.S. and other allied contributions. When pressed, however, they will acknowledge that U.S. contributions in intelligence and refueling were ultimately more important than transport, which they were able to procure on the international market (although reliance on Russia for such enablers comes with its own drawbacks). The impact of the U.S. KC-135 refueling aircraft was particularly crucial to the initial stages of the operation, because opening the door to more complete close air support allowed French forces to move fast at lower risk. French officers judged U.S. intelligence contributions to be equally important when viewed over the course of the operation as a whole.[28]

French needs will change over time. The need for transport capability will decline significantly as the French fleet of Airbus long-range transport aircraft, A400Ms, the first of which was delivered in September 2013, grows. Even with a heavy, 30,000-kilogram load, the A400M can reach Bamako from Paris.[29] U.S. drone capabilities will become less important to France as the French acquire their own fleet of twelve MQ-9 Reapers – nearly all of which will likely be stationed in Africa. Some French officers have called for an enlargement of the so called "Five Eyes" intelligence sharing arrangements to include France, but others are more skeptical and favor special U.S.-French bilateral intelligence sharing arrangements. Improvements on this front – whatever the format – are desirable, and operations like *Serval* may nudge the United States away from habitual cautiousness on the issue. France is eventually planning to purchase more tankers, but not soon. Refueling will therefore continue to be an area where the United States can leverage its own capabilities to facilitate French combat operations.

Both sides were also very positive about the working relationship. As one U.S. official noted, "there was no Gaullist reflex here, just a real, deep sense that 'if it wasn't for the Americans we couldn't have done it.'"[30] Several French officials themselves expressed their deep appreciation for the importance of the U.S. and other allied contributions, which were critical to allowing France first to maintain the initiative and then to root al Qa'ida out of the Ifoghas. The positive experience also lessened French resistance to U.S. Africa Command, once viewed as an imperious American encroachment on French turf. General Carter Ham, who commanded U.S. forces in Africa and made a significant effort to establish close and early communication with his counterparts in France, deserves much of the credit for this positive evolution in Franco-American cooperation, as does his successor General Rodriguez, who took over the command in April 2013 as French operations were underway.

The only real complaint from the French was that the United States was unaccustomed to playing a supporting role in operations. "The question is how can you participate in operations according to a French model," said one general.[31] U.S. allies frequently plug into U.S. operations, but it is rare – if not unprecedented – that the U.S. plugs into an allied operation. Such individuals stressed the difference between the French approach and that of not just the United States, but also the British and Australians – the Anglo-Saxons, who, according to the French at least, tend to be less willing to take risks and more reliant on a big footprint with lots of support structures.[32]

The French would like to see *Serval* become a model for future Franco-American security cooperation in Africa, and with good reason. In cases where France is prepared to provide the bulk of the forces, pay most of the bill, and take on most of the risks, the model of cooperation achieved in *Serval* can and should be welcomed by the United States. To a degree, President Obama's decision to limit U.S. participation in allied operations over Libya in 2011 to those "unique capabilities" that only the United States possessed set the stage for cooperation on this model in Mali. In Libya, however, the United States was still in a leading role in many respects, politically through the North Atlantic Council and the international Contact Group for Libya, and militarily when it came to the logistical backbone of the operation. In Mali, however, U.S. support was far more limited and included only logistics and intelligence. The French were entirely in command of the operation, with allies in a decidedly supporting role.

The French want to keep it this way. Looking ahead, one French general said, the "danger is an American policy that competes with the French. There should not be any competition between us," he said, when it comes to African security issues.[33] Given America's historical disinterest in the continent, this seems unlikely to become a problem.

THE ROAD AHEAD

After Serval, al Qa'ida in the Islamic Maghreb was forced to rebuild. They lost foot soldiers in large numbers and in the future may have to compete with other Salafist organizations – especially as ISIS – for recruits. The death of Abu Zeid deprives at least his *katiba*, which was the most important of those that remained loyal to Droukdal, of a strong leader. In addition, as noted, Mali's experience with *shari'a* has not endeared its population to the Arab jihadists from Algeria. Meanwhile, some modest progress strengthening the militaries of Mauritania and Niger has been made, and the longer al Qa'ida in the Islamic Maghreb goes without a major attack, the more its legitimacy will diminish – something that the leaders are no doubt aware of.

Nevertheless, if *Serval* was a blow to regional jihadist groups it obviously did not eliminate them. The underlying operating environment for violent groups in Africa remains dismayingly favorable and in North Africa, the environment for violent jihadist groups is particularly good. The states in the region are weak and their populations vulnerable. The regional supply of arms is depressingly large, and accessing small arms will not be a problem for jihadi or other insurgent groups seeking to acquire them in the future. In Libya the political and security situation is extremely poor and conducive to jihadists of many shades and stripes, including al Qa'ida, ISIS, *Murabitun*, Ansar al Shari'a, and descendants of the Libyan Islamic Fighting Group. The situation in Egypt is better, but far from perfect. Tunisia has managed to keep these groups at bay, but may find it difficult to do so indefinitely without improvements elsewhere in the region. Not least, the continued legitimacy of global jihad, be it al Qa'ida affiliates like al Nusrah or its competitors like ISIS, allows these groups to link to a broader narrative and espouse higher goals. The thousands of foreign fighters that have made their way from Europe and America to Syria and Iraq may prefer the living conditions in the Middle East to those in the Sahel, but if the world manages to clamp down on the problem in the Middle East, African jihad will be a suitable second choice.

In short, the problem of Salafi jihadism in Africa is very real and needs continued attention. Whether in Afghanistan, Iraq, Syria, Yemen, or Mali, the spread of these groups is a problem that cannot be fixed quickly or easily, and perhaps not even in this era. In Africa, the problem will need to be addressed through a regional strategy that combines long-term political, economic, and financial support to governments and populations with security cooperation and military action when necessary. In the Sahel, the strategy will require economic development, strengthening governance, and empowering states to address the threat of takeover by jihadist groups. In Mali, development projects that improve access to basic services in Tuareg and other areas on the margins of society are essential. This means improving access to water and energy, as well as education and health services. If Mali's government and those of its neighbors do not provide these goods, outsiders may, usurping the legitimacy of the state. It also means a continued effort to strengthen and professionalize the military and especially police forces of the region and calls for better cooperation between these and other development efforts. As discussed throughout this book, continued efforts to address underlying political conflicts such as that between the Tuareg and Bamako in Mali are also essential.

These are tall tasks, to be sure. The Sahel is and will, for the foreseeable future, remain one of the poorest regions of the world. Agricultural weakness makes food crises frequent, and malnutrition ravages whole populations, killing hundreds of thousands of children a year. Development and stability are further threatened by a demographic boom, which will continue to put pressure on food and other resources, complicating politics. Thus relying solely on state-building and development to address the problem is unlikely to succeed. Military force will be needed.

A cooperative regional military approach bringing together the countries of the region, France, and the United States is desirable. Here, Operation *Barkhane* will be an important contribution. As the jihadists move across uninhabited spaces, French forces will be free to conduct direct strikes against them with strike fighters, close air assets, and special operations teams. The French acquisition of Reaper from the United States will improve situational awareness and should allow these strikes to be more effective than ever. Algeria, with a military that is 300,000 strong, a long frontier with Mali, and aspirations for regional leadership, has a key role to play and real capacity to help, especially when it is willing to cooperate with France. Some initial steps have been taken to build structures to strengthen regional cooperation, including a joint operational headquarters that brings together Mauritania, Niger, and Mali, in Tamanrasset, Algeria, along with a fusion cell that involves Algeria and other regional players. These need outside support.

France and the United States would do well to build on the model of cooperation that emerged in 2013. The United States will have to consider how it can help France. Possibilities include facilitating French operations as it did with *Serval*, taking on more financial and training responsibility for ensuring the readiness of African forces, conducting operations itself or alongside the French, and keeping military and other state-building efforts going. Funding to support the overall effort will be a critical need – and no doubt bone of contention – for the countries concerned.

The United States should also investigate the means of deploying forces in smaller sizes, similar to those the French deployed in *Serval*. The Marine Corps is well positioned to provide such a capability to U.S. leaders, but the U.S. Army could also do so, if it wanted to. Small-medium footprint operations like *Serval* could then become an important part of a larger political and diplomatic strategy aimed at addressing the problem of Salafi jihadism where it arises over time.

In the longer term, policymakers should also bear in mind that military action against groups like al Qa'ida in the Islamic Maghreb – for all its advantages – tends to narrow the horizons for reconciliation. Dead-enders may never reconcile, and hence may always need to be eliminated from the equation by military means. Other members of the kind of jihadist groups that took over northern Mali in 2012 may be reconcilable, and attention needs to be given to ensuring that these young men have a visible alternative to continued participation in violent jihad. Again, political progress on north-south reconciliation – as in Iraq and Afghanistan – is ultimately a precondition for a lasting solution to the country's jihadist problem.

Because Africa is so vast and the resources available for addressing the problems it faces so limited, jihadist groups in Africa seem destined to remain a malignant growth for many years. They will undermine international efforts to strengthen governance and improve the lives of other Africans. Moreover, if the direct threat of attacks in Europe and the United States is limited in comparison with the threat posed in the Bin Laden era, these groups will continue to target U.S. and European interests in Africa itself when and if they can. Even if most groups do not currently invest heavily in attacking the West, they are highly unpredictable, can be extremely violent, and would almost surely target the West if given the opportunity to do so. The threat posed by the foreign fighters that have flocked to Iraq and Syria is already beginning to replicate itself in Libya. Conflict with the West, sadly, is deeply rooted in their creed, as is conflict with the more secular Arab and African governments that they target on a regular basis.

A central goal and challenge of counterterrorism strategy in Africa must be to ensure that these jihadists groups do not obtain the means to target the United States. This means not inviting them to do so, but it also means denying them safe haven, and preventing them from growing strong or ambitious enough that they begin to think and act more globally. The possibility that African groups could attack in Europe should not justify alarmism, or enable unnecessarily aggressive counterterrorism strategies that could backfire, but it is a reason for sustained vigilance and concerted, long-term, cooperative effort – both military and civilian, both French and American – to undercut African jihad.

ANNEX 1

Annex 1. Key Salafi-Jihadist Groups in North Africa

Name of Group	Base of Operations	Years
Al Qa'ida in the Islamic Maghreb (AQIM), previously Groupe Salafiste pour la Predication et le Combat (GSPC)	Algeria, Mali	1998–present
Al Takfir wal al Hijrah	Egypt (Sinai)	2011–present
Al Mulathamun (Mohktar Belmohktar)	Mali, Libya, Algeria	2012–2013
Al Murabitun (Mohktar Belmohktar)	Mali, Libya, Algeria	2013–present
Ansar al Shari'a Egypt	Egypt	2012–present
Ansar al Shari'a Libya	Libya	2012–present
Ansar al Shari'a Mali	Mali	2012–present
Ansar al Shari'a Tunisia	Tunisia	2011–present
Egyptian Islamic Jihad (EIJ)	Egypt	1978–2001
Groupe Islamique Arme (GIA)	Algeria	1993–2004
Harakat al Shuada'a al Islamiyah (IMM)	Libya	1996–2007
Harakat Ansar al Din	Mali	2011–present
Islamic State of Iraq and al Sham (ISIS)	Libya, Egypt	2014–present
Jaish al Islam (aka Tawhid and Jihad Brigades)	Egypt (Sinai)	2005–present
Jamaat Ansar Bayt al Maqdis	Egypt (Sinai)	2011–present
Libyan Islamic Fighting Group (LIFG)	Libya	1990–present
Moroccan Islamic Combatant Group (GICM)	Morocco	1998–present

(continued)

185

Annex 1. (*continued*)

Name of Group	Base of Operations	Years
Movement for Tawhid and Jihad in West Africa (MUJAO)	Mali	2011–2013
Muhammad Jamal Network (MJN)	Egypt	2011–present
Mujahideen Shura Council of the Environs in Jerusalem (MSC)	Egypt (Sinai)	2011–present
Salafia Jihadia (As-Sirat al Moustaquim)	Morocco	1995–present
Tunisian Combatant Group (TCG)	Tunisia	2000–2011

NOTES

1 France, Mali, and African Jihad

1 Interview with U.S. Defense Department official, December 3, 2013, Washington, DC.
2 Interview with senior French Defense official, January 20, 2013, Paris.
3 Interview with senior U.S. Defense Department official, January 12, 2013, Washington, DC.
4 Interview with senior French Defense official, January 20, 2013, Paris.
5 Interview with senior U.S. Defense Department official, February 20, 2013, Washington, DC.
6 Interview with senior U.S. Defense Department official, February 20, 2013, Washington, DC.
7 Writing a book about a problem like Salafi jihadism in Africa quickly and inevitably draws the researcher into a broad range of academic subjects and debates. In the case of *Serval*, these include Mali's social and political history, the anthropology and culture of the Tuaregs, French colonial history, and a number of more technical operational military concerns. With regard to these subjects, this account attempts to draw on the best available literature, but without seeking to challenge of build much on it. This is also not a book about the domestic aspects of French counterterrorism policy, or "homeland defense" in U.S. parlance. On this subject, see Frank Foley, *Countering Terrorism in Britain and France: Institutions, Norms and the Shadow of the Past*, Cambridge: Cambridge University Press, 2013.
8 Claude Angeli, "Un Afghanistan Africain au Sud de l'Europe," *Le Canard Enchaîné*, April 11, 2012, p. 5.
9 The causes of terrorism and the role of poverty in particular have been much debated. There seems to be a lack of evidence for the theory that poverty directly causes radicalization. At best, it is only one possible cause among many. Poverty, however, does engender weak states and create incentives for insurgency, both of which are conducive to terrorist groups. For scholarly work

that favors a link between economic conditions and terrorism or insurgency, see James D. Fearon and David Laitin, "Ethnicity, Insurgency, and Civil War," *American Political Science Review*, Vol. 97 no. 1 (February 2003), pp. 75–90; Paul Collier and Anke Hoeffler, "Greed and Grievance in Civil War" *Oxford Economic Papers*, Vol. 56, No. 4 (2004), pp. 563–595. On terrorism specifically, see Paul S. Brock Blomberg, Gregory D. Hess, and Akila Weerapana, "Economic Conditions and Terrorism," *European Journal of Political Economy*, Vol. 20 No. 2 (2004), pp. 463–478; Kostas Drakos and Andreas Gofas, "In Search of the Average Transnational Terrorist Attack Venue," *Defence and Peace Economics*, Vol. 17, No. 2 (2006), pp. 73–93. Scholarship that does not support the link between poverty and terrorism includes Alan B. Krueger and David D. Laitin, "Kto Kogo?: A Cross-Country Study of the Origins and Targets of Terrorism" in Philip Keefer and Norman Loayza, *Terrorism, Economic Development, and Political Openness*, Cambridge: Cambridge University Press, 2008, pp. 148–173; Alan B. Krueger, *What Makes a Terrorist: Economics and the Roots of Terrorism*, Princeton, NJ: Princeton University Press, 2007; Alberto Abadie, "Poverty, Political Freedom, and the Roots of Terrorism," *American Economic Review (Papers and Proceedings)*, Vol. 96, No. 2 (2006), pp. 50–56. See also Ethan Bueno de Mesquita, "The Political Economy of Terrorism: A Selective Overview of Recent Work," *The Political Economist*, Vol. 10, No. 1 (2008), pp. 1–12.

10 For an overview, see Peter Bergen, Bruce Hoffman, and Katherine Tiedemann, "Assessing the Jihadist Terrorist Threat to America and American Interests," *Studies in Conflict & Terrorism*, Vol. 34, No. 2 (2011), pp. 65–101. See also Seth G. Jones, *A Persistent Threat: The Evolution of al Qa'ida and Other Salafi Jihadists*, Santa Monica, CA: RAND Corporation, RR-637-OSD, 2014.

11 For an account, see David D. Kirkpatrick, "A Deadly Mix in Benghazi," *The New York Times*, December 28, 2013.

12 See Christopher S. Chivvis and Andrew Liepman, *North Africa's Menace: AQIM's Evolution and the U.S. Policy Response*, Santa Monica, CA: RAND Corporation, RR-415-OSD, 2013.

13 Nicholas Kulish, "Investigation Moves Slowly in Kenyan Mall Seige," *The New York Times*, October 11, 2013, p. A9.

14 Christophe Boltanski and Sarah Halifa-Legrand, "Mali: Un Désastre Français," *Nouvel Observateur*, April 12, 2012.

15 For example, "From Africa to the Middle East, France's New Hawkishness," *AFP*, November 17, 2013.

16 Jean-Dominique Merchet, "Le Mali coutera 647 million d'euros cette année," *l'Opinion*, October 13, 2013.

17 On the frequent abuse of historical analogy in policymaking see Richard E. Neustadt and Ernest R. May, *Thinking in Time: The Uses of History for Decisionmakers*, New York: Simon and Schuster, 1986.

2 Al Qa'ida's North African Franchise

1 Quoted in Seth G. Jones, *Hunting in the Shadows: The Pursuit of al Qa'ida Since 9/11*, New York, NY: Norton, 2012, p. 434. For a leading skeptical view on the significance of Bin Laden's death for al Qa'ida see Bruce Hoffman, "Al Qaeda's Uncertain Future," *Studies in Conflict and Terrorism*, Vol. 36, No. 8, pp. 635–653.

2 For background on radicalization in Algeria see George Joffé, "Trajectories of Radicalization: Algeria 1989–1999," in George Joffé, ed., *Islamist Radicalisation in North Africa: Politics and Process*, New York, NY: Routledge, 2012; Jean-Pierre Filiu, "The Local and global Jihad of al-Qa'ida in the Islamic Maghrib," *Middle East Journal*, Vol. 60, No. 2, Spring 2009, pp. 213–226.

3 E.g., Salima Mellah and Jean-Baptiste Rivoire, "El Para, the Maghreb's Bin Laden," *Le Monde Diplomatique*, English Edition, February 2005.

4 M.A.O., "Hattab et Belmokhtar condamnés à 20 ans de prison," *El Watan*, March 31, 2007.

5 Valentina Soria, "Global Jihad Sustained Through Africa," *RUSI: UK Terrorism Analysis*, No. 2, April 2012.

6 L. Touchard, B. Ahmed, Ch. Ouazani, "Aqmi: Abdelmalek Droukdel, l'émir caché," *Jeune Afrique*, January 10, 2012.

7 Mathieu Guidère, "Une filiale algérienne pour Al-Qaida," *Le Monde Diplomatique*, November 1, 2006.

8 Serge Daniel, *AQMI: L'Industrie de L'enlèvement*, Paris: Fayard, 2012, pp. 121–122.

9 Jean-Pierre Filiu, "The Local and Global Jihad of al-Qa'ida in the Islamic Maghrib," *Middle East Journal*, Vol. 60, No. 2, Spring 2009, pp. 213–226.

10 Mathieu Guidère, "Une filiale algérienne pour Al-Qaida," *Le Monde Diplomatique*, November 1, 2006.

11 Mathieu Guidère, "Une filiale algérienne pour Al-Qaida," *Le Monde Diplomatique*, November 1, 2006.

12 SITE Intelligence Group, "Salafist Group for Call and Combat Announces its New Name as al-Qaeda Organization in the Islamic Maghreb," January 26, 2007, translation of statement by Abu Musab Abdul Wadud issued by the al-Fajr Information Center on January 24, 2007. Available at: www.ent .siteintelgroup.com (accessed July 29, 2014).

13 Jean-Pierre Filiu, "The Local and Global Jihad of al-Qa'ida in the Islamic Maghrib," *Middle East Journal*, Vol. 60, No. 2, Spring 2009, pp. 213–226.

14 See Bruce Riedel, *In Search of al Qa'ida: Its Leadership, Ideology, and Future*, Washington, DC: Brookings, 2008, p. 126.

15 Jean-Luc Marret, "Al-Qaeda in the Islamic Maghreb: A "Glocal" Organization," *Studies in Conflict and Terrorism*, Vol. 31, No. 6, June, 2008, pp. 541–442.

16 Serge Daniel, *AQMI: L'Industrie de L'enlèvement*, Paris: Fayard, 2012, p. 149; Mathieu Guidère, "Une filiale algérienne pour Al-Qaida," *Le Monde Diplomatique*, November 1, 2006.

17 Jean-Pierre Filiu, "The Local and Global Jihad of al-Qa'ida in the Islamic Maghrib," *Middle East Journal*, Vol. 60, No. 2, Spring 2009, pp. 213–226.

18 Ibid.

19 See Christopher S. Chivvis and Andrew Liepman, *North Africa's Menace: AQIM and the U.S. Policy Response*, Santa Monica, CA: RAND Corporation, RR-415-OSD, 2013; Bruce Bruce Hoffman, "Al Qaeda's Uncertain Future," *Studies in Conflict and Terrorism*, Vol. 36, No. 8, pp. 635–653. On links to Europe see Serge Daniel, *AQMI: L'Industrie de L'enlèvement*, Paris: Fayard, 2012, pp. 126–127.

20 On the importance of organizational challenges to addressing terrorist groups see Jacob N. Shapiro, *The Terrorist's Dilemma: Managing Violent Covert Organizations*, Princeton: Princeton University Press, 2013.

21 "An Interview with Abdelmalek Droukdal," *New York Times*, July 1, 2008.

22 See extracts from an interview with captured jihadist "Mouawiya" in Violette Lazard, "Mener le jihad conformément à la méthode adoptée par Oussama ben Laden," *Libération*, January 6, 2012.

23 UNODC, *World Drug Report*, 2013, *passim*; Adam Nossiter, "Leader Ousted, Nation Is Now a Drug Haven," *New York Times*, November 1, 2012.

24 UNODC, *World Drug Report*, 2013, p.vii.

25 Department of State, *Trafficking in Persons Report*, June 2013.

26 Wolfram Lacher, "Challenging the Myth of the Drug Terror Nexus in the Sahel," *WACD Background Paper*, No. 4, 2013.

27 SOCOM-2012-0000019 in Nelly Lahoud et al., *Letters from Abbottabad: Bin Laden Sidelined?*, West Point, NY: Combatting Terrorism Center, May 3, 2012.

28 André Bourgeot, "Des Tuareg en Rebellion" in Patrick Gonin, et al., *La Tragédie Malienne*. Paris: Vendémiaire, 2013, pp. 113–129.

29 Christopher S. Chivvis and Andrew Liepman, *North Africa's Menace: AQIM and the U.S. Policy Response*, Santa Monica, CA: RAND Corporation, RR-415-OSD, 2013, p. 7.

30 Isabelle Lasserre and Thierry Oberlé, *Notre guerre secrète au Mali: Les nouvelles menaces contre la France*, Paris: Fayard 2013, p. 111.

31 "AQIM Demands Afghan Withdrawal in Return for French Hostages," Reuters, November 18, 2010.

32 Serge Daniel, *AQMI: L'Industrie de L'enlèvement*, Paris: Fayard, 2012, p. 43.

33 On this relationship see Jacob N. Shapiro, *The Terrorist's Dilemma: Managing Violent Covert Organizations*, Princeton: Princeton University Press, 2013, esp. 249–256.

3   Hostages, Ransoms, and French Security Policy

1   On French foreign policy traditions see Frédéric Charillon, *La politique étrangère de la France*, Paris: Documentation Française, 2011; Frederic Bozo, *La Politique*

Etrangere de la France, Paris: Editions Flammarion, 2012; Philip H. Gordon, *A Certain Idea of France*, Princeton, NJ: Princeton University Press, 1993; Anton de Porte, "The Foreign Policy of the Fifth Republic," in James F. Hollifield and George Ross, eds., *Searching for the New France*, New York: Routledge, 1991, pp. 250–274; Alfred Grosser, *Affaires Exterieures: La Politique de la France, 1944–1984*, Paris: Flammarion, 1984; David P. Calleo, *The Atlantic Fantasy*, Baltimore, MD: Johns Hopkins University Press, 1970.

2   M. Dominique de Villepin, French Minister of Foreign Affairs, speech delivered to the U.N. Security Council, New York, February 14, 2003.

3   On the crisis in Franco-American relations, see Philip H. Gordon and Jeremy Shapiro, *Allies at War: America, Europe, and the Crisis over Iraq*, New York: McGraw-Hill, 2004.

4   See Frédéric Charillon, *La politique étrangère de la France*, Paris: Documentation Française, 2011, pp. 77–81.

5   See Guillaume Parmentier, "French-American Relations after the Iraq War: How to Redefine the Relationship," in Mairi Mclean, and Joseph Szarka, eds. *France on the World Stage: Nation State Strategies in the Global Era*, New York: Palgrave, 2008, pp. 20–36.

6   See John E. Peters, et al., *European Contributions to Operation Allied Force*, Santa Monica: RAND, 2001, p. 20.

7   Vincent Desportes, "La guerre en Afghanistan et la France: un bien lointain conflit," *Revue Defense Nationale*, No. 740, May 2011, pp. 45–52.

8   Natalie Nougayrède, "De Chirac à Sarkozy: la France redécouvre la guerre d'Afghanistan," *Le Monde*, June 12, 2008, p. 5; Vincent Desportes, "La guerre en Afghanistan et la France: un bien lointain conflit," *Revue Defense Nationale*, No. 740, May 2011, pp. 45–52.

9   On this subject see Frederic Bozo, "Sarkozy's NATO Policy: Towards France's Atlantic Realignment?" *European Political Science*, No. 9, 2010, pp. 176–188.

10 Thomas Withington, "The French Armed Forces in Afghanistan," *Military Technology*, June 2, 2012 pp. 83–89.

11 Theo Farrell, Sten Rynning, Terry Terriff, *Transforming Military Power since the Cold War: Britain, France, and the United States, 1991–2012*, Cambridge: Cambridge University Press, 2013, pp. 255–256.

12 French Defense expert Jean-Dominique Merchet, quoted in Vincent Desportes, "La guerre en Afghanistan et la France: un bien lointain conflit," *Revue Defense Nationale*, No. 740, May 2011, pp. 45–52.

13 Patrick Roger, "En France, le débat s'intensifie sur le renfort des troupes en Afghanistan décidé par M. Sarkozy," *Le Monde*, August 22, 2008, p. 5; Nathalie Guibert avec Guillaume Perrier, "Afghanistan: la réponse tardive de la France à l'OTAN: Paris n'enverra que 80 hommes, bien que M. Obama en demande 1 500," *Le Monde*, February 7, 2010, p. 5.

14 Interview with a senior U.S. intelligence official, Virginia, April, 2013.

15 See Christopher S. Chivvis, "The End of Freedom Fries," *The National Interest*, February 7, 2014.

16 Nicolas Sarkozy, "19th Ambassador's Conference: Speech by Nicolas Sarkozy, President of the Republic," Paris, France, August 31, 2011.

17 Bruno Tertrais, "Leading on the Cheap? French Security Policy in Austerity," *The Washington Quarterly*, Vol. 36, No. 3., Summer, 2013, pp. 47–61.

18 See Tony Chafer, "From Confidence to Confusion: Franco-African Relations in the Era of Globalisation," in Mairi Mclean, and Joseph Szarka, eds. *France on the World Stage: Nation State Strategies in the Global Era*, New York: Palgrave, 2008, pp. 37–56.

19 Senegal, Mali, Niger, Burkina Faso, Togo, Benin, Cameroon, Equitorial Guinea, Gabon, and Congo.

20 French National Assembly, "Rapport d'information sur la situation sécuritaire dans les pays de la zone sahélienne," No. 4431, March 6, 2012.

21 Ibid.

22 Ibid.

23 Jean-Dominique Merchet, "Mali: le COS est bien présent au Sahel … contrairement à ce que dit Laurent Fabius," *Secret Defense*, September 25, 2012.

24 French National Assembly, "Rapport d'information sur la situation sécuritaire dans les pays de la zone sahélienne," No. 4431, March 6, 2012.

25 Interview with a U.S. official, Washington, DC, April 9, 2014.

26 See "U.S. AFRICOM Photo," United States Africa Command, Stuttgart, Germany, February 16, 2011.

27 Interview with a U.S. official, via telephone, Washington, DC, April 14, 2014.

28 Ibid.

29 Interview with a U.S. official, Washington, DC, April 9, 2014.

30 Christophe Châtelot and Nathalie Guibert, "Le défi de la refondation de l'armée malienne," *Le Monde*, February 5, 2013, p. 2.

31 Interview with a senior U.S. military official, Washington, DC, February 21, 2014.

4 Merah and Malistan

1 A permanent resident, though not a citizen, of the United States, of Afghan origin.

2 Peter Bergen, Bruce Hoffman, and Katherine Tiedemann, "Assessing the Jihadist Terrorist Threat to America and American Interests," *Studies in Conflict & Terrorism*, Vol. 34, No. 2, 2011, pp. 65–101.

3 "Tuerie de Toulouse: retour sur les événements," *Le Monde.fr*, March 24, 2012.

4 Matthew Campbell, "Police Stunned by Combat Skills of 'Lone Wolf' Killer," *Sunday Times*, March 25, 2012, p. 22.

5 "Tuerie de Toulouse: retour sur les événements," *Le Monde.fr*, March 24, 2012.

6   Matthew Campbell, "Police Stunned by Combat Skills of 'Lone Wolf' Killer," *Sunday Times*, March 25, 2012, p. 22.

7   Dan Bilefsky, "A Killer's Alienation, Not a Tie to Al Qaeda, Surfaces in Inquiry," *International Herald Tribune*, March 31, 2012 p. 5.; Campbell, "Police Stunned."

8   Campbell, "Police Stunned."

9   Dan Bilefsky and Maïa de la Baume, "Officials See the Terrorist Threat They Feared Most," *International Herald Tribune*, March 23, 2012, p.5.

10 Laurent Borredon et Jacques Follorou, "Bernard Squarcini: 'Nous ne pouvions pas aller plus vite'," *Le Monde.fr*, March 23, 2012; Yves Bordenave et Jacques Follorou, "Mohamed Merah, un membre actif de la mouvance djihadiste international," *Le Monde.fr*, March 22, 2012.

11 "Tuerie de Toulouse: retour sur les événements," *Le Monde.fr*, March 24, 2012; Francois Molins, Press Conference, March 23, 2012.

12 Yves Bordenave et Jacques Follorou, "Mohamed Merah, un membre actif de la mouvance djihadiste international," *Le Monde.fr*, March 22, 2012.

13 Dan Bilefsky, "A Killer's Alienation, Not a Tie to Al Qaeda, Surfaces in Inquiry," *International Herald Tribune*, March 31, 2012 p. 5.

14 Olivier Roy, "Loner, Loser, Killer," *International Herald Tribune*, March 24, 2012, p.6.

15 Campbell, "Police Stunned."

16 Bilefsky, "A Killer's Alienation, Not a Tie to Al Qaeda."

17 Insee, Recensement 2010, exploitation principale.

18 "Quatre personnes interpellées en France," *Le Monde*, February 7, 2013, p. 4.

19 On Africa's broader transitions in this period see Michael Bratton and Nicolas van de Walle, *Democratic Experiments in Africa: Regime Transitions in Comparative Perspective*, Cambridge: Cambridge University Press, 1997.

20 Seymour M. Lipset, "Some Social Prerequisites for Democracy: Economic Development and Political Legitimacy," *American Political Science Review*, No. 53, 1959, pp. 69–105.

21 United Nations, *Human Development Report*, 2013, p. 89.

22 Michael W. Doyle and Nicholas Sambanis, *Making War and Building Peace*, Princeton, NJ: Princeton University Press, 2008, pp. 104–108.

23 French Senate, Rapport d'Information, no. 513, April 16, 2013.

24 Interview with a Malian academic, Bamako, Mali, January 23, 2014.

25 Interview with a senior U.S. official, Bamako, Mali, January 24, 2014.

26 See Naffet Keita, "Y-a-t-il un gouvernement légitime au Mali?" in Patrick Gonin, et al., *La Tragédie Malienne*. Paris: Vendémiaire, 2013, pp. 83–91.

27 Interview with a former senior U.S. official, Washington, DC, February 20, 2014.

28 Elizabeth Bulmiller, "Leon Panetta Says U.S. Has Pledged to Help France in Mali," *New York Times*, January 14, 2013.

29 Bruce Whitehouse, "What's to Love about Mali? Four Things," *Bridges from Bamako*, February 4, 2013.

30 Jean Fleury, *La France en guerre au Mali*, Paris:Jean Picollec, 2013, p. 73; Lasserre and Oberlé, *Notre guerre secrete*, p. 156.

31 Ida Nicolaisen and Johannes Nicolaisen, *The Nomadic Tuareg*, Copenhagen: Rhodos, 1997 (2 vols), p. 42.

32 Nicolaisen and Nicolaisen, *The Nomadic Tuareg*, pp. 119, 292.

33 Nicolaisen and Nicolaisen, *The Nomadic Tuareg*, p. 277.

34 Thurston Clarke, *The Last Caravan*, New York: Putnam, 1978, p. 47.

35 Cited in Clarke, *The Last Caravan*, p. 36.

36 Jules Verne, *Invasion of the Sea*, trans. Edward Baxter, edited with an introduction by Arthur B. Evans, Middletown, CT: Wesleyan University Press, 2001, p. 16.

37 Nicolaisen and Nicolaisen, *The Nomadic Tuareg*.

38 Baz Lecoq, *Disputed Desert: Decolonisation, Competing Nationalisms and Tuareg Rebellions in Northern Mali*, Leiden, Brill Publishers, 2010, pp. 366–367.

39 Nicolaisen and Nicolaisen, *The Nomadic Tuareg*, p. 20.

40 Baz Lecoq, *Disputed Desert*, p. 370.

41 Nicolaisen and Nicolaisen, *The Nomadic Tuareg*, p. 20.

42 For example, Alan Kuperman, "A Model Humanitarian Intervention? Reassessing NATO's Libya Campaign," *International Security*, Vol. 38, No. 1, Summer 2013, pp. 105–136.

43 Interview, Washington, DC, January 3, 2014.

44 Interview with senior U.S. official, Bamako, Mali, January 24, 2014.

45 Malika Groga-Bada, "Mali: AQMI et le Touareg Connection," *Jeuneafrique. com*, December 12, 2011; Jean-Christophe Notin, *La Guerre de la France au Mali*, Paris: Tallandier, 2014, p. 61.

46 Lasserre and Oberlé, *Notre Guerre Secrète*, p. 151.

47 Scott Stewart, "Stratfor: Mali besieged by fighters fleeing Libya," *Defenceweb*, February 3, 2012.

48 Cherif Ouazani, "Rébellion du MNLA au Mali: Ag Najem, ou la soif de vengeance," *Jeune Afrique*, January 27, 2012; André Bourgeot, "Des Tuareg en Rebellion" in Patrick Gonin, et al., *La Tragédie Malienne*. Paris: Vendémiaire, 2013, pp. 113–129.

49 M. Groga-Bada, "Mali: Aqmi et la Touareg Connection," *Jeuneafrique.com*, December 12, 2011.

50 Interview with U.S. official, Washington, DC, April 15, 2014.

51 Quoted in Douglas Porch, *The Conquest of the Sahara*, New York: Farrar, Straus and Giroux, 1984, p. 33.

52 On the growth of Wahabbism and the Arab *Dogha* around Gao see André Bourgeot, "Des Tuareg en Rebellion" in Patrick Gonin, et al., *La Tragédie Malienne*. Paris: Vendémiaire, 2013, pp. 113–129.

53 Interview with French military officials, Paris, France, January 15, 2014; interview with senior U.S. official, January 3, 2014.

54 Scott Stewart, "Stratfor: Mali Besieged by Fighters Fleeing Libya," *Defenceweb*, February 3, 2012.

55 "Clashes between Malian Army and Tuareg Rebels 'Kill 47' – Military Source," *BBC Monitoring Middle East*, January 21, 2012; "Mali Military Says 47 Killed in Northern Clashes," *Defenceweb*, January 20, 2012.

56 Interview with a senior U.S. official, Bamako, Mali, January 24, 2014.

57 Adam Nossiter, "Qaddafi's Weapons, Taken by Old Allies, Reinvigorate an Insurgent Army in Mali," *New York Times*, February 6, 2012, p. 4.

58 Interview with a senior U.S. official, Bamako, Mali, January 24, 2014.

59 Tanguy Berthemet, "Des Touaregs exécutent des soldats maliens," *Le Figaro*, March 14, 2012, p. 7.

60 See, e.g., "Highlights from Malian Press 14 Feb 12," *BBC Monitoring Africa*, February 15, 2012.

61 Interview with a U.S. official, Bamako, Mali, January 24, 2014.

62 "Mali's Amadou Sanogo Emerges from Obscurity to Head Junta," *AFP*, March 26, 2012.

63 Interview with U.S. official, Paris, France, January 15, 2014; interview with French official, Paris, France, January 17, 2014; interview with U.S. officials, Bamako, Mali, January 24, 2014.

64 Interviews, Bamako, Mali, January, 2014.

65 At least one senior U.S. military official watching the coup closely later said he thought that all it would have taken was a concerted effort by the top Malian military leaders and the whole thing could have been brought under control. Interview with senior U.S. official, Washington, DC, January 3, 2014.

66 Interview with a former senior U.S. official, Washington, DC, February 21, 2014.

67 Interview with senior U.S. official, Bamako, Mali, January 24, 2014.

68 Adam Nossiter, "Mali Uprising Proves No Threat to Junta Leader's Vision of Authority," *The New York Times*, May 2, 2012, p. 4.

69 Tanguy Berthemet, "La France en quête d'une solution pour le Mali," *Le Figaro*, September 21, 2012, p. 7.

70 Jean-Philippe Rémy, "Le Mali Sous la Menace des Islamistes," *Le Monde*, April 5, 2012, p. 7.

71 Laserre and Oberlé, *Notre Guerre Secrète*, p. 97.

72 Xan Rice, "The Taking of Timbuktu," *Financial Times*, June 2, 2012, p. 7.

73 Malika Groga-Bada, "Mali: AQMI et le Touareg Connection," *Jeuneafrique. com*, December 12, 2011 ; André Bourgeot, "Des Tuareg en Rebellion" in Patrick Gonin, et al., *La Tragédie Malienne*. Paris: Vendémiaire, 2013, pp. 113–129.

74 Quoted in Borzou Daragahi, "West Grows Fearful of North Africa Militants," *Financial Times*, May 11, 2012, p. 3.

75 Xan Rice, "The Taking of Timbuktu," *Financial Times*, June 2, 2012, p. 7.

76 Ibid.

77 Rukmini Callimachi, "In Timbuktu, al Qa'ida Left Behind a Manifesto," *Associated Press*, February 14, 2013.
78 Rukmini Callimachi, "$.60 for cake: al-Qaida records every expense," *Associated Press*, December 30, 2013.
79 Centre de Doctrine et d'Emploi des Forces, "Synthese RETEX de l'operation Serval au Mali, Janvier-Mai 2013," November 2013.
80 "General Ham Discusses Security Challenges, Opportunities at George Washington University," Washington, DC, December 3, 2012.
81 Report of the Secretary General on the Situation in Mali, S/2012/894, November 28, 2012.
82 Tanguy Berthemet, "La France en quête d'une solution pour le Mali," *Le Figaro*, September 21, 2012, p. 7.
83 Natalie Nougayrède, Christophe Châtelot, "Le Mali en appelle à l'ONU pour reconquérir le Nord," *Le Monde*, September 26, 2012, p. 3.

5 Leading Africa from Behind

1 Interview with a senior French official, Washington, DC, December 5, 2013.
2 Ibid.
3 Interview with senior French official at the Elysée Palace, Paris, France, January 20, 2014.
4 Interview with a senior French military official, Paris, France, January 14, 2014.
5 Laserre and Oberley, *Guerre Secrete*, pp. 20–26.
6 French Senate, Rapport d'Information, no. 513, April 16, 2013, pp. 10, 91.
7 Interview with a senior French official, Paris, France, January 17, 2014.
8 Interview with Dioncounda Traoré, Bamako, Mali, January 24, 2014.
9 Ibid.
10 Ibid.
11 Interview with senior French official at the Elysée Palace, Paris, France, January 20, 2014.
12 Ibid.
13 Berthemet, Tanguy, "Mali: Fabius juge probable l'usage de la force," *Le Figaro*, July 13, 2012, p.6.
14 Interview with senior French official at the Elysée Palace, Paris, France, January 20, 2014.
15 Ibid.
16 Ibid.
17 Scott Stewart, "Stratfor: Mali Besieged by Fighters Fleeing Libya," *Defenceweb*, February 3, 2012.
18 Isabelle Mandraud, "La diplomatie souterraine de l'Algérie sur la crise au Mali," *Le Monde*, July 3, 2012, p. 5.

19 Isabelle Lasserre and Thierry Oberlé, "Mali: la France en pointe contre Aqmi," *Le Figaro*, September 24, 2012, p. 7.

20 Natalie Nougayrède and Christophe Châtelot, "Le Mali en appelle à l'ONU pour reconquérir le Nord," *Le Monde*, September 26, 2012, p. 3.

21 Christophe Châtelot, "Le Burkina Faso parie sur l'option diplomatique pour sortir le Mali de la crise," *Le Monde*, August 9, 2012, p. 3.

22 Interview with a former senior U.S. official, Washington, DC, February 20, 2014.

23 David Baché, "Le Mali a enfin un gouvernement d'union nationale," *Le Figaro*, August 23, 2012, p. 8.

24 "Discours du Président de la République à l'occasion de la XXème Conférences des Ambassadeurs," Paris, August 27, 2012.

25 Isabelle Lasserre and Thierry Oberlé, "Mali: la France en pointe contre Aqmi," *Le Figaro*, September 24, 2012, p. 7.

26 Interview with senior French official at the Elysée Palace, Paris, France, January 20, 2014.

27 Ibid.

28 M. Francois, Hollande, president of the French Republic, speech delivered to the 67th United Nations General Assembly, New York, NY, September 25, 2012.

29 Interview, Washington, DC, December 5, 2013.

30 Interview with French military officials, EMA, Paris, France, January 15, 2014.

31 Natalie Nougayrède, Christophe Châtelot, "Le Mali en appelle à l'ONU pour reconquérir le Nord," *Le Monde*, September 26, 2012, p. 3.

32 Interview with U.S. Official, Washington, DC, March 28, 2014.

33 See Johnnie Carson, "Addressing Developments in Mali: Restoring Democracy and Reclaiming the North," Testimony Before the Senate Committee on Foreign Relations Subcommittee on African Affairs Washington, DC, December 5, 2012.

34 Interview with a former senior U.S. official, Washington, DC, January 3, 2014.

35 Patrick Gonin, Marc-Antoine Pérouse de Montclos, "Mali, l'intervention difficile," *Le Monde*, July 10, 2012, p. 18.

36 Interview with a former senior U.S. official, Washington, DC, February 20, 2014.

37 As of January 2014, Sanogo's class picture still hung on the wall to the left of the entrance of the *Ecole de Mantien de la Paix* in Bamako.

38 Alexandra Geneste, "Multiplication d'obstacles pour une opération au Mali," *Le Monde*, December 7, 2012, p. 6.

39 Colum Lynch, "Rice: French Plan for Mali Intervention is 'Crap'," *Foreignpolicy.com*, December 11, 2012.

40 Interview with former senior U.S. official, Washington, DC, February 20, 2014; Lynch, "Rice: French Plan for Mali Intervention is 'Crap'."

41 Alexandra Geneste, "Multiplication d'obstacles pour une opération au Mali," *Le Monde*, December 7, 2012, p. 6.

42 Interview with senior French official, Elysée, Paris, France, 2014.

43 Multiple interviews, Paris, France, January, 2013. On French military traditions see Jean Doise and Maurice Vaïsse, *Diplomatie et outil militaire, 1871–1991*, Paris: Editions du Seuil, 1992.

44 Interview with French military officers, EMA, Paris, France, January 15, 2014.

45 Interview with a French military officer, January 17, 2014.

46 On this subject see Douglas Porch, "Bugeaud, Gallieni, Lyautey: The Development of French Colonial Warfare" in Peter Paret, ed., *Makers of Modern Strategy: from Machiavelli to the Nuclear Age* (Princeton: Princeton University Press, 1986), pp. 376–407.

47 Theo Farrell, Sten Rynning, Terry Terriff, *Transforming Military Power since the Cold War: Britain, France, and the United States, 1991–2012* (Cambridge: Cambridge University Press, 2013), pp. 220–226.

48 See Peter Apps, "With Multiple Missions, U.S. Military Steps Up Africa Focus," *Reuters*, June 27, 2013.

6 Crisis and Opportunity

1   Interview with senior French MOD official, Paris, France, January 20, 2014.

2   Jean-Philippe Rémy, "A Gao, ex- "capitale" du Mujao, la mort a frappé sans prévenir," *Le Monde*, February 2, 2013, p. 6

3   Interview with senior French MOD official, Paris, France, January 20, 2014.

4   Interview with Dioncounda Traoré, Bamako, Mali, January 24, 2014.

5   Lasserre and Oberlé, *Notre Guerre Secrète*, p. 90.

6   Interview with Dioncounda Traoré, Bamako, Mali, January 24, 2014.

7   Interview with French military officer, Elysée, Paris, France, January 20, 2014.

8   Interview with French military officer, Paris, France, January 17, 2014.

9   Interview with French security expert, Paris, France, January 13, 2014.

10 Interview with security expert, Paris, France, January 14, 2014.

11 Interview with senior French MOD official, Paris, France, January 20, 2014.

12 Ibid.

13 Interview with French security expert, Paris, France, January 16, 2014.

14 Interview with senior French MOD official, Paris, France, January 20, 2014.

15 Interview with French military official, Paris, France, January 17, 2014; interview with senior U.S. official, Bamako, Mali, January 24, 2014.

16 Interview with high-level Malian official, Bamako, Mali, January 24, 2014.

17 Interview with French military officials, EMA, Paris, France, January 15, 2014.

18 Interview with senior French MOD official, Paris, France, January 20, 2014.

19 Interview with senior U.S. official, Bamako, Mali, January 24, 2014.

20 Interview with senior French official, Elysee, Paris, France, Januray 20, 2014.

21 Ibid.

22 Ibid.
23 Ibid.
24 France Ministry of Defense, *Mali: lancement de l'operation Serval,* January 12, 2013; Gros et al., 2013, p. 9.
25 Interview with senior French official, Elysee, Paris, France, January 20, 2014.
26 Declaration du Président de la République, Situation au Mali, January 11, 2013.
27 All information about French deployments and troop movements are from French Ministry of Defense daily updates on *Serval,* unless otherwise noted.
28 Philippe Gros, Jean-Jacques Patry, and Nicole Vilboux, "Serval: bilan et perspectives," Fondation pour la Recherche Stratégique (FRS), No. 16/13, June 2013.
29 French MOD daily updates.
30 Jean-Philippe Rémy, "A Markala, l'armée française se prépare à l'affrontement," *Le Monde,* January 19, 2013, p. 4.
31 Centre de Doctrine et d'Emploi des Forces, "Synthese RETEX de l'operation Serval au Mali, Janvier-Mai 2013," November 2013.
32 Thierry Oberlé, "La stratégie des militaires français au Mali," *Le Figaro,* January 24, 2013, p. 8.
33 Centre de doctrine d'emploi des forces (CDEF), RETEX, p. 40.
34 French MOD daily updates.
35 Ibid.
36 Ibid.
37 Interview with General de Saint-Quentin, Paris, France, January 21, 2014.
38 Interview with senior French official, Elysee, Paris, France, January 20, 2014.
39 Nicolas Prissette, "Baromètre JDD: petit "effet Mali" sur la popularité d'Hollande," *Le Journal du Dimanche,* January 19, 2013; IFOP-JDD, "Les indices de popularité," Janvier 2013.
40 Gaël Vaillant, "La guerre au Mali profitera-t-elle à Hollande?" *Le Journal du Dimanche,* January 14, 2014.
41 G.V., "Mali: l'opposition ne parle pas d'une seule voix" *JDD.com,* January 21, 2013.
42 Alain Frachon, ""Opération Serval" au Mali ou le choix du moindre mal," *Le Monde,* January 14, 2013; Pierre Rousselin, "La France dans son rôle au Mali," *Le Figaro,* January 15, 2013, p.1; Nicolas Demorand, "Tumeur," *Libération,* January 14, 2013.
43 "David Cameron Welcomes French Military Involvement in Mali," *Telegraph,* January 12, 2013.
44 "Germany Considers Options to Aid Mali Intervention," *Deutsche Welle,* January 14, 2013.
45 "Intervention de la France au Mali: le président de l'UA 'aux anges'," *AFP,* January 11, 2013.

46 See Orb International, "New Poll: Nearly 8 in 10 Malians Support International Military Intervention in the North," January 24, 2013. Available at: www.orb-international.com/article.php?s=new-poll-nearly-8-in-10-malians -support-international-military-intervention-in-the-north

47 There was less support in the Middle East. See Pew Research, "As Mali Votes, Mixed Reception to French Intervention from Publics in Africa and Middle East," July 25, 2013. Available at: http://www.pewglobal.org/2013/07/25/ as-mali-votes-mixed-reception-to-french-intervention-from-publics-in -africa-and-middle-east/

48 Multiple interviews, Paris, France, January 2013.

49 Alexandre Lemarié, "Le chef de l'Etat n'a pas de stratégie claire," *Le Monde*, February 19, 2013.

50 *France 24*, "Politiques," January 17, 2013.

51 Dominique de Villepin, "Non, la guerre ce n'est pas la France," *Journal du Dimanche*, January 12, 2013.

52 Quoted in Daveed Garenstein-Ross, "Send Lone Wolves to Strike Inside of France," *Gunpowder and Lead*, January 17, 2013.

53 Matthew Campbell, "Motorbike Killer's Video Exposes Threat as France Goes on Alert," *The Sunday Times*, January 20, 2013, p. 13.

54 Baba Ahmed, "Un Mission: Mali Jihadist Spokesman Killed," *AP*, March 14, 2013.

55 Jean Guisnel, "Somalie: l'otage Denis Allex tué lors d'un assaut français," *Le Point*, January 12, 2013; Jean Guisnel, "Somalie: le raid pour libérer Denis Allex a été conduit depuis le Mistral," *Le Point*, January 13, 2013.

56 Interview with senior French MOD official, Paris, France, January 20, 2014.

57 Simon Tisdall, "France's Lonely Intervention in Mali," *The Guardian*, January 14, 2013.

58 Interview with a senior French military officer, Paris, France, January 21, 2014.

59 Thierry Oberlé, "La stratégie des militaires français au Mali," *Le Figaro*, January 24, 2013, p. 8.

60 Présidence de la République, "Conférence de presse du Président de la République à Dubai," January 15, 2013.

61 Republique de la France, Ministère des Affaires Etrangères et Européennes, "Entretien du ministre des affaires étrangères, M. Laurent Fabius, avec «Le Grand Jury RTL-LCI-Le Figaro» – Extraits – Paris, 13 janvier 2013," *Declarations officiels de politique étrangere*, January 14, 2013.

62 Quoted in Jean-Christophe Notin, *La Guerre de la France au Mali*, Tallandier: Paris, 2014, p. 271.

7 *Serval*

1 Interview with a French officer, Paris, France, January 20, 2014.

2 Rick Atkinson, *An Army at Dawn*, New York, NY: Picador, 2002, p. 37.

3 Correspondence with General Barrera, April 9, 2015.

4 Interview with a senior French military officer, Paris, France, January 16, 2014.

5 Isabelle Lasserre and Thierry Oberlé, "Mali: la France en pointe contre Aqmi," *Le Figaro*, September 24, 2012, p. 7.

6 Interview with a senior French military officer, Paris, France, January 21, 2014.

7 Interview with a French security expert, Paris, France, January 17, 2014.

8 Jean-Christophe Notin, *La Guerre de la France au Mali*, Paris: Tallandier, 2014, pp. 125–126.

9 François Heisbourg, "A Surprising Little War: First Lessons of Mali," *Survival: Global Politics and Strategy*, Vol. 55, No. 2, April–May, 2013.

10 Philippe Gros, Jean-Jacques Patry, and Nicole Vilboux, "Serval: bilan et perspectives," Fondation pour la Recherche Stratégique (FRS), No. 16/13, June, 2013.

11 Interview with a UN military officer, Bamako, Mali, January 23, 2014.

12 Interview with a U.S. official, Paris, France, January 14, 2014.

13 Interview with a French officer, Paris, France, January 16, 2014.

14 Alexandre Duyck, "Grégoire de Saint-Quentin: missions très spéciales," *Le Journal du Dimanche*, September 30, 2013.

15 Correspondence with General Barrera, April 9, 2015.

16 Multiple interviews with French officials, Paris, France, January 2013.

17 Ch. Ly, "Contacts avec la Belgique," *La Libre Belgique*, January 14, 2013.

18 Interview with a U.S. official, Paris, France, January 14, 2014.

19 David Pugliese, "Harper Acknowledges Canadian Forces Committed to Short-Term Aid to Malian Military," *Ottawa Citizen Online*, January 13, 2013.

20 Alain Lallemand, "La Belgique « est prête », mais dans le cadre européen," *Le Soir*, January 12, 2013, p. 14; Ch. Ly, "Contacts avec la Belgique," *La Libre Belgique*, January 14, 2013; "Belgium offers C-130s, helicopters to France's Mali campaign," *Agence France Presse – English*, January 15, 2013.

21 Interview with senior U.S. Department of Defense official, Washington, DC, February, 20, 2013.

22 See Christopher S. Chivvis, *Toppling Qaddafi: Libya and the Limits of Liberal Intervention*, New York, NY: Cambridge University Press 2013, pp. 139–143.

23 Interview with a senior French military official, Paris, France, January 16, 2014.

24 Interview with a senior French military official, Paris, France, January 14, 2014.

25 Interview with a U.S. official, Washington, DC, December 3, 2013.

26 Interview with a U.S. official, Paris, France, January 14, 2014.

27 Nathalie Guibert, "Le Pentagone a envoyé son drone Global Hawk au Mali," *Le Monde*, January 27, 2013, p. 5.

28 Nathalie Nougayrede, "La relation franco-américaine à l'épreuve du Sahel," *Le Monde*, January 27, 2013, p. 5.

29 "US Military Sending Air Tankers to Refuel French Jets over Mali," *Associated Press*, January 27, 2013.

30 Interview with a senior French military officer, Paris, France, January 21, 2014.

31 Interview with a former senior U.S. military official, Washington, DC, January 3, 2014.

32 Jean Fleury, *La France en guerre au Mali*, Paris: Jean Picollec, 2013.

33 Interview with a senior French defense official, Paris, France, January 20, 2014.

34 Ibid.

35 Interview with U.S. Defense Department official, Washington, DC, December 3, 2013.

36 Interview with a senior U.S. official, Washington, DC, January 3, 2014.

37 Ibid.

38 Interview with a Danish military official, by telephone from Washington, DC, June 12, 2014.

39 Ibid.

40 Interview with a senior French defense department official, Paris, France, January 20, 2014.

41 Sénat, Rapport d'Information, "au nom de la commission des affaires étrangères, de la defense et des forces armées par le groupe de travail 'Sahel', en vue du débat et du vote sur l'autorisation de prolongation del'intervention des forces armées au Mali." No. 513, April 16, 2013.

42 Interview with a French military officer, by telephone, from Washington, DC, April 17, 2014.

43 Gros, Philippe, Jean-Jacques Patry, and Nicole Vilboux, "Serval: bilan et perspectives," *Fondation pour la Recherche Stratégique (FRS)*, No. 16/13, June 2013, p. 8.

44 Interview with a French military officer, by telephone, from Washington, DC, April 17, 2014.

45 Notin, *La Guerre de la France au Mali*, pp. 314–315.

46 CDEF, RETEX, p. 42.

47 Ibid.

48 Interview with a French military officer, by telephone, from Washington, DC, April 17, 2014.

49 Interview with a French military officer, Paris, France, January 17, 2014.

50 CDEF, RETEX, p. 45.

51 Jean-Philippe Rémy, "Soldats et jihadists pris dans les sables au nord du Mali," *Le Monde*, February 1, 2013, p. 6.

52 "Hollande Visits Mali to Push for African Takeover," AFP, February 2, 2013.

53 "Slideshow: Mali Welcomes Hollande in Timbuktu and Bamako," RFI English, February 4, 2013.

54 "Hollande au Mali: le plus dur reste à faire," *Le Monde*, February 2, 2013.

55 Interview with a senior U.S. official, Washington, DC, January 3, 2014.

56 Isabelle Lasserre, "La guerre éclair des Français dans le Sahel," *Le Figaro*, January 29, 2013, p. 6.

57 Interview with a French military officer, by telephone from Washington, DC, April 17, 2014.

58 Isabelle Lasserre, "La guerre éclair des Français dans le Sahel," *Le Figaro*, January 29, 2013, p. 6.

59 Jean-Philippe Rémy, "Au Mali, un attentat atteste de la permanence de la menace djihadiste," *Le Monde*, February 10, 2013, p. 5.

60 Thierry Oberlé, "Gao en état de siège après l'offensive des djihadistes," *Le Figaro*, February 12, 2013, p. 9.

61 Jean-Philippe Rémy, "Soldats et jihadists pris dans les sables au nord du Mali," *Le Monde*, February 1, 2013, p. 6.

62 Theirry Portes, "Hollande va prêcher la concorde à Bamako," *Le Figaro*, February 2, 2013, p. 6.

63 Interview with senior French military official, by telephone, June 4, 2014.

64 Ibid.

65 Ibid.

66 Bernard Barrera, *Opération Serval: Notes de Guerre, Mali 2013*, Paris: Editions de Seuil, 2015, p. 304.

67 Correspondence with General Barrera, April 9, 2015.

68 Interview with a French military officer, by telephone from Washington, DC, April 17, 2014.

69 Interview with a French military officer, by telephone from Washington, DC, April 17, 2014.

70 Ibid.

71 Ibid.

72 Barrera, *Opération Serval*, pp. 144–151.

73 Interview with a senior French military officer, by telephone, June 4, 2014.

74 Interview with a French military officer, by telephone, April 17, 2014.

75 Interview with a senior French military officer, Paris, France, January 21, 2014.

76 Barrera, *Opération Serval*, p. 193 (et passim).

77 "Serval, Quand l'Armée Film sa Guerre," *Envoyé Spécial*, October 17, 2014.

78 Ibid.

79 Interview with a French military officer, Paris, France, January 17, 2014.

80 Barrera, *Opération Serval*, p. 210.

81 Interview with senior French military officer, Paris, France, January 21, 2014.

82 Correspondence with General Barrera, April 9, 2015.

83 CDEF, RETEX; "Serval, Quand l'Armée Film sa Guerre," *Envoyé Spécial*, October 17, 2014.

84 Notin, *La Guerre de la France au Mali*, pp. 467–469.

85 Barrera, *Opération Serval*, p. 164.

86 CDEF, RETEX, p. 58.

87 CDEF, RETEX, p. 62.

88 Barrera, *Opération Serval*, p. 309.

89 Interview with senior French military officer, Paris, France, January 21, 2014.

90 Interview with senior French official, Elysée, Paris, France, January 20, 2014; Interview with senior French military officer, Paris, France, January 21, 2014.

91 U.S. Senate, Committee on Armed Services, Subcommittee on Emerging Threats and Capabilities, "Hearing to Receive Testimony on Department of Defense Programs and Policies with Respect to Emerging Counterterrorism Threats in Review of the Defense Authorization Request for Fiscal Year 2014 and the Future Years Defense Program," April 9, 2013.

92 David Baché, "Mali: le chef des forces oust-africaines sur la defensive," *Le Figaro*, April 16, 2013, p. 5.

93 UN Security Council, "Report of the Secretary-General on the situation in Mali," March 26, 2013, S/2013/189.

94 Ibid.

95 United Nations Security Council, S/RES/2100, 2013; Theirry Tardy, "Mali: The UN Takes Over," *EUISS Alert*, No. 10, May 2013; Isaline Bergamaschi, "MINUSMA: Initial Steps, Achievements and Challenges," *NOREF Policy Brief*," September 2013.

96 Rémi Carayol, "Mali: Minusma, c'est flou," *Jeune Afrique*, July 5, 2013; Isaline Bergamaschi, "MINUSMA: Initial Steps, Achievements and Challenges," *NOREF Policy Brief*, September 2013.

97 Rémi Carayol, "Mali: Minusma, c'est flou," *Jeune Afrique*, July 5, 2013.

98 Adam C. Smith, "Pitfalls of Force Generation Await UN Peacekeeping Operation in Mali," *International Peace Institute Global Observatory*, May 24, 2013.

99 "Security Council Unanimously Approves New UN Peacekeeping Mission in Mali," UN News Centre, April 25, 2013.

100 United Nations Security Council, S/RES/2100, 2013.

101 Interview with senior French military official, via telephone, June 4, 2014.

102 French army figures provided to author.

103 Interview with senior French military official, via telephone, June 4, 2014; French army figures provided to author.

8 The Elusive "Political" Dimension

1 See Christopher S. Chivvis and Jeffrey Martini, *Libya After Qaddafi: Lessons and Implications for the Future*, Santa Monica, CA: RAND Corporation, RR-577-SRF, 2014.

2 Interview with Dioncounda Traoré, Bamako, Mali, January 24, 2014.

3 Interview with senior French official, Elysee, Paris, France, January 20, 2014.

4 Interview with U.S. official, Paris, France, January 15, 2014.

5 Interview with European Union Training Mission (EUTM) staff, Bamako, Mali, January 23, 2014.

6 Christophe Châtelot and Nathalie Guibert, "Le défi de la refondation de larmée malienne," *Le Monde*, February 5, 2013, p. 2.

7 Internal French MOD figures provided to author; author interview with EUTM staff, Bamako, Mali, January 23, 2014. On EUTM see also Thierry Tardy, "Mali : restaurer la paix dans un pays en guerre" *EUISS Alert*, no. 8, February 6, 2015.

8 Interview with EUTM staff, Bamako, Mali, January 23, 2014.

9 Mohamed D. Diawara, "L'accord proposé par Ouagadougou: le Niet de Dioncounda aux médiateurs," *Info-Matin* (Bamako), June 14, 2013; "Mali: les grandes lignes de l'accord signé à Ouagadougou," *RFI*, June 19, 2013.

10 "Accord Preliminaire à l'Election Presidentielle et Aux Pourparlers Inclusifs de Paix Au Mali," June 2013.

11 Interview with senior U.S. official, Bamako, Mali, January 24, 2014.

12 "Report of the Secretary-General on the situation in Mali," S/2013/582, October 1, 2013.

13 Ibid.

14 Charlotte Bozonnet, "'IBK', nouvel homme fort du Mali," *Le Monde.fr*, July 31, 2013; Cyril Bensimon, "Au Mali, le nouveau president face à d'immenses defies," *Le Monde.fr*, September 4, 2013; ICG, "Mali: Reform or Relapse," *Africa Report*, no. 210, January 10, 2014.

15 Jean-Herve Jezequel, "Le Mali après Serval: éviter la rechute," *Jeune Afrique*, January 29, 2014.

16 ICG, "Mali: Reform or Relapse," *Africa Report*, no. 210, January 10, 2014. See also Stephanie Pezard and Michael Shurkin, *Achieving Peace in Northern Mali: Past Agreements, Local Conflicts, and the Prospects for a Durable Settlement*, Santa Monica, CA: RAND, 2015.

17 ICG, "Mali: Reform or Relapse."

18 (n.a.) "Azawad: le chef coutumier de l'Adrar des Ifoghas quitte le MNLA et rejoint le HCA," *RFI*, May 19, 2013.

19 "Mali: le Haut Conseil de l'Azawad met en place ses instances," *RFI*, May 20, 2013.

20 Remi Carayol, "Mali: jihadistes sur le retour," *Jeune Afrique*, September 9, 2013.

21 Saharamedias.net, "Azawad: Agreement Between Arab and Tuareg Armed Groups," August 9, 2013.

22 Jean Dominique Merchet, "Mali: cet étrange général Ag Gamou," *L'Opinion*, June 2, 2014.

23 For example, Abdoulsalam Hama and Joe Penney, "Mali Must Disarm the Militias," *New York Times*, June 18, 2015.

24 Remi Carayol, "Mali: jihadistes sur le retour," *Jeune Afrique*, September 9, 2013.

25 Charlotte Bozonnet and Jacques Follorou, "La reprise de la violence au Mali force le president 'IBK' à écourter sa visite à Paris," *Le Monde.fr*, October 1, 2013.

26 Rukmini Callimachi, "Al-Qaida Takes Responsibility for Reporters' Death," *Associated Press*, November 6, 2013; Andrew McGregor, "Merger of Northern Mali Rebel Movements Creates Political Distance from Islamist Movements," *Jamestown Terrorism Monitor*, Vol. 11, No. 21, November 14, 2013; Jacques Follorou, "Mali: trois des ravisseurs des journalists de RFI étaient connus des services de reseignement français," *Le Monde.fr*, November 5, 2013.

27 Jeremy Binnie, "Analysis: UN peacekeepers struggle against IEDs in Mali" *IHS Jane's 360*, January 6, 2015.

28 Cyril Bensimon, "Paris attribute le double assassinat de Kidal à AQMI," *Le Monde.fr*, November 4, 2013.

29 Jean-Dominique Merchet, "La France reorganize son dispositive militaire au Sahel autour de quatre bases," *l'Opinion*, January 21, 2014.

30 Jean-Herve Jezequel, "Le Mali après Serval: éviter la rechute," *Jeune Afrique*, January 29, 2014.

31 Francis Fukuyama, *Statebuilding: Governance and World Order in the 21st Century*, Ithaca: Cornell University Press, 2004.

32 Interviews, Bamako, Mali, January 2014.

9 The Road Ahead

1 Interview with senior French MOD official, Paris, France, January 20, 2014.

2 Nicolas Beau, *Papa Hollande au Mali: Chronique d'un fiasco annoncé*, Paris: Balland, 2013. See esp. pp. 213–218.

3 Stephen W. Smith, "In Search of Monsters," *London Review of Books*, February 7, 2013. See also, "Behind France's Foray Into Mali," *Current History*, May 2013, pp. 163–168.

4 Michel Onfray, "M. Hollande ne comprend rien aux guerres idéologiques du XXIe siècle," *Le Monde*, April 23, 2013.

5 Marc Antoine Perouse de Montclos, "Dans l'œil du cyclone" in Gonin et al., *La tragédie Malienne*, Paris: Vendémiaire, p. 12.

6 Olivier Roy, "Vaine stratégie française au Mali," *Le Monde*, February 5, 2013.

7 For example, Robert A. Pape, "When Duty Calls: A Pragmatic Standard of Humanitarian Intervention," *International Security*, Vol. 37, No.1, Summer, 2012, pp. 41–80.

8 See Taylor Seybolt, *Humanitarian Intervention: The Conditions for Success and Failure*, Oxford: Oxford University Press, 2007, pp. 30–45.

9 Interview with senior French military officer, June 4, 2014.

10 On Zaid's importance see, Gros, 2013; Geneva Center for Training and Analysis of Terrorism, "Celui qui parlait au desert: Abdulhamid Abou Zaid, nécrologie du silence," March 23, 2013.

11 Romain Mielcarek, "Où sont passés les jihadistes qui ont combattu au Mali?" *RFI.com*, October 23, 2013; "Les jihadistes d'Aqmi en Tunisie sont des vété-rans du Mali," *AFP*, August 5, 2013.

12 As translated in Andrew Lebovich, "Of Mergers, MUJAO, and Mokhtar Belmokhtar," *al-Wasat*, August 23, 2013.

13 François Heisbourg, "A Surprising Little War: First Lessons of Mali," *Survival: Global Politics and Strategy*, Vol. 55, No. 2, April–May, 2013. See also Etienne de Durand, "Does France have an Exit Strategy in Mali?" *Foreign Affairs*, February 20, 2013.

14 Interview with a senior French military officer, Paris, France, January 21, 2014.

15 Interview with General de Saint-Quentin, Paris, France, January 21, 2014.

16 Interview with a senior French military officer, Paris, France, January 21, 2014.

17 Interview with several French security experts, Paris, France, January, 2014.

18 Interview with a senior French military officer, Paris, France, January 21, 2014.

19 Christopher S. Chivvis, "Preserving Hope in the Democratic Republic of Congo," *Survival*, Vol. 49, No. 2, Summer 2007, pp. 21–42.

20 On this issue see also, Bruno Tertrais, "Leading on the Cheap? French Security Policy in Austerity," *The Washington Quarterly*, Vol. 36, No. 3, 2013. For back-ground see Kenneth Neal Waltz, *Man State and War*, New York, NY: Columbia University Press, 1959.

21 Jean Fleury, *La France en guerre au Mali*, Paris: Jean Picollec, 2013, p. 49.

22 Interview with senior French military officer, Paris, France, January 16, 2014.

23 Ibid.

24 Jean-Dominique Merchet, "Le Mali coutera 647 million d'euros cette année," *L'Opinion*, October 13, 2013.

25 Interview with a French security expert, Paris, France, January 16, 2014.

26 Interview, Washington, DC, December 5, 2013.

27 Interview with a former senior French military officer, Paris, France, January 14, 2014.

28 Interview with a senior French military officer, Paris, France, January 21, 2014.

29 See Airbus Defense and Space, "The Versatile Airlifter of the 21st Century."

30 Interview with a U.S. official close to the operation, Paris, France, January 14, 2014.

31 Interview with a senior French military official, Paris, France, January 16, 2014.

32 Ibid.

33 Ibid.

BIBLIOGRAPHY

"Accord Preliminaire à l'Election Presidentielle et Aux Pourparlers Inclusifs de Paix Au Mali," June 2013.

Airbus Defense and Space, "The Versatile Airlifter of the 21st Century." As of August 4, 2014: http://www.airbusmilitary.com/aircraft/a400m/a400mabout.aspx.

"An Interview with Abdelmalek Droukdal," *The New York Times*, July 1, 2008.

Angeli, Claude, "Un Afghanistan Africain au Sud de l'Europe," *Le Canard Enchaîné*, April 11, 2012.

Atkinson, Rick, *An Army at Dawn*, New York: Picador, 2002.

"Azawad: Agreement between Arab and Tuareg Armed Groups," *Saharamedias.net*, August 9, 2013.

"Azawad: le chef coutumier de l'Adrar des Ifoghas quitte le MNLA et rejoint le HCA," *RFI*, May 19, 2013.

Baché, David, "Le Mali a enfin un gouvernement d'union nationale," *Le Figaro*, August 23, 2012.

Barrera, Bernard, *Opération Serval: Notes de Guerre, Mali 2013*, Paris: Editions de Seuil, 2015, p. 304.

"Mali: le chef des forces oust-africaines sur la defensive," *Le Figaro*, April 16, 2013.

Beau, Nicolas, *Papa Hollande au Mali: Chronique d'un fiasco annoncé*, Paris: Balland, 2013.

"Belgium Offers C-130s, Helicopters to France's Mali Campaign," *Agence France Presse – English*, January 15, 2013.

Bensimon, Cyril, "Au Mali, le nouveau president face à d'immenses defies," *Le Monde.fr*, September 4, 2013.

"Paris attribute le double assassinat de Kidal à AQMI," *Le Monde.fr*, November 4, 2013.

Bergamaschi, Isaline, "MINUSMA: Initial Steps, Achievements and Challenges," *NOREF Policy Brief*, September 2013.

Bergen, Peter, Bruce Hoffman, and Katherine Tiedemann, "Assessing the Jihadist Terrorist Threat to America and American Interests," *Studies in Conflict & Terrorism*, Vol. 34, No. 2, 2011.

Berthemet, Tanguy, "Des Touaregs exécutent des soldats maliens," *Le Figaro*, March 14, 2012.

"La France en quête d'une solution pour le Mali," *Le Figaro*, September 21, 2012.

"Mali: Fabius juge probable l'usage de la force" *Le Figaro*, July 13, 2012.

Bilefsky, Dan, "A Killer's Alienation, Not a Tie to Al Qaeda, Surfaces in Inquiry," *International Herald Tribune*, March 31, 2012 p. 5.

Bilefsky, Dan and Maïa de la Baume, "Officials See the Terrorist Threat They Feared Most," *International Herald Tribune*, March 23, 2012, p. 5.

Boltanski, Christophe and Sarah Halifa-Legrand, "Mail: Un Désastre Français," *Nouvelle Observateur*, April 12, 2012.

Bordenave, Yves and Jacques Follorou, "Mohamed Merah, un membre actif de la mouvance djihadiste international," *Le Monde.fr*, March 22, 2012.

Borredon, Laurent and Jacques Follorou, "Bernard Squarcini: 'Nous ne pouvions pas aller plus vite'," *Le Monde.fr*, March 23, 2012.

Bozonnet, Charlotte, "'IBK', nouvel homme fort du Mali," *Le Monde.fr*, July 31, 2013.

Bozonnet, Charlotte and Jacques Follorou, "La reprise de la violence au Mali force le president 'IBK' à écourter sa visite à Paris," *Le Monde.fr*, October 1, 2013.

Bratton, Michael and Nicolas van de Walle, *Democratic Experiments in Africa: Regime Transitions in Comparative Perspective*, Cambridge: Cambridge University Press, 1997.

Bulmiller, Elizabeth, "Leon Panetta Says U.S. Has Pledged to Help France in Mali," *The New York Times*, January 14, 2013.

Callimachi, Rukmini, "Al-Qaida Takes Responsibility for Reporters' Death," *Associated Press*, November 6, 2013.

"In Timbuktu, al Qa'ida Left Behind a Manifesto," *Associated Press*, February 14, 2013.

"$.60 for cake: al-Qaida records every expense," *Associated Press*, December 30, 2013

Campbell, Matthew, "Police Stunned by Combat skills of 'Lone Wolf' Killer," *Sunday Times*, March 25, 2012, p. 22.

Carayol, Rémi, "Mali: jihadistes sur le retour," *Jeune Afrique*, September 9, 2013.

"Mali: Minusma, c'est flou," *Jeune Afrique*, July 5, 2013.

Carson, Johnnie, "Addressing Developments in Mali: Restoring Democracy and Reclaiming the North," Testimony Before the Senate Committee on Foreign Relations Subcommittee on African Affairs Washington, DC, December 5, 2012.

Châtelot, Christophe, "Le Burkina Faso parie sur l'option diplomatique pour sortir le Mali de la crise," *Le Monde*, August 9, 2012.

Châtelot, Christophe, and Nathalie Guibert, "Le défi de la refondation de l'armée malienne," *Le Monde*, February 5, 2013.

Chivvis, Christopher S., "Preserving Hope in the Democratic Republic of the Congo," *Survival: Global Politics and Strategy Summer 2007*, Vol. 49, No. 2, June 1, 2007, pp. 21–42.

Toppling Qaddafi: Libya and the Limits of Liberal Intervention, New York: Cambridge University Press, 2013.

Chivvis, Christopher S., and Andrew Liepman, *North Africa's Menace: AQIM's Evolution and the U.S. Policy Response*, Santa Monica, CA: RAND Corporation, RR-415-OSD, 2013.

Chivvis, Christopher S., and Jeffrey Martini, *Libya after Qaddafi: Lessons and Implications for the Future*, Santa Monica, CA: RAND Corporation, RR-577-SRF, 2014.

Clarke, Thurston, *The Last Caravan*, New York: Putnam, 1978.

"Clashes between Malian Army and Tuareg Rebels "Lill 47" – Military Source," *BBC Monitoring Middle East*, January 21, 2012.

Daniel, Serge, *AQMI: L'Industrie de L'enlèvement*, Paris: Fayard, 2012.

Daragahi, Borzou, "West Grows Fearful of North Africa Militants," *Financial Times*, May 11, 2012.

DeDurand, Etienne, "Does France Have an Exit Strategy in Mali?" *Foreign Affairs*, February 20, 2013.

Diawara, Mohamed D., "L'accord proposé par Ouagadougou: le Niet de Dioncounda aux médiateurs," *Info-Matin* (Bamako), June 14, 2013.

"Discours du Président de la République à l'occasion de la XXème Conférences des Ambassadeurs," Paris, August 27, 2012.

Doise, Jean, and Maurice Vaïsse, *Diplomatie et outil militaire, 1871–1991*, Paris: Editions du Seuil, 1992.

Doyle, Michael W., and Nicholas Sambanis, *Making War and Building Peace: United Nations Peace Operations*, Princeton, NJ: Princeton University Press, 2006.

Duyck, Alexandre, "Grégoire de Saint-Quentin: missions très spéciales," *Le Journal du Dimanche*, September 30, 2013.

Farrell, Theo, Sten Rynning, and Terry Terriff, *Transforming Military Power since the Cold War: Britain, France, and the United States, 1991–2012*, Cambridge: Cambridge University Press, 2013, pp. 220–226.

Filiu, Jean-Pierre, "The Local and Global Jihad of al-Qa'ida in the Islamic Maghrib," *Middle East Journal*, Vol. 60, No. 2, Spring 2009.

Fleury, Jean, *La France en guerre au Mali – Les combats d'AQMI et la révolte des Touareg* Paris, France: Picollec, 2013.

Follorou, Jacques, "Mali: trois des ravisseurs des journalists de RFI étaient connus des services de reseignement français," *Le Monde.fr*, November 5, 2013.

French Ministry of Defense, *Mali Operations*. As of June 23, 2014: http:// www.defense.gouv.fr/operations/mali/actualite/mali-lancement-de-l -operation-serval.

French Senate, "Rapport d'Information, no. 513," April 16, 2013.

"From Africa to the Middle East, France's New Hawkishness," *AFP*, November 17, 2013.

Foley, Frank, *Countering Terrorism in Britain and France Institutions, Norms and the Shadow of the Past*, Cambridge: Cambridge University Press, 2013.

Fukuyama, Francis, *Statebuilding: Governance and World Order in the 21st Century*, Ithaca: Cornell University Press, 2004.

"General Ham Discusses Security Challenges, Opportunities at George Washington University," Washington, DC, December 3, 2012.

Geneste, Alexandra, "Multiplication d'obstacles pour une opération au Mali," *Le Monde*, December 7, 2012.

Gonin, Patrick, and Marc-Antoine Pérouse de Montclos, "Mali, l'intervention difficile," *Le Monde*, July 10, 2012.

Gonin, Patrick et al., eds., *La tragédie malienne*, Paris : Vendémiaire, 2013.

Groga-Bada, Malika, "Mali: AQMI et le Touareg Connection," *Jeuneafrique.com*, December 12, 2011.

Gros, Philippe, Jean-Jacques Patry, and Nicole Vilboux, "Serval: bilan et perspectives," *Fondation pour la Recherche Stratégique (FRS)*, No. 16/13, June, 2013.

Guibert, Nathalie, "Le Pentagone a envoyé son drone Global Hawk au Mali," *Le Monde*, January 27, 2013.

Guidère, Mathieu, "Une filiale algérienne pour Al-Qaida," *Le Monde Diplomatique*, November 1, 2006.

Hama, Abdoulsalam and Joe Penney, "Mali Must Disarm the Militias" *New York Times*, June 18, 2015.

"Highlights from Malian press 14 Feb 12," *BBC Monitoring Africa*, February 15, 2012.

Heisbourg, François, "A Surprising Little War: First Lessons of Mali," *Survival: Global Politics and Strategy*, Vol. 55, No. 2, April–May, 2013.

Hoffman, Bruce, "Al Qaeda's Uncertain Future," *Studies in Conflict and Terrorism*, Vol. 36, No. 8, 2013.

"Hollande au Mali: le plus dur reste à faire," *Le Monde*, February 2, 2013.

Hollande, M. Francois, President of the French Republic, speech delivered to the 67th United Nations General Assembly, New York, September 25, 2012.

"Hollande Visits Mali to Push for African Takeover," *AFP*, February 2, 2013.

ICG, "Mali: Reform or Relapse," *Africa Report*, No. 210, January 10, 2014.

Insee, Recensement 2010, exploitation principale. Available at: http://www.insee.fr/fr/default.asp

Jezequel, Jean-Herve, "Le Mali après Serval: éviter la rechute," *Jeune Afrique*, January 29, 2014.

Joffé, George, "Trajectories of Radicalization: Algeria 1989–1999," in George Joffé, ed., *Islamist Radicalisation in North Africa: Politics and Process*, New York: Routledge, 2012.

Jones, Seth G., *A Persistent Threat: The Evolution of al Qa'ida and Other Salafi Jihadists*, Santa Monica, CA.: RAND Corporation, RR-637-OSD, 2014.

Hunting in the Shadows: The Pursuit of al Qa'ida Since 9/11, New York: Norton, 2012.

Kirkpatrick, David D., "A Deadly Mix in Benghazi," *The New York Times*, December 28, 2013. As of July 1, 2014: http://www.nytimes.com/projects/2013/benghazi/#/?chapt=0

Kulish, Nicholas, "Investigation Moves Slowly in Kenyan Mall Seige," *The New York Times*, October 11, 2013, p. A9.

Kuperman, Alan, "A Model Humanitarian Intervention? Reassessing NATO's Libya Campaign," *International Security*, Vol. 38, No. 1, Summer 2013.

"L'islamiste algérien Rachid Ramda définitivement condamné à la perpétuité," *Le Monde*, June 15, 2011.

Lacher, Wolfram, *Challenging the Myth of the Drug-Terror Nexus in the Sahel*, Kofi Annan Foundation, 2013. As of July 2, 2014: http://www.wacommissionondrugs.org/wp-content/uploads/2013/08/Challenging-the-Myth-of-the-Drug-Terror-Nexus-in-the-Sahel-2013-08-19.pdf

Lahoud, Nelly, et al., *Letters from Abbottabad: Bin Laden Sidelined?*, West Point, NY: Combatting Terrorism Center, May 3, 2012.

Lallemand, Alain, "La Belgique « est prête », mais dans le cadre européen," *Le Soir*, January 12, 2013.

Lasserre, Isabelle, "La guerre éclair des Français dans le Sahel," *Le Figaro*, January 29, 2013.

Lasserre, Isabelle, and Thierry Oberlé, "Mali: la France en pointe contre Aqmi; Paris et ses alliés planchent sur une intervention pour débarrasser la région de la menace terroriste.," *Le Figaro*, September 24, 2012.

Notre guerre secrète au Mali: Les nouvelles menaces contre la France, Paris: Fayard 2013.

Lazard, Violette, "Mener le jihad conformément à la méthode adoptée par Oussama ben Laden," *Libération*, January 6, 2012.

Lebovich, Andrew, "Of Mergers, MUJAO, and Mokhtar Belmokhtar," *al-Wasat*, August 23, 2013.

Lecoq, Baz, *Disputed Desert: Decolonisation, Competing Nationalisms and Tuareg Rebellions in Northern Mali*, Leiden: Brill Publishers, 2010.

"Les jihadistes d'Aqmi en Tunisie sont des vétérans du Mali," *AFP*, August 5, 2013.

Lipset, Seymour M., "Some Social Prerequisites for Democracy: Economic Development and Political Legitimacy," *American Political Science Review*, No. 53, 1959.

Ly, "Contacts avec la Belgique," *La Libre Belgique*, January 14, 2013.

Lyman, Princeton N., and J. Stephen Morrison, "The Terrorist Threat in Africa," *Foreign Affairs*, January 1, 2004.

Lynch, Colum, "Rice: French Plan for Mali Intervention is 'Crap'," *Foreignpolicy.com*, December 11, 2012.

M.A.O., "Hattab et Belmokhtar condamnés à 20 ans de prison," *El Watan*, March 31, 2007. As of July 15, 2014: http://www.algeria-watch.org/fr/article/mil/sale_guerre/hattab_belmokhtar.htm

"Mali conflict: French ransom cash 'funded militants'," *BBC News Africa*, February 8, 2013. As of July 1, 2014: http://www.bbc.com/news/world-africa-21391518

"Mali: le Haut Conseil de l'Azawad met en place ses instances," *RFI*, May 20, 2013.

"Mali: les grandes lignes de l'accord signé à Ouagadougou," *RFI*, June 19, 2013.

"Mali military says 47 killed in northern clashes," *Defenceweb*, January 20, 2012.

"Mali's Amadou Sanogo emerges from obscurity to head junta," *AFP*, March 26, 2012.

Mellah, Salima, and Jean-Baptiste Rivoire, "El Para, the Maghreb's Bin Laden," *Le Monde Diplomatique*, English Edition, February 2005.

Mandraud, Isabelle, "La diplomatie souterraine de l'Algérie sur la crise au Mali," *Le Monde*, July 3, 2012.

Marret, Jean-Luc, "Al-Qaeda in Islamic Maghreb: A "Glocal" Organization," *Studies in Conflict and Terrorism*, Vol. 31, No. 6, June 2008, pp. 541–552.

McGregor, Andrew, "Merger of Northern Mali Rebel Movements Creates Political Distance from Islamist Movements," *Jamestown Terrorism Monitor*, Vol. 11, No. 21, November 14, 2013.

Merchet, Jean Dominique, "La France reorganize son dispositive militaire au Sahel autour de quatre bases," *l'Opinion*, January 21, 2014.

"Mali: cet étrange général Ag Gamou," *l'Opinion*, June 2, 2014.

"Le Mali coutera 647 million d'euros cette année" *l'Opinion*, October 13, 2013.

Mielcarek, Romain, "Où sont passés les jihadistes qui ont combattu au Mali?" *RFI.com*, October 23, 2013.

Molins, Francois, Press Conference, March 23, 2012.

Nicolaisen, Ida, and Johannes Nicolaisen, *The Tuareg*, Rhodos, 1997.

Nicolaisen, Johannes, and Ida Nicolaisen, *The Pastoral Tuareg: Ecology, Culture and Society*, 2 vols, New York: Thames and Hudson, 1997.

Nossiter, Adam, "Leader Ousted, Nation Is Now a Drug Haven," *The New York Times*, November 1, 2012.

"Mali Uprising Proves No Threat to Junta Leader's Vision of Authority," *The New York Times*, May 2, 2012.

"Qaddafi's Weapons, Taken by Old Allies, Reinvigorate an Insurgent Army in Mali," *The New York Times*, February 6, 2012.

Notin, Jean-Christophe, *La Guerre de la France au Mali*, Paris: Tallandier, 2014.

Nougayrede, Nathalie, "La relation franco-américaine à l'épreuve du Sahel," *Le Monde*, January 27, 2013.

Nougayrède, Natalie, and Christophe Châtelot, "Le Mali en appelle à l'ONU pour reconquérir le Nord," *Le Monde*, September 26, 2012.

Oberlé, Theirry, "Gao en état de siège après l'offensive des djihadistes," *Le Figaro*, February 12, 2013.

Onfray, Michel, "M. Hollande ne comprend rien aux guerres idéologiques du XXIe siècle" *Le Monde*, April 23, 2013.

Ouazani, Cherif, "Rébellion du MNLA au Mali: Ag Najem, ou la soif de vengeance," *Jeune Afrique*, January 27, 2012.

Pape, Robert A., "When Duty Calls: A Pragmatic Standard of Humanitarian Intervention," *International Security*, Vol. 37, No.1, Summer, 2012, pp. 41–80.

Pezard, Stephanie and Michael Shurkin, *Achieving Peace in Northern Mali: Past Agreements, Local Conflicts, and the Prospects for a Durable Settlement*, Santa Monica, CA: RAND, 2015.

Porch, Douglas, *The Conquest of the Sahara*, New York: Farrar, Straus and Giroux, 1984.

Portes, Theirry, "Hollande va precher la concorde à Bamako," *Le Figaro*, February 2, 2013.

Pugliese, David, "Harper Acknowledges Canadian Forces Committed to Short-Term Aid to Malian Military," *Ottawa Citizen Online*, January 13, 2013.

"Quatre personnes interpellées en France," *Le Monde*, February 7, 2013.

Rémy, Jean-Philippe, "Au Mali, un attentat atteste de la permanence de al menace djihadiste," *Le Monde*, February 10, 2013

"Le Mali Sous la Menace des Islamistes," *Le Monde*, April 5, 2012.

"Soldats et jihadists pris dans les sables au nord du Mali," *Le Monde*, February 1, 2013.

"Report of the Secretary-General on the situation in Mali," S/2013/582, October 1, 2013.

"Report of the Secretary General on the Situation in Mali," S/2012/894, November 28, 2012.

Rice, Xan, "The Taking of Timbuktu," *Financial Times*, June 2, 2012.

Riedel, Bruce, *In Search of al Qa'ida: Its Leadership, Ideology, and Future*, Washington, DC: Brookings, 2008.

Roy, Olivier, "Loner, Loser, Killer," *International Herald Tribune*, March 24, 2012.

"Vaine stratégie française au Mali," *Le Monde*, February 5, 2013

"Security Council Unanimously Approves New UN Peacekeeping Mission in Mali," *UN News Centre*, April 25, 2013.

Sénat, Rapport d'Information, "au nom de la commission des affaires étrangères, de la defense et des forces armées par le groupe de travail 'Sahel', en vue du débat et du vote sur l'autorisation de prolongation del'intervention des forces armées au Mali." No. 513, April 16, 2013.

"Serval, Quand l'Armée Film sa Guerre," *Envoyé Spécial*, October 17, 2014.

Seybolt, Taylor, *Humanitarian Intervention: The Conditions for Success and Failure*, Oxford: Oxford University Press, 2007.

Shapiro, Jacob N., *The Terrorist's Dilemma: Managing Violent Covert Organizations*, Princeton, NJ: Princeton University Press, 2013.

"Slideshow: Mali Welcomes Hollande in Timbuktu and Bamako," *RFI English*, February 4, 2013. As of June 27, 2014: http://www.english.rfi.fr/africa/20130203-slideshow-mali-welcomes-hollande-timbuktu-and-bamako

Smith, Adam C., "Pitfalls of Force Generation Await UN Peacekeeping Operation in Mali," *International Peace Institute Global Observatory*, May 24, 2013.

Smith, Stephen W., "Behind France's Foray Into Mali," *Current History*, May 2013, pp. 163–168.

"In Search of Monsters," *London Review of Books*, February 7, 2013.

Soria, Valentina, "Global Jihad Sustained through Africa," *RUSI: UK Terrorism Analysis*, No. 2, April 2012.

Stewart, Scott, "Stratfor: Mali Besieged by Fighters Fleeing Libya," *Defenceweb*, February 3, 2012.

Tardy, Theirry, "Mali: The UN Takes Over," *EUISS Alert*, No. 10, May 2013.

"Mali : restaurer la paix dans un pays en guerre" *EUISS Alert*, no. 8, February 6, 2015.

Tertrais, Bruno, "Leading on the Cheap? French Security Policy in Austerity," *The Washington Quarterly*, Vol. 36, No. 3, 2013.

Trafficking in Persons Report, June 2013, United States Department of State, 2013.

Touchard, L., B. Ahmed, Ch. Ouazani, "Aqmi: Abdelmalek Droukdel, l'émir cache," *Jeune Afrique*, January 10, 2012.

"Tuerie de Toulouse: retour sur les événements," *Le Monde.fr*, March 24, 2012.

United Nations, *Human Development Report*, 2013.

United Nations Development Programme, *Human Development Report 2013, The Rise of the South: Human Progress in a Diverse World*, 2013.

United Nations Security Council, "Report of the Secretary-General on the situation in Mali," March 26, 2013, S/2013/189.

United Nations Security Council, S/RES/2100, 2013.

UNODC, *World Drug Report 2013*, United Nations Publication, Sales No. E.13.XI.6, 2013.

"US military sending air tankers to refuel French jets over Mali," *Associated Press*, January 27, 2013.

U.S. Senate, Committee on Armed Services, Subcommittee on Emerging Threats and Capabilities, "Hearing to Receive Testimony on Department of Defense Programs and Policies With Respect to Emerging Counterterrorism Threats in review of the Defense Authorization Request for Fiscal Year 2014 and the Future Years Defense Program," April 9, 2013.

Verne, Jules, *Invasion of the Sea*, trans. Edward Baxter, edited with an introduction by Arthur B. Evans, Middletown, CT: Wesleyan University Press, 2001.

Waltz, Kenneth Neal, *Man State and War*, New York: Columbia University Press, 1959.

Whitehouse, Bruce, "What's to Love about Mali? Four Things," *bridgesfrombamako.com*, February 4, 2013.

World Bank, "World Development Indicators," 2014. As of July 16, 2014: http://data.worldbank.org/data-catalog/world-development-indicators

INDEX